BOOKS
in search of
CHILDREN

BOOKS
in search of
CHILDREN

Speeches and Essays by

LOUISE SEAMAN BECHTEL

Selected and with an Introduction by
Virginia Haviland

The Macmillan Company · Collier-Macmillan Ltd., London

FIRST PRINTING

Permission to reprint essays by Louise Seaman Bechtel is gratefully acknowledged to the following publishers and copyright holders:

The Atlantic Monthly, Boston, Massachusetts, for "The Giant in Children."

Catholic Library Association for "Padraic Colum: A Great Storyteller of Today," reprinted from *The Catholic Library World,* December, 1960.

D. C. Heath and Company for "Thinking About Children's Classics," reprinted from *The Packet,* Fall, 1955.

The Horn Book, Inc., for essays originally published in *The Horn Book Magazine* and copyrighted by The Horn Book, Inc., Boston, on the dates indicated— "The A.I.G.A. Children's Book Show" (Aug., 1958), "Berta and Elmer" and Their Picture Books (Aug., 1928), "Books Before Five" (Sept., 1941), "Boris Artzybasheff, 1899–1965" (April, 1966), "Can Writing Be Taught?" (Nov., 1940), "Elizabeth Coatsworth: Poet and Writer" (Jan., 1936), "Gertrude Stein for Children" (Sept., 1939), "Helen Sewell, 1896–1956, The Development of a Great Illustrator" (Oct., 1957), "Margaret Wise Brown, 'Laureate of the Nursery'" (June, 1958), "Rachel's Gifts" (July, 1942), "Tribute to an Artist-Wanderer" (Oct., 1950).

Library Journal (published by the R. R. Bowker Co.) for "Dorothy Lathrop: Artist and Author," reprinted from *Library Journal,* June 15, 1938, Copyright 1938 by R. R. Bowker Co.; and for "The Children's Librarian," reprinted from *Library Journal,* October 15, 1950, Copyright 1950 by R. R. Bowker Co.

National Council of Teachers of English for "A Tribute to Margery Bianco," reprinted from *The Elementary English Review,* June, 1935.

The New York Times Company for "The Art of Illustrating Books for the Younger Readers," reprinted from *The New York Times Book Review,* Nov. 10, 1940.

W. C. C. Publishing Company, Inc., for "From Dr. Dolittle to Superman" and "Imagination's Other Place" (a review), reprinted from *New York Herald Tribune Book Review* Sept. 25, 1949, and Nov. 13, 1955, respectively.

For

Elizabeth Coatsworth Beston
with loving gratitude for
the special friendship that has
brightened every year since
college

Contents

OF CHILDREN AND BOOKS

OF TIMES AND TRENDS

Louise Seaman Bechtel

A tenth-anniversary celebration of the establishment of Macmillan's "First Children's Department in Book Publishing" was observed in the August, 1928, issue of *The Horn Book Magazine*. Here the editor stated:

> In the year 1919 two important and far-reaching events occurred in the publishing of books for young people: — (1) The Macmillan Company created a separate children's department; and (2) the President of that firm, Mr. George P. Brett, one of the ablest and wisest men in the publishing profession, selected the peculiarly right young *woman* as head of the new department.

That young woman was Louise Seaman (later to be Mrs. Edwin DeTurck Bechtel) who was appointed to the department in 1919, after a year in other departments of Macmillan. She had graduated from Vassar and spent three years teaching in a private school in New Haven.

These magazine pages summed up that ten years of publishing:

No amateur at the business of publishing could present such a list (as that of the tenth year). No average person could ever bring together these books. Miss Seaman could not have done it in her early years. . . . We have said that this tenth year of Miss Seaman's publishing is richer than her early years. But the output of her early years was so different from the regulation publishing that it was notable and noticeable to other publishers as it was to booksellers and librarians. . . .

Four years later Doubleday, Page & Co. followed the Macmillan example and since that time four other New York publishing houses and one Boston house have created children's departments with properly qualified women at their head.

(Note: these houses were E. P. Dutton & Company; Longmans, Green; Harper & Brothers; Frederick A. Stokes; and Little, Brown & Company.)

Proof of the quality of this publishing is to be seen in those early Macmillan Children's Book Catalogs—the selection of books to be published and the tailoring of the whole to make a list in tune with basic principles. The creator of the catalogs, who found she must face the challenge of designing her own books, reveals here also a graphic skill.

The first catalog in 1920 listed some 250 titles, about half of them from England, about half produced at Macmillan by earlier editors. The catalog grew to eighty-eight pages, with color illustrations, photographs of authors, and little essays and quotations. Pages from the 1928 Fall Announcement Catalog were reproduced in *The Horn Book*. Prominently promoted were the Macmillan Children's Classics and the equally attractive Little Library volumes of "lesser classics." Alongside George Macdonald's charming *The Light Princess* here were such new titles as Rachel Field's *Little Dog Toby* and Elizabeth Coatsworth's *The Cat and the Captain* (both of these were story-hour favorites when told by John Cronan at the Boston Public Library). Also on early lists were the striking editions of Mme. d'Aulnoy's *The White Cat* with Elizabeth Mac-

Kinstry's illustrations and the "Big Pinocchio" (as the children always called it) which was printed in Italy—the new English translation carefully fitted among the many pictures. It was one of the dozen or so books Miss Seaman had printed in Europe.

Eunice Blake, Louise Seaman's assistant 1927–1932 (later to become head of her own department for children's books at the Oxford University Press in New York and then at Lippincott's), has, like others, pointed out that Louise Seaman was ahead of her time. This was to be seen in her recognition of developments affecting children, her awareness that changes of taste develop around the classics. In "A Rightful Heritage" and "Thinking About Children's Classics" she expressed these deep concerns in pieces written nearly three decades apart.

Louise Seaman was not only a "first" here at Macmillan's— forming new methods, learning new techniques—but, as *The Horn Book* tribute pointed out, she was an exception in many special ways. Pondering the question of what made this editor exceptional —what elements of background, circumstance, or personality contributed to the making of this career—one can find answers in the papers included here, for they reveal the dynamic intellect and energy she brought to her work and unique intensities of interest that directed it.

Her experience of teaching young children in an atmosphere of progressive thinking and experiment led to a continuing deep interest in the child and in progressive experimental education. This interest was related to an emphasis on the role of trade books, including many kinds of nonfiction, in the classroom. In many of her writings she stressed the importance of the informational book. Such books she herself published and in some notable instances she was responsible for a teacher's submission of a manuscript including the histories by Gertrude Hartman, the plays from the Shady Hill School in Cambridge, *Buried Cities* from the

A READING LIST OF FAIRY TALES

Such famous books as these need no defense in a modern world. There will always be parents, aunts and uncles, boys and girls, who enjoy together the humor and magic, the human understanding, the superb prose style of such writers as George MacDonald, Lewis Carroll, Hans Christian Andersen, James Stephens and William Bowen.

ENGLISH FAIRY TALES. Ed. by F. A. Steele. Ill. by Arthur Rackham. The Children's Classics. $1.75. (Ages 6-8).

HOUSEHOLD TALES from the Brothers Grimm. Ed. by Lucy Crane. Ill. by Walter Crane. The Children's Classics. $1.75. (Ages 6-8).

THE GOOSE GIRL and Other Stories from Grimm. Ill. by Einar Nerman. The Little Library. $1.00. (Ages 6-8).

THUMBELINA. By H. C. Andersen. Ill. by Einar Nerman. The Little Library. $1.00. (Ages 6-8).

THE FAIRY BOOK. Ed. by Mrs. Craik. (D. M. Mulock.) Ill. by Warwick Goble. $2.50. (Ages 6-8).

SALLY GABBLE AND THE FAIRIES. By Miriam C. Potter. Ill. by Helen Sewell. The Little Library. $1.00. (Ages 6-8).

THE PETER PAN PICTURE BOOK. Ed. by Daniel O'Connor. Ill. by Alice Woodward. The Little Library. $1.00. (Ages 6-8). (*See Peter Pan, index, for various editions of this title.*)

THE ADVENTURES OF A BROWNIE. By Mrs. Craik. Ill. by Mary Seaman. The Little Library. $1.00. (Ages 6-8).

THE LITTLE LAME PRINCE. By Mrs. Craik. With the old illustrations. The Little Library. $1.00. (Ages 6-8).

THE LIGHT PRINCESS. By George MacDonald. Ill. by Dorothy Lathrop. The Little Library. $1.00. (Ages 6-8).

THE KINGDOM OF THE WINDING ROAD. By Cornelia Meigs. $1.75. (Ages 6-10).

THE ENCHANTED FOREST. By William Bowen. Ill. by Maude and Miska Petersham. $2.00. (Ages 6-10).

THE KING OF THE GOLDEN RIVER. By John Ruskin. Ill. by Mary Seaman. The Little Library. $1.00. (Ages 8-10).

THE ROSE AND THE RING. By William M. Thackeray. Ill. by the author. Duplicate of English miniature edition. The Little Library. $1.00. (Ages 8-10).

MOPSA THE FAIRY. By Jean Ingelow. Ill. by Dugald Walker. The Children's Classics. $1.75. (Ages 8-10).

THE PRINCESS AND THE GOBLIN. By George MacDonald. Ill. by Francis Bedford. The Children's Classics. $1.75. (Ages 8-10).

THE PRINCESS AND CURDIE. By George MacDonald. Ill. by Dorothy Lathrop. The Children's Classics. $1.75. (Ages 8-10).

AT THE BACK OF THE NORTH WIND. By George MacDonald. Ill. by Francis Bedford. The Children's Classics. $1.75. (Ages 8-10).

WATER BABIES. By Charles Kingsley. Ill. by Warwick Goble. $2.50. (Ages 8-10).

GRANNY'S WONDERFUL CHAIR. By Francis Browne. Ill. by Emma Brock. The Children's Classics. $1.75. (Ages 8-10).

From Field: ELIZA AND THE ELVES

From the 1929 catalog of Macmillan Books for Boys and Girls

Frances Parker School in Chicago, and *The Goldsmith of Florence* from storytelling at the Cleveland Museum of Art. Often in articles she cited the contribution made by Lucy Sprague Mitchell, calling attention to the fresh insight provided in the latter's first two *Here and Now* storybooks and defending her in the controversy raging over "milk bottles" versus "Grimm" for the pre-school child. She published two "story-geographies" by Mrs. Mitchell, *North America* and *Manhattan Now and Long Ago*.

Of her teaching in New Haven, Eunice Blake recalls that she had been "an adoring pupil in the seventh grade." And, she adds, "I think that she was a born teacher. She brought enthusiasm and originality to her teaching as she did to her editing. She always expected more of her authors and her employees than they thought they had in them, and usually she brought out abilities that one did not know one had."

Louise Seaman's attention was often focused on what makes reading an experience for children. She never forgot the child: she knew their interests, knew that they find excitement both in fantasy and in machines and the everyday world around them. She stressed that "there is poetry in jet planes and space ships and atoms" and again that books on machines can be beautiful as well as informative. She was, irresistibly, what the library calls a "readers' adviser." Her eagerness to bring book and reader together is reflected in the list making for her publishing catalogs and in later lists. While on the *New York Herald Tribune Book Review* (1949–1957) she produced numerous selective lists which the *Book Review* sent out in response to inquiries. There were lists of nature books, books on religion, and a general list entitled "Too Good to Miss." She was a strong advocate of reading aloud to children and sharing books in the home, and in her book reviews and speeches almost inevitably promoted these, ever urging parents to expose their children to the best. In 1927 she wrote in the

Atlantic Monthly her article "The Giant in Children" (see page 141) in which she insisted that there should be no "childish" books—"nothing which will have to be outgrown."

Macmillan's children's lists 1919–1934 reflect another of Louise Seaman's individual intensities of interest—in the graphics of book production. Her mother and sister were artists and she herself naturally achieved distinction in dealing with the graphic arts. She was often sought to express herself on book art and design: by *The New York Times* in 1926 to write on new illustrators of children's books, by her own *New York Herald Tribune* to review adult books about such artists as Arthur Rackham and Beatrix Potter, and by the American Institute of Graphic Arts to serve on their juries. She served first in 1933, again for the 1937–1941 show of "Five Years of Children's Books" (when Anne Carroll Moore and Boris Artzybasheff also served, and she spoke for the jury), for the 1942–1943 children's book show when she wrote "The Jury Reports," and for the 1955–1957 show, which she also reported. Her grasp of graphics was cultivated in working with her artists and it was put to an exacting test in these collaborations with other jurors.

That she wrote with a sure critical sense about illustration and book design was pointed out by Anne Carroll Moore in her "Three Owls' Notebook" (in *The Horn Book Magazine,* December, 1957):

> Louise Seaman Bechtel has written of Helen Sewell with such clarity, sensitivity to personality, and acuteness of observation of her work. . . . She has illuminated her study of the artist's growth and development by her selection and arrangement of reproductions from the books she has illustrated. . . . From the frontispiece chosen from *A First Bible* to the endpiece from *The Dream Keeper,* the arrangement of the illustrations is in such harmony with what Mrs. Bechtel is telling the reader as to affirm its truth to the life and the work of an artist who was her friend. To those who knew Helen Sewell she lives in this revealing tribute.

The fifteen years of Louise Seaman's publishing reveal how much she contributed to the establishing of standards. Imbedded in her own tribute to May Massee, who at Doubleday in 1922 became the second editor to head a children's book publishing department, is her view of publishing children's books (*The Horn Book,* July, 1936):

> I don't think other book editors can understand the way a children's book-maker feels about her list. Each title means so much more than just an editor's O.K. on a manuscript. More frequently than on other lists, it means the actual conception of the book by the editor and the difficult pursuit of the right author and artist. Always it means detailed supervision of book-making, knowledge of types, often the actual pasting up of pictures and pages, often not only literary editing of the manuscript but a struggle over each stage of the proof-reading, and certainly supervision of all one's own proofs. How often it means a happy friendship with author and artist, and thereby a deep concern for their welfare. All this demands an expense of time, emotion, money, beyond any hours or salary or common sense. It could not be otherwise, and it's fun, because it is indeed "living" books.
> . . . It is no "ivory tower" sort of job. It means thinking of new kinds of promotion, seeking ideas for it from others, being alert to the special opportunities of each book, encouraging each selling experience that develops in the field. It demands an imaginative understanding of all kinds of people behind desks and counters far away, and either seeing them personally or writing material they will be moved by.

The "happy friendship" and "deep concern" in relationships with her authors is revealed in testimony from them. Elizabeth Coatsworth, her classmate at Vassar and longest of all a friend, has written of what she calls a "heady" experience:

> I think always of work with her as challenging. She herself was meeting a great challenge in her own work as the head of a department for children's books when there were few precedents, and all through her years at Macmillan she was pioneering new

forms and new methods. I remember how impressed I was when she began to discuss her books over the radio, which no one had up to that time done.

At all events, just as she was challenged daily by her work, so she challenged her writers. . . . We were young and had been friends long before we were editor-and-author. We worked together without fear or favor and I hope Louise enjoyed the association as much as I did. I can imagine no better training for a young author than she gave me.

Cornelia Meigs, another of her authors, was one who found those early days a "landmark in my writing life. They were of unalloyed pleasure and advantage to me. She taught me much from the very beginning for she brought to her work not only a sparkling personality, but a dynamic force of enterprise and interpretation that were immediately effective. . . . She had a full amount of firm common sense on which to base her decisions so that one did not question her authority or her ideas."

The selection of Louise Seaman Bechtel's writings compiled here—both lectures and articles—comes chiefly out of her two careers: from the publishing years and from the later period, 1949–1956, when she served as Editor, "Books for Boys and Girls" for the *New York Herald Tribune Book Review*. Others come from the also active years between.

Those in-between years were not spent in retirement. Living in Mt. Kisco, she served (1935–1962) as a trustee of the local library in Bedford and from her own home here, up to World War II (when the automobile transport of children was limited) lent books to local boys and girls, from her great children's literature collection in "Mr. Winkle's Room." This provided the valuable direct contact with children that she so much enjoyed and that so enhanced her criticism. During this period also she did much traveling and speaking, which included in the summers of 1940 and 1941 the teaching of writing for children at the Rocky Mountains Writers' Conference.

Her own books for children, *Brave Bantam*, illustrated by Helen Sewell, and *Mr. Peck's Pets*, illustrated by Berta and Elmer Hader, appeared in 1946 and 1947. She obviously enjoyed writing these, but she has said that she feels her best "books" are the bound copies of her Macmillan Children's Book Catalog. However, both of these "fond and entirely true records" which came out of her life in the country were given a certain praise by the reviewers. Alice M. Jordan considered *Brave Bantam* to be "A story for little children in which the author has something to say and says it with humor and imagination." Of the second book, this *Horn Book* reviewer wrote, "A good book to read aloud to older children and adults who will appreciate the humor of the situation."

Louise Seaman Bechtel's contribution as a critic-reviewer as well as, of course, publisher, was due to highly developed critical faculties, which were quickly recognized. That she covered the entire output of children's books singly (as was done by her successor, Mrs. Margaret Sherwood Libby, but is almost impossible today) gave special validity to her selection and forcefulness to the making of comparative judgments.

She wrote about books not only for the *New York Herald Tribune* and *The Horn Book Magazine*, but also for the *Saturday Review, The New York Times*, and *The Bookman*, and was one of a committee of three concerned with children's books for the United States Quarterly Book List published by the Library of Congress. In the last-named, from September 1948 through September 1954, except for a few issues, she was listed as a contributor in the March and September issues, which covered children's literature. This highly selective medium of unsigned reviews was designed "to help persons wishing to keep abreast of current contributions of the United States." (On the Advisory Committee for this quarterly appeared the names of Frederic G. Melcher and Frances Clarke Sayers.) From her balanced selecting, one is aware again of breadth of interests, good taste, and acumen in comment.

Nonfiction as well as fiction and folklore were included and picture books of enduring value.

Through her speaking and her library visits as well as through the gifts of good publishing, she became a great friend of librarians and they of her. She considered the children's librarian in several senses the great "defender of books" (see her Bowker Lecture—until now the only such lecture devoted to children's books). In her years as a publisher she found Alice M. Jordan, head of work with children at the Boston Public Library, "sane, humorous, learned, with a remarkable knowledge of the old children's books, with plenty of wise watching of a wide range of children—no wonder the publishers paid attention to her judgments" (*The Horn Book*, February, 1941). To her she often sent manuscripts to be criticized.

She was much at home in Boston, where she served *The Horn Book Magazine* as an Associate Editor from the October, 1939, issue until December, 1957, when her title on the masthead was changed to "Director." For its pages she wrote many pieces. From my own association with the magazine, when I joined the reviewing staff as co-editor with Jennie D. Lindquist of the bi-monthly Booklist, it was my own good fortune to become acquainted with Mrs. Bechtel and to comprehend her vitality in the reviewing picture. Here in *The Horn Book* family were Louise Seaman Bechtel, Bertha Mahony Miller, Alice M. Jordan, and Anne Carroll Moore—all vitally interested in the issues and controversies within the children's book world. It was stimulating, and salutary, for me as a novice reviewer, to see that differences in opinion were inevitable, and good. We felt Mrs. Bechtel's sound, vigorous approach to books and enjoyed it.

During the first half of the 1950's Mrs. Bechtel regularly surveyed children's books for children's librarians of New England— in the lecture hall of the Boston Public Library where Alice M.

Jordan, our admired teacher of courses in children's literature and library work for children, had earlier become famous for her annual summaries. We were held spellbound by Mrs. Bechtel's gaiety, forcefulness, and contagious conviction of importance in the books she singled out for attention.

A chronology of her speaking and writing schedules shows that during all her active years she was sought frequently as speaker for women's clubs, teachers' associations, P.T.A.'s, booksellers, and radio. In her publishing years she was the "story lady" in a weekly series on Newark's Station WJZ, to discuss the exciting books she was producing. This was the first time a radio station had featured a program devoted to children's books. She also addressed writing classes, library schools, and library associations. On bookselling trips in the early twenties, she went from coast to coast, before any other woman did this sort of selling.

The measure of her ability to interpret is seen in the number of anniversary occasions when she was the one chosen to sum up the significances and the trends of an era (see "Books on the Ladder of Time," pages 239–255). It was she whom the children's librarians in their national association asked to address them in 1950 on their fiftieth anniversary, a speech in which was heard a salute to the important relationship between children's librarians and good publishing for children.

For the Bowker Lecture Series, endowed by Frederic G. Melcher and given annually at the New York Public Library on some phase of publishing, she was the editor invited to talk in 1946 about the publishing of children's books—a lecture subsequently republished a number of times, as J. Donald Adams in *The New York Times* (February 10, 1946) had heartily recommended, for the benefit of all who work with children's books.

On September 25, 1949, one found in the *New York Herald Tribune Weekly Book Review* for its twenty-fifth anniversary her article "From Dr. Dolittle to Superman: New Trends in Children's Books." Here again she summarized many "beginnings" that were significant in the children's book world in general after World War I.

In 1960 the New York Public Library chose her to be their speaker on the occasion of the fiftieth anniversary of their annual exhibition of "Children's Books Suggested as Holiday Gifts."

Four decades are viewed in the papers gathered here. Brought together on the fiftieth anniversary of Macmillan's Children's Book Department, these writings highlight the movements, advances, the growth in American publishing for children in general during those years that followed its pioneer venture. They reveal the career of the one editor-critic who in developing the first juvenile department worked with some of the "greats" in American children's literature of the twentieth century. To her then we owe a slice of literary history.

VIRGINIA HAVILAND

Of the Making of Books

Finding New Books
for Boys and Girls

From School and Home, *January, 1933.*

What happens to manuscripts that come to a publishing house? What about those intended specially for children? How does the publisher decide which to publish? Does he (or she) have other ways of getting books except by mail?

Your editor asked me to answer these questions. Trying to do so has caused me such soul-stirring and conscience-searching that I could hardly write at all. How can one explain the *why* of over six hundred books? For that is the number I have published so far, and each has its own story.

Sometimes half, sometimes all of my days are spent looking at manuscripts, talking to people who have written manuscripts, giving contributions back to authors or artists, or discussing ideas that might be books. Frankly, I wish that this pressure were not so great, and that more time were free to go out to find material; to roam about in fine schools and libraries, in many different kinds of places, to watch what children like, and hear what they need. That is the tantalizing part of publishing—that its detail ties one to a desk, and its essence demands continuous contact with life. Yet if one of those visitors or those manuscripts is neglected, sometimes a chance at something very fine is gone forever.

What happens to the book proposition, picture book, typed text, or outlined idea, either mailed to, or left with, a publisher? It is recorded in two places—on a general house list, and in the department in which it has special consideration. It is read or looked at by at least two people—the department reader and the head of the department. It then goes on a formal list where recommendation is made for its having an "outside" paid reading, or being declined, or being returned with suggestions. Perhaps it is being returned for the third or fourth time to that list, and has a recommendation for a contract. Each list is taken up and discussed officially with the president or the board of the house. In some cases formal "decline" notes are sent, in some, detailed letters with suggestions. In my department, we handle between fifty and one hundred manuscripts a week, varying with the time of year. The depression has greatly increased the number we receive.

The reading within the house is of course done very fast, but it cannot be done carelessly. It doesn't take long to discover that some things are very bad, or to decide that some are not "our kind" of publication, or others are duplicates of something we have already done. It does take long to decide that something is good and worth further thought.

Outside "readers" include experienced people in libraries and schools, writers and reviewers, a few outstanding good booksellers, a few parents, people at Boy Scout and Girl Scout Headquarters, etc. They are paid according to the length of the manuscript, and also in accordance with their own standing. To persuade a busy and famous history professor at a university to go over a manuscript is more expensive than to get an opinion from an impecunious reviewer, though the opinions may be of equal value. Sometimes as many as five opinions are taken before we settle what we shall do with a single proposition.

Of course, what dominate the actions taken are the attitude of the publishing house, the opinions of the individual editor, the amount being invested in children's books at the time, and the list as a whole, its proportion and the trend of its development.

So, suppose I tell you some personal stories of manuscripts that did become books. Let us take three that have won the Newbery Medal as the best contributions to literature for children of their year.

When Rachel Field and Dorothy Lathrop walked down Eighth Street and saw *Hitty* in the window of an antique shop, they knew they wanted to own her. They told me about this extraordinary doll, and I, very obtuse, said, "How interesting!" Later they bought her and started working on the book in secret. At last they had an outline, a chapter, a drawing, and I was allowed to look and listen. "This book," said Miss Field, "is going to win the Newbery Medal on its text, and be one of the fifty best made books of the year, for its pictures and make-up!" She may have been joking, but both prophecies came true. Sealed bids were taken from several publishers, and fortunately we *won*. Every detail of the book was settled by the indefatigable author and artist, who even went to the Metropolitan Museum to choose a calico pattern of the right period for the binding and jacket designs. Here was a book where the publisher had little to do, and deserves very little credit for perspicacity! *Hitty* has proved both a best seller and a "classic" that everyone approves and loves. It is just slightly to my credit that I knew these already outstanding bookmakers and stood in their good graces.

Mr. Kelly's book *The Trumpeter of Krakow* came in the mail, with a letter from the author. It had already been turned down by at least one other house. He was not sure whether it was a novel

FAMOUS DOLL STORIES

THE LITTLE WOODEN DOLL. By Margery Bianco. Ill. by Pamela Bianco. The Little Library. $1.00. (Ages 4-8).

SUSANNA'S AUCTION. The story of a little French girl and her doll Josephine. Ill. by Boutet de Monvel. The Little Library. $1.00. (Ages 4-8).

THE MEMOIRS OF A LONDON DOLL. Being the famous English story of Maria Poppet by "Mrs. Fairstar," (R. H. Horne). Introd. by Clara W. Hunt. Ill. by Emma Brock. The Little Library. $1.00. (Ages 8-12).

HITTY: Her First Hundred Years. By Rachel Field. Ill. by Dorothy Lathrop. $2.50. (Ages 8-12).

PINOCCHIO. By Collodi. Translated by della Chiesa. Ill. by Mussino. The Italian edition. $6.00. (Ages 8-10).

PINOCCHIO. Same translation, with a selection from the Mussino pictures. The Children's Classics. $1.75. (Ages 8-12).

KASPERLE'S ADVENTURES. By Josephine Siebe. Translated by Florence Geiser. Ill. by Frank Dobias. $2.50. (Ages 8-10).

ANCIENT AND MODERN DOLLS. A picture book in which dolls tell their own stories. By Gwen White. (Imp.) $2.00. (Ages 6-8).

TOYS AT THE ZOO. By Gwen White. (Imp.) $2.00. (Ages 6-8).

PEEPS AT THE WORLD'S DOLLS. By H. W. Canning-Wright. (Imp.) $1.00. (Ages 8-12).

PINOCCHIO UNDER THE SEA. Ed. by John W. Davis. Transl. by Carol della Chiesa. $1.25. (Ages 8-10).

From HITTY, *Her First Hundred Years*

From the 1929 catalog of Macmillan Books for Boys and Girls

or a book for young people. It was discovered by my assistant, who thought it a thrilling tale. One library reader suggested certain cutting and a few changes. When it was contracted for, Mr. Kelly procured the pictures from an artist he knew in Krakow. He also procured the loan of one of the trumpets from St. Mary's tower, which blew that beautiful call from coast to coast in America and created a stirring friendship between young Americans and the city fathers across the sea.

The story of *The Cat Who Went to Heaven* is a record of a friendship. In my Vassar days, one of the most dramatic and interesting people on the campus was Elizabeth Coatsworth. When I became a publisher, our talks turned on books from a new angle, and, not only did she contribute unusual titles to my list, but gave inspiring advice and suggestions on other lines than those of her own writing. Out of our talks grew this presentation of an Oriental point of view, this unique weaving of tales of the Buddha into a tender, moving, human story appealing to young and old.

There are so many other books I'd like to tell you about. I remember the day when Mr. Bronson walked into the office with a small glass bottle containing the one extant specimen of a "fish with hands," from the Sargasso Sea. From that visit grew *Fingerfins* and, later, *Paddlewings* and *Pollwiggle,* his new tadpole story. He came with a letter to someone in the firm who sent him down to me—it was as easy as all that to discover one of our most interesting artist-authors in the field of natural history.

Out of my contact with schools has come a procession of unusual titles of which I am very proud: from the Shady Hill School, Cambridge, Massachusetts, *The Shady Hill Play Book,* edited by the head of that school, Katharine Taylor, also *Building a Model Railroad* by Albert Coolidge. From the Lincoln School, New York, *Working with Electricity* by Katharine Keelor and *City Stories,* a first book of writing and art by the children themselves. From the

Francis Parker School, Chicago, *Buried Cities* by Jennie Hall. From Teachers College and Horace Mann, New York, *The Little Wooden Farmer* and *The Blue Teapot* and other books by Alice Dalgliesh. Recommended by the curriculum planner in Los Angeles public schools, *The Merry Ballads of Robin Hood* by Dietrich and Walsh. From the former editor of Progressive Education Magazine, *The World We Live In* and *These United States* by Gertrude Hartman. From Lucy Sprague Mitchell, of City and Country School, and her own training school, *North America,* the outstanding storybook geography.

Some very unusual books have come from museums. The Robinsons' *Beasts of the Tar Pits* originated in work at the Los Angeles Museum. Gibson's *The Goldsmith of Florence* grew out of storytelling at the Cleveland Museum of Art. So did Alice Howard's *Sokar and the Crocodile* and *Ching Li and the Dragons.*

More books than you can guess come from cooperation with the splendid group of children's librarians who, through their enthusiasm and pioneer work, laid the foundations for this whole movement of the *new* children's bookmaking. Since I am writing for school people, I have emphasized their books, but I must mention one of my first best sellers, *The Memoirs of a London Doll,* brought to me by Miss Hunt of Brooklyn, a precious little old first edition which she found in the dust of the old library when they moved. She thought children of today would like it—and she was right.

So, you see, there are some books one searches and asks for, there are others that "fall in one's lap"; some come in the mail, others develop in conversation. And all the while one has in mind real children, the fascinating, varied, irritating, nonclassified lot of them. Some love derricks and machines; some are loyal to fantasy and fairy tales; some want romance; and all need variety in their reading. One can draw up schedules of what should be published; the subjects, the ages, the new approaches on old themes that

BOOKS FOR BOYS AND GIRLS AGES SIX TO EIGHT
FICTION

From The Memoirs of a London Doll

THE MEMOIRS OF A LONDON DOLL

Written by Herself. Edited by Mrs. Fairstar. Introduction by Clara W. Hunt. Ill. by Emma Brock. *Dec. cloth, 16mo, $1.25.*

This delightful little book was first published in Boston in 1852. A copy was discovered by Miss Hunt during a "moving time" at the Brooklyn Public Library. She has written a charming introduction telling of her discovery and suggesting to boys and girls some of the quaint and interesting things in this delightful story of Maria Poppet, the wooden doll made by a famous London doll maker about one hundred years ago. The book is of historical importance, for it gives a very vivid picture of life in London in the early 19th Century.

THE MAGIC FOREST

By Stewart Edward White. Author of The Blazed Trail, etc. *Ill., 12mo, cloth, $1.25.*

Johnny, five years old, walked off a Pullman into the heart of the Canadian woods. The Indians took care of him and taught him many things all little boys want to know about Indian life, before they took him back to his parents. Mr. White's power of describing woodland life is all in this book, and yet it remains truly for children. Especially good to read to little boys.

GREY WOLF, Indian Mystery Stories of Coyote, Animals and Men

By Bernard Sexton. Ill. by Gwenyth Waugh. *Dec. boards, 12mo, $1.50.*

As Grey Wolf, Bernard Sexton is well known to boys and girls. Many have read his stories in papers and magazines, and many even luckier ones have heard him tell his tales by camp fires on far hillsides. This group of his favorite stories from old Indian legends has the strangeness of their very ancient folklore, also their simplicity and intimacy with nature.

From Grey Wolf

CARROTS, JUST A LITTLE BOY

By Mrs. Molesworth. Ill. by Walter Crane. *Cloth, 12mo, $1.00.*

Long ago in England little folks began to love the quaint, simple, delightful tales of Mrs. Molesworth. They have stood the test of time and of the affections of children in many lands. Carrots is a special favorite with little children. And their mothers love to read aloud the story of this very small boy and the merry little sister who took care of him. The pictures are from those of Walter Crane for the original edition.

THE CUCKOO CLOCK

By Mrs. Molesworth. Ill. by Walter Crane. *Cloth, 12mo, $1.00.*

Mrs. Molesworth's once-upon-a-time stories, with their old-fashioned flavor, are as popular to-day as they were in 1877. Partly it is because children always recognize the true fairy lover. But the chief reason is the reality of her little boys and girls. Little Griselda, who came to live with her two aunts in the house that held the cuckoo clock, is like any lonely little girl of any time or place. How the cuckoo cheered her, and how he found a real new friend for her, makes a story for little girls.

From the 1922 catalog of Macmillan Books for Boys and Girls

ought to be handled as the Soviets have done. But, like them, one finds it hard to keep to such schedules; the right author and artist do not turn up at the right moment. Meantime, there is the occasional luck of a great writer doing a fine book which no one could order, or ever guess at, such as John Masefield's *The Midnight Folk,* or Padraic Colum's *The Forge in the Forest,* or Cornelia Meigs's *The Willow Whistle.*

Need I say that among all these books, a publisher keeps to standards which should be obvious to one who knows his list? A *good book*—so many descriptions of it, so many opinions of it! Well, the list must speak for itself—I simply cannot tell you here exactly what I think is a good book!

When a Publisher Makes a Catalog

*From a speech given at the American Library
Association Convention, New Haven, 1929.*

To the true bookworm the arrival of a book catalog is an exciting event. He sniffs its very ink smell eagerly, and his eye travels voraciously up and down the pages.

But a book record for professional use is one thing, and a catalog for a wide public is another. The public of a children's book catalog is peculiarly difficult in its great girth: it includes the trained children's book librarian who has, before she opens it, prejudices, sympathies, critical opinions. Next, the teacher, who may know very little of modern children's book values, but needs them for definite purposes. Next, the bookshop person, who, except in a few rare cases, knows the books only commercially as merchandise. Next, the parent, who reluctantly tries to perform a duty, or eagerly approaches it from a very personal point of view. Last, the poor child himself, who occasionally gets a look, and who knows, quickest of the lot, just what he wants.

It is a hard thing for the publisher to make all these appeals at one time. In most publishing houses, there are regular official spring and fall lists in which all books of all departments must be included. There are also trade order lists. Generally, in addition to these, which have very wide distribution, weekly bulletins go out, and also special cards to libraries. So the children's catalog has the advantage or disadvantage of repeating announcements already made. It has a chance to do something very different. On the other hand, it may be the only catalog in the field to reach some people. So it needs to follow the usual rules for any catalog. Boring though they may be, let us go over them. Surprisingly enough, I have found trade catalogs which do not observe them.

1. Arrangement clear, type not only artistic but clear and simple in its general effect.

2. Classification following one of several useful points, subject, age, author. Index and price list essential.

3. Shape, pleasant to handle, whether it is large or small.

4. Contents should indicate whether it is a complete or partial list of the firm's publications; if partial, exactly where a complete list is to be procured.

5. Information about each book complete, including its size, kind of binding, illustrations in color or black and white. Description should include age appeal, either by years or by careful analysis, as well as real information as to the contents. A commendation or review is not sufficient unless it also makes these clear.

6. Since pictures are an essential part of these books, sample pictures should be included. These samples cannot be too small, or they are unfair to the artist and misleading as to the appeal of the book.

To fulfill these points for a list of any size means a booklet of relatively large cost per copy. There is a wide variety in publishers' uses of a children's catalog. One publisher tells me hers is confined to libraries and bookshops. Another, that hers is aimed entirely at special mail order. Another, that the salesmen think it is a good thing so they make it, but that the firm really believes it is wasted except as general publicity. Naturally, we wish very much that we knew just what effect our catalogs have, and just how many sales they produce. It is very hard to find out.

My own experience in catalog-making has been that of continuous experiment. Catalog Number 1 from my department was a tall, thin list, to fit into a salesman's pocket, also into big letter envelope mailing. With the greatest glee in the world I selected quotations to head each group of books. Here was my inheritance of books from England and from America as well.

Over the list of school and college stories, I quoted John Dewey: "Growing is not something which is completed in odd moments; it is a continuous leading into the future."

Over our various editions of Alice, I put some lines by E. V. Lucas.

> The Grownup and the Prillilgirl
> Were walking hand in hand;
> They were as pleased as Punch to be
> Alone in Wonderland:
> "If there were other books like his,"
> They said, "It would be grand."

Over the books on exercising, games, camping, etc., one of my great favorites from Hilaire Belloc, M.D.

> The vulture eats between his meals,
> And that's the reason why
> He very, very rarely feels
> As well as you or I.
> His eye is dull, his head is bald,
> His neck is growing thinner
> Oh, what a lesson for us all,
> To only eat at dinner.

There were pictures from many books, with rather long captions, that led you from the picture really into the story, such as the one for Cornelia Meigs's *The Pool of Stars:* "It was by this pool that the owner of the ruined house told Betsey and David tales of bygone days, so that they started planning how they might help her. Here, they conquered some of the hardest tasks in their college entrance work. But at more exciting moments, the pool was the center of a mystery. When the most important part of a great invention disappeared, David—read and find out how the mystery was solved."

The whole was bound together by frequent use of those very characterful and beautiful initials done by Rackham for his King Arthur. And I was terribly awfully proud of it. All these 250 titles were published before my time.

In the years following, it changed in many ways. First, there came the wave of demand for aging books, which I think was much influenced by a bright salesman's invention for use of The Ladder Library. That year the "ladder" man motto, "Let your children climb through books," increased our business noticeably and he made a catalog that exactly fitted the steps of his ladder.

The next year the manager of the department made her own catalog again, and kept the age listings for the general list at the back, but presented the new books without such hard and fast age groupings on the first pages.

Then came a catalog in which I planned a separate section for photographs of outstanding authors and artists and brief biographies.

In 1929, a departure was made in the form of Reading Lists. Remembering a very distinguished speech at an A.L.A. convention in which Miss Elizabeth Wisdom of Brooklyn described "reading sequences" in children's various interests, I spent the most enormous amount of time creating such reading sequences out of my own list. To lead from Mother Goose up to Masefield's *Salt-Water Poems and Ballads,* from Grimm and Andersen up to James Stephens, from *Nanette of the Wooden Shoes* and *Little Tonino* up to Shackleton and Stefansson, from Katharine Adams and Augusta Seaman to Cranford and Jane Austen—all this seemed to me valuable, and a rather different sort of list-making.

However, the 1929 catalog did not seem to turn the world upside down, even though its color work was printed by the Jean Berte watercolor process, and even though it included these invaluable lists.

So, in 1930 I returned to the personality of the authors and artists as a key note. Several librarians wrote that they much preferred this arrangement. In any case, as usual, after cutting every bookshop request in half, and trying to save enough for library school classes, we still did not have enough for the demand, which has been true every year from the beginning. What people do with catalogs may be a question. The fact that they want them, we cannot doubt.

Also in 1930, our school book and children's book departments combined in making a complete graded supplementary list for schools which has proved tremendously useful in the school field and which we intend to keep in print. For this list I wrote entirely different new descriptions of all my titles included, judging as best I could the rather different needs of that field.

With the increased interest in books of travel, and the demand definitely expressed for lists of books on different countries, I made this spring a reading list called Travel Books, binding it up in some fortunately leftover gay covers of our 1930 Reading Lists. Twenty-four countries are represented, with over two hundred books. I was very lucky to find, for a tail-piece to my Travel Books, a verse written by Elizabeth Coatsworth, and used in her book *The Sun's Diary*.

> I lie in my bed in this walled room
> And at my head is the north pole,
> And my two feet stretch toward the tropics.
> To my left are the old cities of Europe
> And to my right the older cities of Asia.
> Below me, with the world between us,
> Is the sun,
> And above me, the moon.

Now, for 1931, catalog Number 12 of my department, I have still another plan. Since everybody's catalog but mine is evidently finished, I don't mind telling it. I am trying to lead into the new books in a new way, by very brief conversations, which occur in large type under pictures and over book descriptions and give the whole more the feeling of feature advertising of an informal sort. These bits of book propaganda are excessively hard to write, but if they can be done well, I feel they are an approach to selling an idea of reading before you are offered title, price, and author. I hope the new type arrangement and the increased number of pictures will make it all look like a gay, informal picture book about books, rather than the usual catalog. The complete list, with rather broad age groupings, alphabetically by author, comes at the back.

There is my experience, put as briefly as possible. I should say it proved nothing, except that the adventure of variety has been a cause both of suffering and of great pleasure to me personally. I have always written my own catalogs myself, from the purely selfish reason that I enjoy doing them. I suppose this is the place to say that I have never seen any reason to put my name on a catalog—it is the books that count—I must make them speak, and my wholehearted tribute as a catalog-maker goes to the authors and artists, that extraordinary, helpful, inspiring, ingenious, nonsensical, poetical, long-suffering band who make the making of catalogs such a delight.

I really love catalogs and I read a tremendous number of them from all over the world. Among those I treasure particularly are the John Gilpin Flyers from the Vassar Bookshop, the broadsides from the New York Children's Bookshop, the glorified catalog which we may dare call *The Horn Book,* the little book lists on special subjects from the Cleveland Public Library, the occasional lists by Mrs. Palmer from Kindermart in Minneapolis, the excellent book cards of Wilhelmina Harper; well, there are too many to mention.

What is there about them that one enjoys? Sometimes a personal quality, sometimes a certain enthusiasm of style, sometimes the very concentrated definite information. Who can say? After all, a catalog is like a book, just as vaguely different for each of us in its appeal as any single book would be. Thank goodness there doesn't have to be just one great perfect catalog, that we all fall down and worship as the best to follow.

I would like to end with a very impertinent question. How do libraries present new books to boys and girls? They are evidently very glad to use such an amusing publicity stunt as Stokes's annual children's newspaper. Our big black and white posters are much in demand, so are jackets. At one time, our set of lantern slides moved about rather vigorously. Displays of foreign dolls and of originals from new books have been sent throughout New England by our Boston office. Of course, in Children's Book Week new books are shown, generally under glass. Many libraries have very effective and attractive new book lists, for which they borrow cuts from publishers. Still I feel a bit dissatisfied.

Storytelling, puppet shows, annual displays, do not seem to me half enough to cover adequately the luring of the child into what he may or ought to like, if he could find it. When a book that you think good enough to buy does not get worn out, what do you do about it? I think of the inside of a children's room just as I think of

꧁ALL the best friends of the children are giving them fine new books this year. Among their "top favorites" is Cornelia Meigs, the author who finds stories in her great-uncle's sea chests, and her great-grandfather's trunks. She loves the prairie, the pioneers, and the friendly Indians whose traditions have lasted in the Middle-West. Her books cultivate the best of the American tradition, and give young people a living feeling about the past of their own country.

The Willow Whistle

By CORNELIA MEIGS

Illustrated by E. BOYD-SMITH. *Cloth,* 8½ x 7½ *in.,* $2.00

You meet Mary Anne, and John who made her the willow whistle; you meet the old Indian who is their friend, and who takes Mary Anne to visit his tribe. There is a thrilling race between John and an Indian boy when Mary Anne and the tribe are lost; there is a grand buffalo hunt when John and his Indian pony get their first buffalo. In the second half of the book, comes the building of the schoolhouse, the first in that part of the West. The Indians misunderstand this kind of medicine, and you will be as surprised and delighted as was Mary Anne when the one person appeared who could dispel all dark imaginings of the Indians, and could also make Mary Anne and John like their first reader.

It is all written with Miss Meigs' particular charm, and her usual fidelity to place and people. How pleased we all are to have the well-loved Mr. Boyd-Smith making his pictures again, and remembering his own share in many scenes of the old West. We have printed the book in large type, and made it a companion volume in size to the popular "Wonderful Locomotive." It is good for reading aloud to seven- and eight-year-olds, good for reading alone if you are nine or ten, a tale of the opening of the West.

The Wonderful Locomotive

By CORNELIA MEIGS

Illustrated by BERTA *and* ELMER HADER. *Cloth,* 8½ x 7½ *in.,* $2.00

One of the best-loved books in America. A small nephew who liked engines, inspired this story of "No. 44," and the boy who lived near a roundhouse and knew an engineer. Thousands of boys of six to nine have thrilled when Peter first took the throttle and made the record run from New York to San Francisco. The pictures on every page show everything he did. Of course it was a dream—but even fathers and uncles have told us that it is every boy's dream. The right book for fathers and small sons to share.

OTHER BOOKS BY CORNELIA MEIGS

The Kingdom of the Winding Road
Cloth, $1.75

Miss Meigs' first book, an unusual collection of brief fairy tales about a wandering minstrel and his adventures bringing happiness to others. (*Ages* 6-10.)

Master Simon's Garden
Cloth, $1.75

Down the years in colonial New England, the plot centering in the home of Master Simon, an idealist and patriot. One of the best stories ever written, to give young people a true sense of the shaping of our country. (*Ages* 12-15.)

The New Moon
Cloth, $1.75

Story of an Irish boy, his lucky six-pence, his dog, his trip to America, and life as a pioneer and friend of the Indians. (*Ages* 10-12.)

As the Crow Flies
Cloth, $1.75

Up the Mississippi with a young lieutenant in pioneer days; an excellent adventure story. (*Ages* 12-15.)

Rain on the Roof
Cloth, $1.75

A vacation and a mystery, on the New England coast. (*Ages* 10-12.)

The Windy Hill
Cloth, $1.50

A boy and a girl, a mystery, and how some old tales helped to solve it. (*Ages* 12-15.)

The Pool of Stars
Cloth, $1.75

Another story of a girl on vacation, a boy who came strangely into a mystery plot, and some bits of history that touched their modern lives. (*Ages* 12-15.)

From the 1931 catalog of Macmillan Books for Boys and Girls

THIS is how one of your favorite authors, Cornelia Meigs, looked when she was very young. There was lots of story-telling in that family, that is where her love of stories started. All her nieces and nephews are friends and critics of her books today.

THIS is how the Indians tried to burn down the new school house out on the prairie, and how the hero of Willow Whistle fought to save it.

the inside of my catalog, as a place where somebody who didn't know he wanted something must be surprised into finding himself irresistibly persuaded that *this* is what he wants. A row of books doesn't accomplish this, any more than a list of titles. I feel that, even at the risk of dignity, a few more signs and shouts, a few more controversial questions in big type, a few more "dares" pasted up for the undoubtedly eager crowds that flock to you after three o'clock every day, will get a greater variety of books read. We can still do it much better than it ever yet has been done in catalogs, and the same kind of experiment, with even more immediate fun in the result, can still be worked with the books themselves.

"A Rightful Heritage"

From a speech given at the Pittsburgh Public Library,
Book Week, 1953.

The words of this title are a ringing challenge to all of us gathered here. We come to celebrate the famous book week which draws together readers young and old. We would like to do at least two things in our brief time together—remember and revive and decide to reread some very enjoyable books; and also bite into the edges of the questions raised by the title, such as what books live on and why, and what is a children's classic.

The title comes from Part III of *A Critical History of Children's Literature,* edited by Cornelia Meigs, written by her and three other specialists in this field. It is this period, that of 1890 to 1920, in which many of us grew up and for those books we have the most fond memories. Specialists must read all of these six hundred pages. Those who read for pleasure at least should not skip Miss Nesbitt's section, "A Rightful Heritage." Here is charming writing and real literary criticism.

Tonight we are thinking of books we do not want children to miss—of those landmarks in publishing here on exhibit. We search for a touchstone difficult to find. A heritage of culture is a complicated matter. The reading child brings to his books a personality of today. Naturally he turns most easily and quickly to things of today and to what his present world has shaped for an atmosphere of interest. His is not yet a world influenced by books and a sense of history: it is molded by today's papers, movies, TV, comics (ninety million comics sold in one month); by his parents' talk (of family economic pressure, of war, of national scandals); and, of course, by the school where so much of his waking life centers.

But even when he is very small, in picture books, music, pictures on the wall, songs sung to him and with him, other atmospheres, other aspects of the world can surround him, comfort him, amuse him. Lovely *words*, words seldom used by journalists or comic writers or writers of informational books, can enchant him. And he can find out very early in life that the world of the inner mind is a far bigger world than the tangible world about him, and that each interprets the other.

The sense of miracle, the moments of revelation, seldom are put into words by a child. Nor can he ask for the book that gives it—he must depend on a variety of books being available. He must wait for some moment in storytelling at a library, in a parent's reading aloud, or until he is roaming among books not too carefully "graded," to find his key to larger worlds. Of course, his sense of miracle may come from facts. What is more wondrous than the blade of grass? As Francis Thompson said,

> O little blade, clay caught,
> A wind, a flame, a thought—
> Inestimably naught—

Or the atom—which has greatly held our modern children's imaginings and fears? It is, however, necessary that children know the world *whole,* not just today with its atoms, not just the miracles of facts, but parts of the long procession of history and literature—the thoughts of men of the past and their best words, as well as deeds. A rightful heritage is an odd mingling of fact, romance, ideas, things, legends, heroes.

. . . .

A book which most beautifully expresses for children and grownups an essence of our English heritage is Kenneth Grahame's *The Wind in the Willows.* Mr. Grahame was a beloved figure in the London of the nineties, a tall, fair, handsome man who worked at the Bank of England. He wrote casually, for pleasure, interpreting his own childhood in books called *Dream Days* and *The Golden Age,* which were very popular in England and here. He married happily and had a son to whom he told stories that were continued in letters when Alastair went to the seashore. It took Mr. Grahame ten years to make these letters into a book. The manuscript was not too well thought of; it was different from his popular *Dream Days.* It was doubtful whether it belonged to young or old. There was much argument about the title. The author first wanted "Mr. Toad," then "The Wind in the Reeds." It came out in America in 1908 as *The Wind in the Willows,* a modest book with only a frontispiece. As it became more and more popular, it had editions with pictures by several artists: a beautiful edition with type designed by Bruce Rogers was illustrated by Arthur Rackham, his last book work. Mr. Grahame died in 1932 at the age of seventy-three; he knew well how much joy his book was giving all over the world, and it has gone on to ever larger and larger audiences.

Here a family can share laughter and tears, adventure and beauty. There is something for everyone—comfortable details of home life, "messing around in boats," longing for an automobile, heroism, a boaster brought low, the moving mystery of the great chapter called "The Piper at the Gates of Dawn." The superb prose has the variety and flexibility of one steeped in the greatest English writers, but using his proud inheritance gaily.

Toad, Ratty, Mole, Otter, Badger, are animal-people whom we know as we do people in a good novel; we understand ourselves better because we feel with them and for them.

If you start to quote, you are lost. Here's Toad expatiating on the joy of life in a caravan, and Rat telling why he loves his river in summer, and Rat and Mole looking in people's lighted windows, and the sea rat's tale of adventure, and the great fight with the Wild Wooders for Toad Hall. "O bliss! O poop-poop! O my! O my!" said Toad. And so say I. What happier Christmas could we wish every family in America, than to reread *The Wind in the Willows?*

. . . .

An interesting study could be made of the change in taste as to what are called Children's Classics. When I started publishing in the early 1920's, Macmillan had the largest number of classics of any American publisher, and most of them were imported from England. It was one of my tasks to group them into a classics series. Within ten years, there were forty-six titles in the famous Children's Classics, and thirty-two in the pocket series of minor classics called The Little Library. The classics, in one catalog of mine, were divided into groups: Folk Tales and Epics; the Bible; Fairy Tales; Stories from France, from England, from America; and Poetry.

But times change, and taste in bookmaking improves, and now, quite properly, Macmillan is revising both these famous classics series. In the twenties, we were apt to use smaller type in books expected to be read aloud; now there has to be big type, for reading aloud has gone out—it has to be right for the children to read themselves.

Every one of those classics titles brings me a vivid memory of a

THE LITTLE LIBRARY

From Memoirs of a London Doll

A series of "little classics," mostly old, some new, all distinguished, and deserving a place on the small child's very first book shelf. *Bound in durable cloth of a gay color, decorated end papers, color jacket, 16mo. Each, $1.00.*

MEMOIRS OF A LONDON DOLL

Written by Herself. Edited by Mrs. Fairstar (Richard Hengist Horne). Introduction by Clara Whitehill Hunt. Illustrated by Emma Brock. *$1.00*.

Any doll-loving little girl of six or eight will take this book with all its quaint descriptions to her heart, and will ponder its fascinating adventures and feel as if she herself had owned the poppet!— *N. Y. Evening Post Literary Review.* (Ages 6-8.)

THE LITTLE LAME PRINCE

By Dinah Marie Mulock (Mrs. Craik). Pictures from first edition, with new colored frontispiece by Raoul Barré. *$1.00*. (Ages 6-8.)

THE ROSE AND THE RING

By William Makepeace Thackeray, with his own illustrations. Sheets imported from London. *$1.00*.

> "Fairy roses, fairy rings
> Turn out sometimes troublesome things." (Ages 8-10.)

THE MAGIC FOREST

By Stewart Edward White. Many sketches of Indian things. *$1.00*.

An extraordinarily good story for young boys. The magic and charm with which Mr. White invests savage and woodland life have been given to this story and yet it remains childlike. The author calls it a "modern fairy story."—*Bull. Am. Inst. for Child Welfare.* (Ages 6-8.)

THE PETER PAN PICTURE BOOK

From the English edition approved by Sir J. M. Barrie. Four full color pictures by Alice Woodward. Various full-page line drawings; music *$1.00*. (Ages 6-8.)

CHARLIE AND HIS KITTEN TOPSY

By Helen Hill and Violet Maxwell. Illustrated by the authors. *$1.00*.

Stories of just the right length and kind to read aloud to four and six year olds, boys or girls. On rainy days it will be a great help in keeping sunshine on their faces.—*The Farmer's Wife.*

The real and imaginary adventures of a little boy in which his kitten Topsy often has a share. For very little children.—*A. L. A. Booklist.* (Ages 4-6.)

From The Rose and the Ring

From the 1923 catalog of Macmillan Books for Boys and Girls

bookmaking experience. It is hard to choose. Take Pinocchio, one that certainly has lived on. In the twenties, he was not so well known here as now, though there had been a few cut versions translated. One day, roaming in the Children's Room of the New York Public Library, I found a little gang of boys, aged anywhere from six to twelve, their heads clustered low over a book I couldn't see. I asked Miss Power what was the absorbing book. "Oh, that's our big Italian Pinocchio." "My goodness," said I, "are they reading Italian?" "Oh no, those are not Italian boys. They're just crazy about the pictures." So I waited to see it myself. I felt the way the boys did. I started negotiating with Bemporad, the Italian publishers, to print that book in Italy with an English translation. I had a new translation made by an Italian American, Carol della Chiesa. Then I had it edited by Margery Bianco, and she and I had to fit it into those four hundred pages, every one of which had one or two pictures. It went on for years, partly because interrupted by the advent of Mussolini (he stopped all children's book publishing to do propaganda in school books), and partly because Bemporad simply would not pay one of the many English in Florence to do proofreading. At last it arrived in sheets which cost us about one dollar a volume to bind. But, such were the times. We priced the book at five dollars nevertheless, and we sold three orders of it— I would say about twelve thousand copies. It was the text from that book which I put into my Children's Classics with as many of the line cuts as we could afford. To get the color, I remember taking photos of eight pages, reducing them to line, then making flat color tracings myself. I was told that Disney used the big one as his source material, but considering the results, it is hard to believe. The Disney version is, as usual, a caricature. The Italian book has Italy itself in reality, on every page.

By 1933, when I retired, many titles popular in the series in the early twenties were already declining in sales.

I would say the obvious declines were in the three George Macdonald fairy tales, in the Walter Crane edition of Grimm, in Mrs.
Molesworth's *The Cuckoo Clock* and *The Tapestry Room,* Jean
Ingelow's *Mopsa the Fairy,* Charlotte Yonge's *The Book of Golden
Deeds, The Prince and the Page,* and other fine historical tales,
Maria Edgeworth's *Simple Susan,* and *Don Quixote.* (You may be
amused to know that when I was last in Madrid, after the last
war, I found that few Spanish children read *Don Quixote,* except
in their readers. Among many handsome modern Spanish books, I
found only one indifferent "easy" edition of *Don Quixote* retold
for children.)

What is a classic, after all? It is a book so widely loved that it
lives on long in print and in people's hearts. It doesn't have to be
great literature. And what is literature? It is *all* the writing of a
given era, the good and the bad. A "literate" person simply means
one able to read. Perhaps, like Mr. Hutchins of Chicago, we of the
children's book world should help establish our standards by making
lists of *great* books.

Each publisher who puts out sets of "classics" uses what he owns
as its core. So the classics sets go on from what they own to use
what is out of copyright, and thus we get the repetition of so much
that is banal and out of date, the eternal Heidis and Black Beauties.
And because copyrights are rightly guarded, classics like *The Wind
in the Willows* or *Hitty* are not in a series or set. Children's sense
of values—and our own too—are muddled by the use of the word
"classic." For if you reread some of these ancient favorites, you will
see that for today's children they are not great books, in a *critical*
literary sense.

One development of the thirties was the increase in books of
tall-tale American folklore. Are these classics? I wouldn't know.
But they brought a refreshing new note in children's books. Paul
Bunyan with his ox and his ax, Pecos Bill with his exaggerated
western doings—they accomplished much for American children.

They were Superman heroes who fitted right into the comics world. They were really funny. They gave a sense of great spaces of our own country. They combined down-to-earth adult doings (so different from the children's doings in so many children's books) with down-to-earth, folksy language. Besides, they stimulated the imagination in new ways. *Yankee Doodle's Cousins* tells how a New England teacher used these tales as a bridge between comics and epics. It can be done! For Finn MacCool and Grettir the Strong and Odysseus are folk heroes too; they just happen to belong to *all* the world, whereas Paul and Pecos belong to us. Children need all of them. They *all* offer tales of crudity and cruelty, with some nonsense, but the Old World ones offer the nobility the American ones lack.

It is the right to that heritage of a larger world which we need to insist upon, so that the children grow up with comparative values. If, while still young, they meet writers whom they will even more greatly enjoy as adults, if they read their own language, not retellings made easy, but possibly rearranged as to paragraphs and chapters selected, put in larger type (such a job of editing for instance as Padraic Colum did for Swift's Gulliver), then they are reading toward their rightful adult heritage. The authors would include Hawthorne, Lamb, Kingsley, Dickens, Stevenson, Kipling, Blake, Christina Rossetti, Swift, W. H. Hudson, De la Mare, Masefield, Van Loon.

Whenever lists of classics, of best books, of landmarks appear, it is fascinating to think by what slim chance a child may or may not come upon such books. For there is a great tendency today to let what is most popular prevail, to let choice of books to buy depend on what children say they like best, or vote for as their favorites.

There is always that contrast between the "best" as intelligent adults see it, and the best seller. There have been the Pollyanna books, the Dotty Dimple books, the Elsie books, the Wizard of Oz books, the Tom Swift, the Bobbsey Twins, the Black Stallion books; some of the older series go mechanically on and on even though the authors are long since dead.

As against such trifles, we want children to know the wine-dark seas of Homer and the deeds and wonders of the days when gods talked with men; to enter worlds so very different from our own crowded, fearful, bristling, journalistic, factual times, that they cannot help but challenge and stretch the imagination. We want them to enter that body of classical literature which is truly everyone's heritage of imagination. For the great old stories provide images, characters, scenes, phrases, names of places which, when they are grown, will interpret much in the world around them today and in the world of books.

There are some favorite, very popular books which will make children trust your sense of humor and understanding. Books like *The Peterkin Papers, Homer Price, Rabbit Hill*, the *Rootabaga Stories, Dr. Dolittle, The Jack Tales*—these are classics of today. For those a bit older, ready for history, adventure, romance, we have illumination of America's past in books like *Hitty, Master Simon's Garden, Johnny Tremain*. For those on the doorway to adult reading, you find Van Loon's *Story of Mankind*, and that remarkable anthology of world religion, *The Tree of Life*.

Some books, rightly called landmarks, are not necessarily a rightful inheritance, however popular. Their extraordinary long life is only possibly significant of children's devotion, and I would call these perhaps sub-literature: *Tom Brown's School Days, The Dutch Twins, Heidi, Lassie Come Home, The Call of the Wild, The Secret Garden*. They do get votes, but who cares! When boys vote, the category of sports books always comes either first or second, and where are the sports books on classics lists? Girls always put romance first. Well, we have *Little Women* for that. *Little Women* is one of the most widely read classics all over the world. It is translated, and, like Alice, has dozens of editions now that it is out of copyright. Actually, it is hard to find many modern American girls over twelve who will admit to being keen on it, at least until a movie has "introduced" them to it.

A happier example of true favorites from another era is that of Tom Sawyer and Huck Finn. It is fascinating to recall that in their early life as books, they were kept from children by libraries. Such *bad* boys! But in fifty years, library attitudes have changed, and now we find sixth, seventh, and eighth grade boys and girls everywhere voting for Tom and Huck as their favorite reading. Here is a case where popularity and rare literary value meet.

One thing to remember this year is that all the new fact books and historical series books will not satisfy *bright* children. They will be bought in quantity by schools where a bright child will read two a day. They will, many of them, open the minds of both bright and slow children to many new vistas, but these openings will wait to be filled with longer, more satisfactory books.

In any case, there is no use deploring the modern child's love of facts and of history, and of taking the easiest book first. In our times, culture is spread wide and thin. It is up to us to build again, till the pyramid rises higher and imagination flowers both in the adult writer and in the children. There is a poetry in jet planes and space ships and atoms which the adult poets have not yet put into words. Mr. Sandburg put machines and skyscrapers into his Rootabaga stories, which have not yet come into their own, though published in the twenties.

One never knows just what will cause the mental awakening which means true inner growth. Those flashes of intuition are different for everyone. They can come from that prickling of the skin or shiver of delight from recognizing a real poem that belongs to you as a revelation. Or they can come from a sort of bursting of light in the mind when certain heretofore unfocused facts come into focus and you realize you are thinking for yourself.

An example of intellectual pleasure combining life and books is hard to find expressed, but I have a rare one. It is the novelist and poet V. Sackville-West writing about her garden in the journal of the Royal Horticultural Society. She says her home is "very English, very Kentish . . . yet it had something foreign about it . . . a faint echo of something that belonged to the Contes de Perrault. La Belle au Bois Dormant—I had been right. That was why figs and vines and roses looked so right, so inevitable. . . . *But I think my deepest stab of pleasure* came when I discovered that the country people gave the name of Rondel to a circular patch of turf surrounded by one of our yew hedges. There was all poetry, all romance, in that name; it suggested Provence and the troubadours and the Courts of Love; but I think I liked it even better when I realized that they were using it as a term far more Kentishly familiar to them: the name they normally gave to the round floor for drying hops inside one of our Kentish oasts."

We should include as landmark books some books of fact which approach literature in their quality, as do some such writers in the adult field—Thoreau, Whitehead, Fabre. For children, we think of books like two of the very first machine books, done by superb artists: *How the Derrick Works* by Wilfred Jones and *The Picture Book of Machinery* by Boris Artzybasheff. They were not well received when I published them in the twenties, nor did they live very long. But they were—they are—beautiful as well as informative, and forerunners of the flood of machine books of today. An easier little book I also published for small boys, Henry Lent's *Diggers and Builders,* has lived on for over twenty-five years.

Other outstanding factual books would be: Genevieve Foster's *Augustus Caesar's World* and *George Washington's World* with their cross sections of world history; Maxwell Reed's *The Earth for*

Sam and *The Stars for Sam;* Katherine Gibson's *The Goldsmith of Florence* and her *Art for Children;* Jennie Hall's *Buried Cities;* Holling C. Holling's *Paddle-to-the-Sea;* Wilfred Bronson's *Paddle-wings* and *Fingerfins,* forerunners of the easier animal books by Dr. Zim.

There must be diversity of taste, or there would be no impulse to such diverse writing as you find in Swift's Gulliver, Bemelmans' *Madeline,* De la Mare's *Three Royal Monkeys, The Little Prince, Smoky, the Cowhorse, Captains Courageous.* Here are many sorts of adventures, simple or complicated, real or fairy, from creative minds that ranged in very opposite directions. Some see facts or history as magic, some as satire, some as deeply felt reality. There is a moment in a child's life when each of these diverse books could give deep satisfaction, if only the book is there for him to discover.

As Mr. Whitehead wrote in *Science and the Modern World:*

> A dangerous gospel is that of Uniformity. When man ceases to wander, he will cease to ascend on the scale of being. Physical wandering is still important, but greater still is the power of man's spiritual adventures—adventures of thought, adventures of passionate feeling, adventures of aesthetic experience. A diversification among human communities is essential for the provision of the incentive and material for the Odyssey of the human spirit.

With poetry, you can expose children most quickly to diversification, with wonderful *words*. It is easiest to quote at odd moments. It most merrily can lead the mind into channels of thinking a step beyond the present. And, it can be sung too. Its words—if it is real poetry—lead on into the words of great literature. When Mr. De la Mare was speaking at an American school, he read a poem later included in his marvelous anthology *Come Hither.* It foretold the minds of boys of today. William Cleland, while he was a schoolboy at St. Andrews, wrote what De la Mare calls one of the unique poems in English. He fell at Kunkeld in 1689, age twenty-eight. One verse of "Hallo, My Fancy":

To know this world's center,
Height, depth, breadth and length,
Fain would I adventure,
To search the hid attractions
Of magnetic actions
And adamantine strength.
Fain would I know, if in some lofty mountain
Where the moon sojourns, if there be tree or fountain;
If there be beasts of prey or yet be fields to hunt in—
Hallo, my fancy, whither wilt thou go?

Then I remember John Masefield, lying on the floor of a house near Yale, making a small boy a pirate alphabet; and later reciting so wonderfully that it seemed the very spirit of England at sea was in the room. And I was able to introduce him to the girl of fourteen whose favorite book in all the world was his long poem *Reynard the Fox*. There are plenty of horse-crazy girls who would love that long poem if only they were helped to discover it, led on to it from their horse romances.

Returning finally to my theme—that the introduction of "great" books and the aim of stimulating the child as to both facts and imaginative literature can be achieved by seeing books and life as one —I think there is a noble example of carrying it out here in the armor exhibit. Here a specialist in medievalism chose beautiful, rare examples of the armorer's art. Young people studied that world and made the astounding background paintings. Inspired display people tied the show in to modern "armor" of war today. The whole was backed by four big steel companies of this great industrial city who helped to print a fine program. And near at hand are the books and the storytellers to make that armor come alive still further for children of all ages. It is an exciting, intelligent venture in education, combining art, history, craft, literature.

Perhaps we should return at the end to heroes. If you wonder how to tell children of today about those old Greeks, those older gods, show the boys first some modern war books, yes, even series books, like Quentin Reynolds on the Battle of Britain, or Margaret Scoggin's true story collection *Battle Stations*. Then refresh your mind by reading the last pages of Paul Hazard's book where he quotes the marvelous English of Charles Kingsley's *Heroes*, a notable book on your list. After Pallas Athene so thrillingly inspires Perseus, Hazard ends the story and the book in his own words:

> Perseus does not wish to be like the cattle that fatten in the meadows; he does not wish death to take him before he has won glory and love. He flies over the sea with his winged sandals, his invincible sword, his shield in which the face of the Gorgon will be reflected. He strikes down the monster. He gives thanks to the Gods, as heroes should do, since without the Gods there is no strength or wisdom. He reigns peacefully over Argos, accomplishing the most difficult task of all, which is to remain true to himself, with spirit resolute and without arrogance, after winning his victory. Then he dies—or at least he seems to die. For in the daytime he stands on the lofty peaks which project beyond the clouds and where the winds no longer blow, in company with the immortals. At evening, he becomes a star; all through the night he can be seen shining in the sky, to guide the sailors who have lost their way.

Can Writing Be Taught?

From The Horn Book Magazine, *November, 1940.*

That is easily answered. Yes, if the writer can teach himself. Yes, if the writer can accept criticism and apply it, generally impossible for adult writers with set habits of thought. Yes, if there is plenty of time, as at school and college, and plenty of patient criticism of plenty of written material.

America today is full of people offering to teach writing by mail, in extension courses, at writers' conferences. I have made no careful survey of such teaching, and I realize it is easy to condemn it wholesale. For the person eager to make money by what we, not too unkindly, call "hack writing," it may serve a purpose. But the person of some innate genius inevitably watches the literary successes of the day with full realization that where a writer really has something to say, the "rules" often go hang.

One of the most interesting experiences of my life was to attend a writers' conference last summer.* Here the question of the title

* The eleventh annual session of the Writers' Conference in the Rocky Mountains, under the auspices of the University of Colorado, at Boulder. Mrs. Bechtel's was the first course in writing for children given there.—Ed.

was uppermost, in spite of the fact that the director's folder insisted that the answer is No, certainly not. In his words, the conference is "a practical experiment in the stimulation of creative writing," a place for people "who want to find out what is wrong with their writing rather than what is right with it." What actually could be accomplished?

Well, the six members of the faculty tried to tell in a radio broadcast, and their very valuable words are preserved on a record which must be unique in the files. As I look over the script, I have this one generalization to make: If over a hundred would-be writers are given three weeks' time to be lectured at, interviewed by, criticized by half a dozen successful authors and editors, none of whom want to increase the number of poor writers in the world, it has to be a very sane, modest, genuine student who comes away still wanting to put pen to paper. They get a rather bitter, salty bath in the realities of the literary life. And surely that is all to the good!

From the purely practical side, many angles of methods of writing, dealing with various markets, nature of publishers, use of agents, earnings, "rights," etc., all were threshed out, not in the classrooms, but mostly in panel discussions. The faculty was supplemented by many visitors, local celebrities, stars at the university, nearby librarians, and the like. Some of the students were stars themselves, winners of prize awards, who lent their own glamour to midnight sessions.

The chief lesson, on this side of the picture, for the hesitant amateur, was in the simple word "work." He or she probably had come with only two or three stories or poems, so slight a sheaf that it availed little as proof of possible variety of material and style for the critic to seize on as hopeful. Such a student, if not widely read, if not deeply inspired by some real thing to say, may have left in a dispirited mental muddle. For instance, I haven't much hope for the two who, having been adversely criticized in several other courses, came to me the last day for fifteen minutes' advice on how to try to write for children! As a last resort!

On the other hand, in my own classes, I did watch several people take notes, take criticism, write and rewrite at midnight, and actually, within three weeks, find a style better suited to their material, or find in their own material subjects better fitted to their own use. These were the exceptions, but they were thrilling. Also, in fairness I must say that at least one-third of my students brought large pieces of finished work, and that several of these were, with little change, ready to go to good publishers. Another group in my class were "listeners," teachers or librarians who were interested in many aspects of children's books and who contributed much to the discussions.

Since my return, Carl Carmer has attacked writers' conferences in the *Saturday Review,* provoking a lot of correspondence, mostly disagreeing with him. I suspect, from the very nature of his attack, that he has been a "literary lion" visitor, and has not had to teach systematically. Conferences differ in every year and every place— none can be ideal; to be even a little more perfect they would have to run for longer sessions and therefore cost more all round. Mr. Carmer's talk of "genius" is nonsense. With the world as it is, genius needs discipline. Too many writers go on too long thinking they are "geniuses." The answer to Mr. Carmer lies in the thousands of "decline" form letters, in the crowded calendars of the editors who "pass on" the genius to bored assistants.

So many problems came up in my survey of writing for boys and girls, I hardly know which to report. The most vital question asked was this: "Shouldn't we study the comic strips and see what they have that we have not?" (I am still working on the answer to that one!) The most puzzling thing about markets was the magazine field, and lack of market there for fiction for older boys and girls. The hardest problems in writing were realistic conversation and style for the very youngest children. In fiction, several puzzlers appeared as to degree of realism possible. The usefulness of one's own childhood memories we tried to work out. But one of my chief aims was to enlarge their conception of subject matter in this so traditional field. Today there are new kinds of children in a new world, and writing has to catch up with them. Of course I had Anne Eaton's *Reading with Children* (Viking, 1940) in one hand, and in the other, Anne Carroll Moore's *My Roads* (Doubleday, 1939). Whatever the subject of my talk, they went along, and were quoted, and their lists were invaluable.

But my students wanted books on "how to write." The best I know is *Do You Want to Write?* by a fellow-faculty, Margaret Widdemer (Farrar & Rinehart, 1937). Written chiefly for amateurs in magazine work, it is amusing, good reading for anyone, and its practical lessons are just as applicable in the children's and in the adult field. I also recommended Mabel Robinson's *Juvenile Story Writing* (Dutton, 1922) and, with reservations, *Writing the Juvenile Story* by May Emery Hall (The Writer, 1940). Miss Hall's lists of markets are very helpful, but her literary examples are queer. They do illustrate her points, but they are badly written. They come mostly from her own published work. I recommended only to special students the four articles by Eric Kelly in *The Horn Book* of 1931. To those writing for the pre-school age, I recommended Alice Dalgliesh's *First Experiences in Literature* (Scribner, 1937) and Lucy Sprague Mitchell's two *Here and Now Story Books* (Dutton, 1936 and 1937). One student has written me that these last two books have made her "listen to children in a new way."

For poetry writers, I urged De la Mare's *Come Hither* (Knopf, 1923), *Sung Under the Silver Umbrella* (Macmillan, 1935), and *Creative Youth* by Hughes Mearns (Doubleday, 1925). I discovered an unusual poetry textbook for colleges, *Understanding Poetry* by Cleanth Brooks, Jr., and Robert Penn Warren, another fellow-faculty (Holt, 1938). No lover of poetry should miss it. At Bertha Mahony Miller's suggestion I was happy to remind them of Quiller-Couch's *On the Art of Reading* (Putnam, 1925) and *On the Art of Writing* (Putnam, 1928). To give all my suggestions would take many pages.

But there is an entirely different aspect of such a conference which should be told. This one of mine was held under the auspices of a great state university, and as part of its enormous summer session. Its students had available not only the writers' conference sessions but also the many very fine conferences on public affairs and education at the university, also the big university library. If they were very strong and willing, they could even take courses at the university. The dormitory put at the disposal of the writers also housed university students—there were "bells," hours of classes were kept, there was just enough planning and discipline so that one felt part of a great studious body. At the same time, any good discussions could be moved entire to one of several lounges, to open courtyards. But the "system" made things fair both to faculty and to students. Appointments had to be scheduled, and the office saw that everyone had his chance.

The particular courses given at "my" conference were in poetry, the novel, short stories, drama, nonfiction articles, and writing for boys and girls. Each of the faculty held lecture classes every second day. Each gave one public address. Extra-distinguished lecturers also came, gave public lectures, attended panel discussions, visited classes, sometimes read manuscripts. The faculty breakfasted apart, but lunched and dined with the students. Since many students submitted material in more than one course, the faculty frequently conferred about them, and several manuscripts demanded more than one opinion, or more than two. At a final faculty meeting, honors were announced in all courses, and scholarships awarded.

The university, too, made it clear that it welcomed the writers. Its president "received" them, addressed them, attended the conference dinner. This put it all on a much more serious level. And for a public speech, open to a whole university, with paid admission, a faculty member of the conference could not rave vaguely, but had to give of his best.

Still I have not reached the "imponderables," those strange steps up the ladder of personal thinking which drew both faculty and students by plane, boat, train, by bus, by flivver. We came from a wheat ranch in Washington, from schools in California, from an attic studio in Brooklyn, from among Mexican children on the Texas border. Eating at one table were a Mormon, a rabbi, a zoology professor, a housewife mother of three sons, a small-town school superintendent, an ex-Metropolitan Opera singer, a last year's Bryn Mawr graduate, a lady engineer who brought her small son and put him in the campus nursery school. Playing croquet together one evening were a Broadway dramatist, the editor of a new experimental writers' magazine in Ohio, a teacher of so-called "children's literature," a Rhodes Scholar novelist, a New York City architect, and I. (Yes, a six-ball game—three to a side. The sports aspect of it all—tennis, mountain climbing, steak fries, etc.—I can't embark on here!) Do you often find this variety of people to talk to? I don't, in three weeks.

Well, writing aside, what did we *all* take home? A vivid, newly critical, newly appreciative attitude toward the world of books and writers. A revival of our love of poetry (had we ever lost it) and a new comfort in the greatest of timeless poetry. New philosophic attitudes, since "the writer as man and citizen" (subject of one address) involves thinking not about style and plot, but about the whole moral aspect of adjustment to the modern world. A revived devotion (had it ever lapsed) to those qualities of character which made it possible for a certain beloved poet to talk on quietly for hours about bull terriers and leave you feeling you had touched the sources of all goodness, wisdom and grace.

To summarize, it was magically comforting to become a student once again, to meet many kinds of Americans on a common level so high as that of intellectual eagerness, to be forced to review and re-value attitudes of mind left a bit shell-shocked by newspaper and radio.

We may feel sure that writing *can't* be taught, yet feel it well worthwhile for writers who deserve it to be "helped." And there *can* be a writers' conference so inspiriting that even a nonwriter might well beg to be allowed merely to listen.

The Art of Illustrating Books for the Younger Readers

From The New York Times Book Review, *November 10, 1940.*

Is there a special "art" for boys and girls? In our great wealth of American children's books have we found new ways of speaking to children pictorially? The answer is definitely no, not yet. Our artistic energies have been too widely diffused. Experiments have been too small and expensive. Fortunately or not, our norm of adult art appreciation stays on the level of the child. Not that of the untouched, truly poetic and creative small child, but that of the "normal," self-conscious twelve-year-old.

So, we lost the Mr. Disney of the original Mickey Mouse and gained the technical wonders and artistic banalities of Snow White. So, our most popular art today is that of the photograph and the comic strip.

Some critics tell us that, especially in painting, there is a true renaissance of American art. If this is true, it must be reflected in our bookmaking, to which many of our best artists contribute. But I have a troubled feeling that the segregation of children's books, and therefore of their pictures, is a phase of an educational mood that will pass and should pass.

For many centuries children shared with the whole community whatever art forms existed, as they share today the movies and the comics. But today we have the special field of children's bookmaking. Relatively, it is a very small drop in the bucket of public expenditure. But we have reason to ask what artists are working specially for children, and whether they are running with the popular tide or saying something special.

These artists inherit a brief tradition that perhaps began with the illustrated books of the 1860's. Mrs. Gatty first did her own pictures, later saw her stories illustrated by Holman Hunt, Burne-Jones, Sir John Tenniel. Later came Walter Crane, Kate Greenaway, and Randolph Caldecott. In America, we had the "parlor gift book" makers, but we also had Howard Pyle.

The happiest years for children's bookmaking came after the First World War, with the influx of books and also of artists from Europe. Then bookmaking stepped away from its tradition. It was a time of sufficient prosperity for American publishers and public to support experimental bookmaking. We found and brought from abroad and created here books whose artwork reflected the gaiety of the Czech peasant, the sophistication of French and Russian art, the best of varied work from many lands, including the U.S.S.R., Sweden, and the Orient. And an artist here doing a book about India or Egypt had the sense and taste either to copy or to imitate closely art forms from those far cultures.

So, within the last twenty years a great variety of beauty has flowered into American bookmaking for boys and girls. It accompanied a sudden expansion of purposeful study of "the child," and the new growth of children's work in public libraries. In spite of it all an overwhelming number of American children still see mostly and prefer the art of the comic strips, and such art as is purely photographic. Yet the audience for our better children's books may be wider than their limited sales figures. And in the schools some children may be reaching toward new conceptions as they paint and draw more freely.

With the swift progress of color lithography the lot of the free-lance artist has not been easy. Many distinguished artists have given their whole time to bookmaking and their return has not been great. But never before has bookmaking been more friendly to them, or more eager to adapt itself and its improving processes to genius.

In black and white, we think first of three men: Robert Lawson (*Ferdinand*), James Daugherty (*Daniel Boone*) and Boris Artzy-basheff (*The Seven Simeons*). Mr. Lawson works in a purely tra-ditional style, with a superb mastery of exact draftsmanship, with a strong pattern delicately expressed. His own new book, *They Were Strong and Good,* is a fine bit of unusual Americana. Mr. Daugherty, much more modern, with his swirling, dynamic pat-terns and bold sweep of heavy line, is always more the painter as opposed to Lawson the etcher. Mr. Artzybasheff can be exquisite, as in *The Seven Simeons,* tonally restrained and realistic, as in *Nansen,* boldly forceful, as in the Aesop, and in the many books of folklore he has treated. Probably he is the most brilliant, power-ful, competent artist in the bookmaking world today. But each of these men is a sincere artist, each has a keen sense of humor, of drama, of detail, none has ever turned out anything cheap or stupid. Also, none of them seems to be considering any special "age," or doing anything "childish."

This is not quite true of the three outstanding women artists I will mention next, who are possibly more popular, who work just as sincerely. Wanda Gág (*Millions of Cats*) has her own biography this fall, a surprise both in words and pictures, a remarkable artist's confession. Dorothy Lathrop (*Hitty, Animals of the Bible*) has a new story of a South American squirrel. Helen Sewell (*A Head for Happy, A Round of Carols*) has a new picture book *Jimmie and Jemima*. These three are all distinguished for splendid black and white. Miss Gág's heavy line is flowing, rich, modern. Miss Lathrop has evolved a delicate realism within a bold design and has also done very beautiful color work. Miss Sewell, again more modern, has a most individualized sculptural treatment which has been widely imitated. It is most perfectly suited to the period pictures for Elizabeth Coatsworth's three Sally books.

If a child owned books illustrated by these six artists alone, what a wealth of inspiration he would have! What a high critical standard of bookmaking, what intelligent, varied suggestion for ways of visualizing life as well as words! How does a child react to these pictures? We cannot generalize, because their taste, even at the youngest ages, always surprises us. Most psychologists have not progressed beyond the fact that most small children like big spaces of bright color. One child may feel that Artzybasheff and Gág are "gloomy," Sewell "stiff," Daugherty "mixey," Lawson and Lathrop his favorites. The next, of the same age, will say the last two are least interesting, and Gág makes him laugh, and he wishes he could draw like Artzybasheff. So, fortunately, we always dare to offer children the best and to continue to experiment. One thing we do know; they have little interest in each other's artwork, or in an artist's attempt to be naive in a child's way.

But this choice of six artists is rather arbitrary. So many others are doing splendid kinds of bookmaking. In color we have the Petershams, the D'Aulaires, the Haders. In black and white there are three famous printmakers: Thomas Handforth, Lynd Ward, Peggy Bacon. Then there are Clare Newberry, William du Bois, Zhenya Gay, Ludwig Bemelmans, Kate Seredy, Kurt Wiese, Valenti Angelo, N. C. Wyeth, Paul Brown, Hilda van Stockum. Robert McCloskey added a cheerful, truly American note this spring with his masterful, supersized comic, *Lentil*.

There are two new artists who step farthest away from traditional styles, who both in method and in imaginative approach are speaking to children in a somewhat new way. Both have a flavor of recent French and Russian bookmaking in their use of flat color combined with bold spaces of black and white. Both have a verve and simplicity which I think eventually will be widely approved by children. Clement Hurd showed himself a master of interpretation when he decorated Gertrude Stein's *The World Is Round.* He also did those gay panorama books of Town and Country, with their poster, toylike continued stories without words (only custom forced the editors to put in a few). Leonard Weisgard has a truly wonderful new *Punch and Judy,* a brilliant capturing of the essence of all puppet shows. Children can play with it too, just as they can release their energies in replying to his nonsense pictures for *The Noisy Book* and *The Country Noisy Book.*

If such a roll-call brings pictures to your mind's eye, think what a contrast they are to those of the many English illustrators we know so well. They are firmly in the old tradition, and also they are firmly entrenched in the hearts of American children, and will live on side by side with these other so much more varied American artists. What would our book world be without Arthur Rackham, Ernest Shepherd, Leslie Brooke, Beatrix Potter, F. D. Bedford? Yet, are we not lucky to have our own varied genius to contrast with them?

With so much that is very fine there is no need for a discriminating parent to spend money on poor bookmaking. I would even say there is no need for a child's fresh eyes to linger over comic strips or movies—but that is another subject, involving morals and literature. Let all that mass of dullness do its worst—at least there does exist a fine, strong store of art in books, always there to be looked at again if they have been bought and are waiting their turn.

The Jury Reports

*Speech representing the Judges—Anne Carroll Moore,
Boris Artzybasheff, L.S.B. and a printer—at the First
Show of Children's Books of the American Institute
of Graphic Arts 1937–1941.*

Tonight I feel deeply in debt to you. You gave me a remarkably interesting week spent among children's books. It seems to me that you, too, should be feeling grateful that you had this idea and put it through. After so many years of being very idealistic, very careful and, shall we say "pure," typographically, you now have let down the bars and let in a four-ringed circus. Maybe you didn't mean to do this—I will explain how it came to be such a trapeze-like event, in a moment. First I must continue to congratulate you. For I believe it is particularly significant, in time of war, that people's eyes should be turned, in their leisure, to books, and to standards of taste, and to a new thoughtfulness and openmindedness about all aspects of creative art.

So much for congratulations. Now for a few confessions. After my first round of the entries, I went home to my small typographical library and dipped into several books. Especially I reread Cobden-Sanderson's *The Ideal Book*. After seeing this show, for your comfort, do go home and reread it. His ideal still holds good.

But children's books are not ready to live up to it, because with a very few exceptions, that subordination of all parts to the whole is not yet accomplished. The illustrator still predominates, and in at least half these books the illustrator is not a bookmaker, and his influence is too loud, too violent, for any except the very cleverest designer to fit him into his proper place. Someday children, too, will have the pleasure of handling books without pictures.

My job tonight is not to prophesy but to persuade you that, in spite of not living up to Cobden-Sanderson, you have here an important show, interesting, provoking, stimulating, well worthwhile. But first, a word as to your jury. It consisted of four people with very definite tastes, very expressive tongues, and absolutely different points of view. They were all vividly conscious of the modern child—and this consciousness I think hampered most the one parent among us, who happened also to be the one printer. Parents seldom can generalize, and who can blame them? But as a jury, we did not generalize, we never said, "Children like this, they hate that." As we know them, children are very much like us four people—that is, violently individualistic in their tastes. What we had to sit upon was our inevitable bias toward subject matter and contents. And it was a blessing indeed for once to be urged to try to forget the author's part of the book.

Of course we could not apply any system of points. Had we done so, it could have given you a very cold, dull show indeed. Instead, we tried to include as many kinds of books, as many different artists, as we could. Within certain limits of actual *bad* printing, we took what was *alive*, first of all—alive and respectably printed and bound, and, by hook or crook, getting three of our four votes, that means pleasing our personal taste. I think not one of us jurors tonight can look at the show with real pleasure—our consciences tell us we needed more time, and that many more books should have been submitted. We longed for either labels or catalog to list both merits and the predominating *de*merits. We beg you to look at the results, if you can, with one eye on your public—that non-typographical public who loves Disney and the comic books, and who has no such standards as yours. They are going to learn from the show by the very fact that the good book stands out so clearly beside the one not so good. They, like you, will have a lot to wonder at!

It still fascinates me to remember some of the things we discarded. Among them were books that might have been conceived in 1890 or even 1850, books whose producers must be living in the mental world of Victoria or Kaiser Wilhelm, books a bit like what Samantha saw at Saratoga, if she saw any book there. Then what a delight to find a modern-minded bookmaker able to create a period atmosphere—of any period, John Newbery's England, gaslit days in New York, the lace valentine era—able to do it delicately, a bit humorously, yet make altogether a book of modern appeal, and a book a modern child would like.

Speaking for myself alone, I found the level of these books very high, very interesting, far above the level of ten years ago. Color printing of course is better, and done in more ways; the format of older fiction is much improved; the adjustment of type to the child's eyes is better; there is a great improvement in front matter and title pages. All the fine work of your other shows and of your book clinics has borne good fruit. Oddly enough, I suspect this show falls down on the photographic book, both in conception and in printing and in layout. Considering the wonderful work shown in the *Camera Year Book,* considering the superb photography in some movies, considering the trend toward this field from every magazine angle, I think this is rather queer. But it really is no loss to the show, since it is the one way of looking at things the public knows most about.

I must speak still more personally of your jury. Our most famous member, Miss Moore, was, as always, full of wisdom and enthusiasm. It was she who could remember how many fine books had *not* been submitted, a matter which, in fairness to all, we could not rectify. Nevertheless, I hope she agrees with us that as to make-up alone you have here most of the outstanding books of the period. And I think, too, she agrees some books not tops in bookmaking have value in the surprise of contrast—the jolt the public will get from the association of very different sorts of things. However, I hasten to add that Miss Moore did not step out of her role as a Maine Yankee—I suspect her many secret thoughts on this show will be somewhere forcibly expressed. It was Miss Moore, I think, who had the kindest heart among us. She would plead for an artist's work to be represented, even if the printer had made a bad job of it. It was she who could leap most quickly to the books she knew the library children loved, and tell us so. And she, when we were sunk with fatigue and very despondent, suddenly remembered that extraordinary book *Dog Can't Bark*. No one had voted for it. She pulled it out, and we hailed it with joy—startlingly fresh and fine it looked; it admitted Roger Duvoisin to the show; we all now felt very pleased with ourselves and cheered up.

Your two men jurors were appallingly conscientious. They took time to be pained at bad work and they enjoyed that pain, it seemed to me. With real gloating, the artist member said, "I threw out one book on *smell*." (It was not the delicious smell of the spice book which upset him.) B. A. wrote on one slip, "Why? It is not for children, and it looks like the Devil"—with a fine sketch of the horned one added. He cried, "What's the matter with people who stain their book tops yellow?" When he found three slips in his own most beautiful *Nansen,* he shrugged sadly. "Boys," said he, "should read Nansen's own story. I like *The Seven Simeons* by this artist much better." He exploded on opening a certain religious book: "Here's God again, the same old man." To this A. C. M.

replied, "But God is the same old man in the story." B. A. it was who wrote on Disney's *Ave Maria,* "No and double no." The rest of us didn't waste our energy that way. Toward the end of the day he moaned, "Oh, if I could find one book with no pictures in it!" And I think many children would agree with him.

Your printer juror once said, "This book is much too charming for boys." To which B. A. replied, "Why shouldn't boys be charmed?" He argued against the Audubon: "Audubon is one of the greatest American artists, and look how awfully he is reproduced on these horrid little pages. And then this other artist draws black and whites that don't go with them!" I argued for the Audubon, until we found it was published in 1936, so our breath was wasted. But the life of Agassiz, almost a duplicate in make-up (how these manufacturers do copy each other!) did get in. B. A. agreed with me in disliking the combination of etchings and wash drawings in the D'Aulaires' *East of the Sun,* but on other scores that fine book had to go in. He said of one woman artist's work, "It's like a little man making a big noise."

By now I'm sure you're all longing to be on a jury with Mr. Artzybasheff. Do, I beg you, use him on any jury you can. You will learn much more than I could report here.

Lastly, do feel pity for the poor printer among us. It was he who left notes like these on his slips: "All but title page and copyright," or "Paper: query weight and opacity," or "Type page good, but title page simply awful." These remarks, of course, had to be reinterpreted as votes, and the poor man really suffered. We hoped to cheer him by allowing him to write the foreword of the catalog, but there, to my surprise, he does not, as he promised, list the many demerits. He is peculiarly mild and kind. That is not how he sounded at that zero hour when dark descended.

Now may I make some more very personal confessions. How I disliked those Heritage Press books, in their gift boxes, with extra-expensive cellophane and tipped-in pictures! How sad I was when the others sat upon my excitement about a little fifty-cent book about a *dam,* which I still love. How I regret letting in the beautiful photos of Whitefoot the Mouse with those terrible pen sketches spoiling them. I still think Reynal and Hitchcock's *What Makes the Wheels Go Round* much more worthy of a place than Rand McNally's uninspired railroad book. I am still sure that Bill Scott did a grand job on his cardboard book poorly titled *Bumblebugs and Elephants.* (Bill, what about calling it "One and One Are Two"?) But I did force in one cloth book and one panorama, so babies have two books in the show anyway.

Of course, I grew very bored with pictures that bleed. I suppose some of your clinics have gone into this problem—the indiscriminate use of the bleed on all four sides of a picture. It generally indicates a desire to have the picture as big as possible, but the artist in most cases seems to have made no provision for the fall of the ax. This is just as irritating on color pictures or line cuts as on photographs.

Then I do not think the problem of size is always happily solved, especially in the picture books. Occasionally it seems as though the artist may not have known the size of the book when he started to work. Some items seem undecided whether to be a picture portfolio or a book. Even a big picture portfolio can be charming, it even can be balanced typographically—see the notes sent along with prints by the Woodcut Society.

But the one juror has gone on too long. I would now like to jump quickly to the personal problem of the children's book editor. Her relation to the manufacturing department is the key to this show, and it is a relation very vivid to my memory. I suppose it is still true, however large or small the publishing house, that this poor woman is ground between the upper millstone of a president who looks only at her cost sheet and the nether millstone of a manufacturing head who groans at her problems. Is it better for her to know nothing and leave all to him? Or, shall she know more than he, neglect his existence, go outside the house for new printers, new designers, new cloths, new color processes, which he has not time or inclination to find for her? In other words, is it war or cooperation? This is at the root of her success, this is what makes the real story behind each of these books fascinating to me. Who, along the line from president to printer, has the courage to say 3000, 4000, 5000, and to relate that number to the retail price? It is still miraculous that so much expensive platemaking, so much really experimental art, sees the light of day. (Now that we are at war, doubtless much of this will again be curtailed as it was in the depression.) The many beautiful books are a tribute to everybody's caring for the health and progress of bookmaking, giving of themselves far above what any nine-to-five day allows. Above all it is a tribute to those girls who have lain awake many a night struggling with that one cent, or ten cents, too much per book, which most of us never hear about. Who knows, ever, where credit lies for a beautiful book?

At this very moment, the new issue of *Print,* that stimulating Rudge magazine, comes out with a leading article on illustration by Mr. Eichenberg. No bookmaker can afford to miss it. He says in part: "Book illustration is an art that has to be fitted in to very special requirements—and that sounds like the very antithesis of art. The illustrator has to guard the integrity of the manuscript he is illustrating, he has to keep in mind that his art is going to be reproduced, printed, looked at between the covers of a book. That takes a lot of self-discipline, to which not many artists like to be submitted." He goes on to discuss the relation of the illustrator to the book designer and all he says is vital.

In the same issue, there is a review of a very beautiful book in this show, *There Was a Horse,* with its tribute to the illustrator Henry Pitz, and its compliment to his present publisher, Knopf, as opposed to his earlier publishers, which happened to include me. It's extraordinary how a good artist, working for a different publisher, appears in such different effect.

Now, just to do the publishers up even browner than I have already roasted them, let us look at their actual names, and their total winning titles. Viking submitted forty books, and you will not be surprised to learn that I would have voted for at least twenty of them. We the jury admitted only nine. You will be surprised to find nine also from Oxford. But Oxford, of course, had not thirty or forty equal to Viking's. Their nine books seem to me remarkably good for a relatively young department, books showing artistic imagination and publishing courage, yet not as good as Viking's though equal in number. Then come seven for Macmillan, but, again, this number of seven, good though they be, have not the character and excitement of say, the five from Knopf's or the four from Holt's which are very interesting. The six from Random House stand out very well. So—numbers don't mean everything. Don't miss the two from William Scott—the best black in the show is the black in his *Punch and Judy,* and in his reprint of *The Log of Christopher Columbus* he has done something very important in presenting source material attractively.

There is no point in talking of individual books when most of you do not know them and they are not in our hands. Perhaps I can generalize a little, however. The group here called Informational seems to me least imaginatively conceived and least well printed. How queer, that with all the brilliant teaching in America, with all the passion for mechanics, with all the boys' hungering for facts, this group both in conception and in printing should be so poor. Here is where the jury stretched a point most often, to lure the fathers and sons and scouts and teachers. Why is there no really superb airplane book? Let's hope for one soon. I call your special attention to the archaeology book from Random House and to the Picture Books for Younger Children—the gayest, most wonderful group. But you suddenly realize that all the rest are picture books, too, or almost all. There are plenty of real picture books for older children. Age levels fortunately are breaking down. Forgetting the text, many of these books would be as happy a gift for a person sixty as for a person six.

In my little bookroom in the country, I have a shelf labeled "Necessary Nonsense for Six to Sixty," and I feel it is a compliment to say that many of these books could go on that shelf. *The Seven Simeons* is there, and *Wee Gillis,* and *Lentil,* and *The Great Geppy.* Because of that shelf I have also had the pleasure of watching adults read for the first time *Little Black Sambo,* and *A Roundabout Turn,* and *The Wind in the Willows.*

Your show as it travels will do the same job of giving adults a new lure to enjoy what is so beautifully offered the children. The catalog offers a grand lot of surprises, all along the line. Here are astronomy, biography, nature and science, folklore, American history, poetry, fiction, animals, travel, detectives, pioneers—the exactly true, the purely imaginative—all so alluringly spread forth, through your efforts, that one would think no child could fail to want to read. If only the words always lived up to the wonderful bookmaking! They so often do not.

I hope this show will go to parts of America where people do not often see, all together, so many new books. I hope that in those far places, some unknown person may linger fascinated and say to himself, "Heavens! That idea I had for a book was not so fantastic after all. Those colors I wanted in my pictures—here are actually printers who could do them. And here are publishers who are certainly eager for new ideas. I'll get to work again." And so he does. And so, besides opening the minds of the book buyers, you will also have created new bookmakers. You are showing them both what can be done—and also how much still needs to be done for our children. Bookmaker, child, and artist are all part of one audience and the creative person must spring from that audience.

The A.I.G.A. Children's Book Show of 1958

From The Horn Book Magazine, *August, 1958.*

The new show of three years of the best-made children's books, sponsored by the American Institute of Graphic Arts, opened at the New York Public Library in May, then started on its travels. The jury were: Jerome Snyder, artist and art director of *Sports Illustrated;* Alvin Eisenman, typographer of the Yale University Press and Professor of Graphic Arts at Yale; and myself, described as "an editor who has also written and reviewed children's books."

Of about 4,500 children's books published in America from 1955–1957, only about 300 were submitted by their publishers. Of these, the jury could have chosen 100, but had difficulty in finding 79 which two of them agreed were worthy. The criteria set up by the A.I.G.A. are for design, typography, manufacture, and concept.

Standards of agreement on good paper, printing, and binding are fairly obvious. Individual taste, however, dominates any judgment on design and concept, which include illustration. So it is not surprising that we agreed at once on about twenty books and had a hard time with the rest. In such a variety of art treatment as we faced, one hesitates to call one book "better" than another and our meetings did not allow much time to debate art values.

It was twenty-five years ago that I first judged an early A.I.G.A. show in this field. With vivid memories of what Frances Sayers calls "the golden twenties of children's bookmaking," I shall courageously try to generalize.

Present standards of typography and book design undoubtedly are higher. More publishers today employ able book-design experts. More artists are able to carry out a unified concept of a book. Better paper is more widely bought. More printing processes are available and more handsome type faces. Yet, with all their technical excellence, I miss in these books an *élan* one found in those of the twenties and early thirties. It is apparent that many publishers of regular trade books are feeling the pinch of rising costs, and not compensating for it with originality. The richly colored end papers of old are practically gone; we have mostly plain white paper there. Jackets are inclined to be dull and unrelated to book design. Bindings are very dull, and generally omit the title from the front cover, using a mysterious small line cut in one poor ink. Where an artist does not letter his own title page, no one seems to have spent much thought on it. Teen-age fiction gets only routine make-up. Most series books are shoddy, with second-rate artwork, except in the standard classics series.

I missed the influence, so obvious between the two world wars, of the brilliant color books from Europe. Where are their descendants? What of such old stalwarts as Bemelmans, McCloskey, Weisgard? They are not at their early best in this show. Françoise is as excellent as ever for the nursery age, but one wishes for a more brilliant treatment of her color. Rojankovsky's lively pages also need better printing. Lynd Ward is here in the life of Lincoln by his wife, with moving realism and superb color. William Pène du Bois is his unique self, the same yet always new, in his funny, exquisite *Lion,* as "modern" as he was long ago, and with handsome end papers too.

It is surprising how many artists of the early thirties still are outstanding today. However, many more artists than in those days are doing uninspired realism, and still more doing imitative, slapdash caricature. The great increase in mass-produced color books possibly blinds one to the excellence of their artwork in some cases. In many, the effect is spoiled by too crowded pages. Besides the Disney atom book and the Homer, these books are represented well by Peattie's *Rainbow Book of Nature,* Art Seiden's *The Story of Noah's Ark,* and the two striking toy books illustrated by Jan Balet.

To leave generalizing, we find that four artists have each three books chosen: Leonard Weisgard, Maurice Sendak, Irene Haas, and Remy Charlip. Charlip has a certain distinction but his oddly static figures do not appeal to me greatly, neither do Sendak's books in this show, though his period piece *Little Bear* is charming. The clear, tiny, humorous figures of Irene Haas always are delightful and she has a flair for odd-shaped format. The most distinguished styles of Mr. Weisgard are missing here, but his line work in the restrained little new edition of *The Wizard of Oz* is superior.

The surprise and distinction I feel generally lacking in these twelve books are quickly seen elsewhere. *See and Say* by Antonio Frasconi is strikingly original and ever so well printed. Colors and arrangement of the words are refreshingly new. James Flora brings a new art style and lively prose to his *The Fabulous Firework Family* and *The Day the Cow Sneezed.* His strong outlines have power; his humor is inexhaustible; his rich colors are unusual and brilliantly reproduced. His work reminds one somewhat of Artzybasheff's early bookwork, but we have yet to see the range of style and power of line of that great illustrator in anyone working on books today.

These three, with *Lion,* I put at the top of my private list; then I add Duvoisin's *Happy Lion* books, though only one of the two got in; the amusing picture story in two-color line of *Harold and the Purple Crayon* by Crockett Johnson; for sheer distinction, Harry Behn's *The Painted Cave,* with his boldly adapted Indian themes; and the gently poetic realism of *Young Kangaroo* with two-color work by Symeon Shimin. Near the top should go Ravielli's wonderfully original *An Adventure in Geometry.* Sturdily outstanding, one of the few books for readers over fourteen worth considering is *Imagination's Other Place,* that remarkable anthology of poems of science and mathematics, with its modern woodcuts by Clare Leighton and its excellent typography. Adding at the end of these private preferences, Disney's *Our Friend the Atom,* with its notable binding, and the Provensens' pictorial version of *The Iliad and the Odyssey,* you have at the core of the show some truly outstanding bookmaking.

Though not so very exciting, or "new" in concept and design, there are other informational books most competently produced that offer their generous visual explanations on big pages. These include *The Rainbow Book of Nature,* illustrated by Rudolf Freund, *Wheels, A Pictorial History* by Edwin Tunis, and *The First Mammals* by William Scheele. A finely made smaller book is *Exploring by Satellite,* with beautiful air-brush pictures by Helmut Wimmer.

The most "modern" books in the show are those illustrated by Bill Sokol, Paul Rand, Nicolas Sidjakov, and Nicolas Mordvinoff with a very new style. Their pictures for me have a nightmare quality, and I doubt that picture-book age children get any artistic message from them. Yet these advanced styles are much more stimulating than the familiar competence of some of the traditional artists. The show would be dull without them, and they will stretch the eyes of any age. I regret that books illustrated by Jean Charlot, Helen Sewell, and Valenti Angelo were voted down by my colleagues. They seemed to me as fine in art concept and production as any in this show.

I have spoken of the books chiefly in terms of their artists. More technical appraisal would take much longer. But it is to be noted that the catalog lists over eighty type faces used, with nineteen books hand-lettered. Good old Baskerville wins, but the range of fascinating new types will delight those who study the books from this angle. It is proof of the creative feeling in the publishing offices where they originated, whether on the part of editor, artist, manufacturing man, or outside book designer.

This show, as it travels, will bring an increase in discrimination to a wide audience, as so many of the Graphic Arts traveling shows have done for many years. It will be studied for different reasons by artists, printers, librarians, book collectors, even by some children. It is a far more interesting way to see a cross section of modern bookmaking than in a bookshop or department store, where many of these books may not be shown at all.

Of Authors and Artists

"Berta and Elmer" and Their Picture Books

From The Horn Book Magazine, *August, 1928.*

The story of Berta and Elmer Hader begins on Telegraph Hill in San Francisco. There Berta, a miniature painter, had a big studio where gathered lots of interesting people. One day Elmer arrived. He had been painting portraits and landscapes, and had taken a "painting-a-minute" vaudeville act across America to Paris. They married and came East to work.

Studio life in New York seemed to them a poor substitute for California. So they explored the suburbs of the city and discovered a wooded hillside on the west bank of the Hudson which no citizen of Nyack thought a good spot for a home. The seclusion, the height, the spring and waterfalls in their front yard, the view over the river—all these appealed to the Haders' imagination, and they drew a picture of a house which would fit it.

Then they built the house themselves. There it stands, with two stories, cellar, gables, large living room, studio—its brown stone and many-paned windows peer down at the river road through the great trees. You look at Elmer, rather slender, with blue eyes twinkling behind his specs, and at Berta, tall and willowy, with great brown eyes and curly brown hair, and refuse to believe that they did that job in four months, with just one week's help from a laborer. As a great circle of people gathers round the large hand-hewn table for Berta's marvelous soup, you wonder whether any book can ever equal in importance or excitement the building of your own home.

But these two are picture-makers first. They have done many kinds of free-lance work. Their full pages in color for the children's pages of women's magazines first brought them to the attention of book publishers. When I held a competition for the first edition of the Happy Hour books, it was the dummy for *The Ugly Duckling*, done by the Haders, that stood out above all the rest of the artists' samples. It was so simple, so childish, so funny; the colors were so clear and bright; the ducks were well drawn; the layout was artistic without being "arty"; the heavy black line meant a keyplate which would live, and a definite rhythm for the eye of the young person. All these qualities appeal to a wide public. I have only to throw one of these *Ugly Duckling* pictures on the screen from a lantern slide, to get a ripple of appreciation, chuckles all over the audience. It is the same response one gets to Boutet de Monvel's *Susanna*, or Lisl Hummel's *The Good-Natured Bear*, or Elizabeth MacKinstry's *Eliza*. I think it is a response to a human quality; it has little to do with appreciation of technique.

During the making of these books, Berta did not appear in New York very often. Elmer brought down sketches, and visited the printers. He informed himself fully on the lithographic process to be used, conferred often with the engravers, and was very aggressive on the subject of inks. The results may be seen in comparing all their titles in these little fifty-cent books: *The Ugly Duckling, Wee Willie Winkie, Hansel and Gretel, Chicken Little* (1927), *The Old Woman and Her Pig, The Three Bears, The Little Red*

Hen (1928). Limited by a black and three-color process in which no ben-day was to be used, and very few spots of overlaid colors, still they have given a variety of color effects, have suggested rather subtle atmosphere and contrast. See the clever use of purple where Goldilocks tiptoes up to the bears' bedroom; see the sun-filled page where the duckling turns into a swan, done with blue and white alone; feel the spring in the end papers of *The Little Red Hen*, with the rows of flower pots, and the wash blowing on the line; and don't miss the country characters in *The Old Woman and the Crooked Sixpence.*

Then there came the big *Picture Book of Travel*. This meant research, and a more complicated layout. Black and five colors, with overlays bringing the effect up to nine colors, were to be used on one whole side of each signature, black and blue on the alternate side, and the vast subject of transportation up to the invention of machinery to be compressed into a sixty-four-page picture book. Dummy, completed black drawings, color keys, text, each came in at exactly the hour stipulated in the contract. Printer and publisher had full time to discuss details and salesmen had a completed book instead of a dummy, from which to do advance selling.

Early in 1928, the new Meigs manuscript, *The Wonderful Locomotive,* demanded an illustrator who drew for small boys, and who knew all about steam engines. We thought such a person didn't exist, for some gloomy weeks. Then one day Elmer heard our moans and said that he had stepped out of the cab of an engine he was driving between Chicago and 'Frisco, to go to art school. Also some of his best friends are the men at the roundhouse near Nyack. So he got the job! Berta reported enthusiasm for the small boy and his dog, and all was well. Miss Meigs reported such enthusiasm in her home among the nephews and nieces, for the Haders' books, that all was even better. And when the sales conference saw the dummy, with the little old 44 puffing away, they voted to double the edition. And when the artists sent in the pictures, there were a third again as many as either contract or publishing plans allowed. But who could leave out one of them—the faces of the brakemen and engineers in the lantern light, the boy and dog peering out of the cab window, the wonderful center spread of the arrival of the circus train—pennies must be counted again, and every picture fitted into its perfect place.

One visitor to the house on the hill who saw the Haders at work on this book reported back to the publishers, "It *must* be a rather wonderful thing, because both of them smile when it's mentioned and I heard Elmer chuckling out loud while he worked on it."

We always come back to the house—as everyone does, and will as long as they are in it. If you can't go, you are cheered by the funniest letters, neatly typed, and decorated with ridiculous pictures in bright colors. No other bills or thank-yous for checks or appointment notes ever carried so many laughs into a publisher's files.

Perhaps this story is more about the books than about the people. What can I add? Berta is an expert cook; she entertains twenty or more people without any fluster and looking like a picture in a peasant apron and handkerchief around her curls. Elmer is a fine dancer and a heroic wood-chopper. They love music and the theater, and one of their favorite authors is James Stephens. I suppose it is natural that people who are so rarely kind to so many friends, and who do so many daily things in that house so beautifully and merrily, should be able to think of the sort of storybook detail, the expansion and concentration of an author's tale that children will always love.

A Tribute to
Margery Bianco

From The Elementary English Review, *June, 1935.*

Probably you are in the midst of reading *The Good Friends*. If not, you soon will be, and chuckling over the pride of Rosie the cow with her ribbons and mirror. You will say, "Only someone who has lived in the country and loves it could write this book."

And that is a very true keynote to a picture of Margery Bianco. Though I have seen her always in New York, yet I think of her inevitably with birds, flowers, animals, sun and clouds and country air. She has lived in the country in America, England, Italy. Before she was twenty-five she had published three novels, now out of print. The one I have read has a background of the New Jersey coast, of strange fisherfolk, of pines, woods, sands, and the great sea now beautiful, now terribly hostile. She makes you feel the tragedy of her characters through the beauty and strangeness of this place, where she spent part of her youth.

Margery Williams, born in England, came to live in America when she was nine years old. Before she was twenty she returned and later married there an Italian, Francesco Bianco. Part of her early married life was spent in London, part outside of Turin in northern Italy. The Captain, as her husband is always called, is an alert, humorous, cultured gentleman with a great knowledge of books. He was for many years a dealer in incunabula—books printed before 1500. He is interested in fine printing, and in all the fine arts, and is a brilliant talker and writer, though he has not written for publication. It was he who, writing from London, answered my questions about Pamela, when I was reviewing *Flora,* and so my friendship with the Biancos began.

When they came to America to live, Pamela and her father and mother and her brother "Cecco," the first great event was a show of Pamela's art work at the Anderson Galleries. A little girl of thirteen with heavy long golden braids showed me her pictures. You know them, as they were so beautifully reproduced in *Flora,* with verses by Walter de la Mare, and you know how stirred and amazed I must have been to have this child tell me about them. I found out that her parents not only had kept her out of school but had kept her away from art lessons and art schools. She liked roller-skating, and riding on bus tops, and poetry and fairy stories. She was eager to see her American cousins.

Her father told me that her drawing had begun when she was very small. He would leave Turin on business trips and tell both children to have a book ready for him when he came home. Pamela's "books" were all pictures, and her very individual talent was apparent at once. In that exhibition, frequently she would say, "That is a portrait of Mummy," or "Here is Mummy again," and I would see, in her very delicate pen lines, an enchanting young face with very big eyes and a dark bang. That was my introduction to Margery Bianco.

We'll skip from Italy and New York of some years ago, to 1934 in a Connecticut village. There I saw Pamela, a mother now, with her baby Lorenzo, and Margery a grandmother, seeming very little older than Pamela. A remarkable oil painting of the baby, standing with his toys between two rose bushes, a glimpse of blue water and sailboats beyond—this showed how Pamela's genius had flowered, and how wise the parents had been to let her work out her talent alone. The Captain's keen understanding of art values, the mother's literary sympathy, had been a rich background.

It is very hard to describe a friend, that is why I am talking first about her family. For of course a good deal of Mrs. Bianco's life has centered on her children. When she first came to America, she brought with her a group of stories she had told them when they were small, stories mostly about their toys. One of these, *The Velveteen Rabbit,* with pictures by the famous English artist William Nicholson, was an immediate success in England and in America. The next year *The Little Wooden Doll* came out in Macmillan's Little Library, with pictures by Pamela, and has gone on and on as a well-loved doll story, excellent to tell aloud. Then *The Skin Horse,* also with Pamela's pictures, and next *Poor Cecco.* This was a long book, a big fat book, with pictures by Arthur Rackham. It was a wonderfully real and exciting tale of nursery toys off on an adventure.

These books all had both critical and sales success and the reason is not hard to find. This kind of imagination, playing not upon fairies but upon the real things a child knows, his toys and his pets, struck a note in the tradition of Mrs. Molesworth, Mrs. Ewing, Mrs. Burnett, a note to which children will always answer. More than that, however, the style was a beautiful English, simple but not babyfied, gentle and beautiful in every line, with a quiet humor, not too subtle for small listeners, and with pathos always inherent. A child might not "pleasurably weep" over them, as some children do over Andersen, but he would feel the tears near, and draw his breath till all comes out well, as of course it always does.

In all these books, there is that touch of the true artist that keeps the most important thing predominant in a dramatic simplification. The Velveteen Rabbit belongs to a Boy—we do not know his name, or what his home looked like, or exactly how many people were in his family, because it doesn't matter to the rabbit's story.

In her later writing, Mrs. Bianco has still published stories in this mood, such as *The Hurdy-Gurdy Man* and *The House That Grew Smaller*. But she has also interpreted America in a new sort of story. We can't call its humor anything at all but American, although I am always tempted to find elements of English influence in her writing. These stories are *The Street of Little Shops* and *The Good Friends*.

Then her love of animals has been given a word in *All About Pets* and *More About Animals*. These books seem to me to strike a new note in "nature" writing for children. An adult would call each chapter a charming essay, but children doubtless read them for the *facts* about the animals they know, and plenty of interesting facts and common-sense advice they find. Mrs. Bianco knows particularly about cats (they still own Common People, whose portrait is the frontispiece of the last book) and Miss Rachel Field's Trotty is the Scotch terrier formerly owned by Pamela. A procession of pets could be listed, dogs, cats, birds, turtles, and Mrs. Bianco's memories of all of them are included in these two books.

If you had ever seen her with a dog, you'd have another key to her character. The firmness results in good training, and the affection means that the dog will love her forever. It is typical of her that in *All About Pets* she advises you to talk to your pets. Read the book and see why. It is also typical of her when I wrote my sorrow at cutting flowers, especially flowers I had grown myself, she wrote back that she always felt that way, and supposed her living room would soon have bunches of carrots and spinach while the flowers nodded on in the garden.

We find book reviews by this author all too seldom in the current press. She has a particular power of analyzing the charm of another author's work, a fine insight into its significance, a wide background of reading, only partly in children's books, and a real ability at editorial criticism. I recall particularly her fine review of *Hitty* for the *Saturday Review*. One wants so good an author always to have time chiefly for her own writing, but we need her also in the field of criticism today. Fine taste, a very fair spirit, and ability to seize on what is right or wrong with a book, are not easy to come by in combination with the power to put it all down in charming English.

You know from her books that she has found unusual friends among "plain people"— the man at the A&P, the gardener, the farmer's wife, the postman. But her friends range also through musicians, artists, authors, critics, in London and New York. I remember rare evenings in the studio on MacDougall Alley, when poets, painters, printers, publishers, came in casually, talked and argued, and went away refreshed. The picture they carried away held the treasured, battered old toys, a living cat and dog, drawings and paintings, the keen alert face of the Captain, the thoughtful, gentle face of Margery, the lovely youth of Pamela, with golden braids wound around her head.

Mrs. Bianco is very modest and hates to make speeches, yet the few times she has spoken are unforgettable. It is a courageous and valiant as well as a poetic and practical person who looks steadily at you and either says something very worth hearing or reads in a delightful voice with an English accent. I hope many of you can some day hear her and meet her. Until then, you have the great delight of her books.

Elizabeth Coatsworth: Poet and Writer

From The Horn Book Magazine, *January, 1936. A later,*
expanded version of this article appeared in Newbery
Medal Books: 1922–1955, *edited by Bertha*
Mahony Miller and Elinor Whitney Field
(Boston, The Horn Book, Inc., 1955).

Not long ago, I had a letter from an old gray house facing the harbor in Hingham. It told of herbs standing green and fragrant on the window sill, of little Meg playing with something "soft as a mouse's ear, Mummie," and of Puss who sent me a strange paper doll—"Tell the auntie it's the snow man's sister." I was thinking of it in the afternoon, when I spoke to a woman's club here in the country, and described *Away Goes Sally*. You should have seen the faces light up as I described the little house on runners, drawn by oxen all the way from Hingham to Maine, the little Sally of long ago and her adventures on this remarkable journey. There was spontaneous applause when I read that poem, "Swift things are beautiful." Everyone responded to that kind of poetry, and I think everyone agreed with me that children today are fortunate to have among them a teller of good stories who could lead from chapter to chapter with good poems. I know only two authors of today who do it successfully, the author of "Sally," and Padraic Colum. And since I think the sense of poetry as interwoven with daily life a thing of tremendous importance to children, I think these authors of unusual significance.

Elizabeth Coatsworth is first and most essentially a poet. She is a storyteller, a scholar, a traveler, a mother, and a housekeeper. She likes to paint. She reads widely in adult writing new and old. Every year she and her husband, Henry Beston, read aloud several plays from Shakespeare. She has hosts of friends, to whom she is helpfully loyal in all sorts of circumstances, and she has a great capacity for enjoying parties and people, for sharing in good talk enthusiastically. She enters the busy town life of Hingham, with frequent visits to nearby Boston, and spends many months on their farm in Maine.

Some of my memories of her include pictures like these: At Vassar, E. C. in her red-lined Italian officer's cape, walking on a bitter winter day to a distant meadow to feed some horses left out in the snow. In New York City, E. C. introducing me to my native heath with a tour to the Statue of Liberty. In my apartment, E. C. composing aloud *The Cat and the Captain* while she posed for a young artist. At Columbia University, where she took an M.A., E. C. arguing learnedly about comparative religions. Expeditions to the Spanish Museum and to the Russian Cathedral. Hours by the fire in Hingham when we talked all kinds of plans for publishing, her interest in the profession being by no means entirely a selfish one, but imaginative and constructive. A visit to a Mr. Lincoln, driving through the New England winter woods, to see his decoys. Her return, with her husband, from a real adventure on Hatteras Island thirty miles off the coast of the Carolinas, our poring over maps and hearing their tales, the old southern chair fastened on the rumble of their runabout. At Hingham again, the big dog Bos'n asleep by the fire, the travel scrapbooks brought out, tales of Morocco, China, Guatemala.

You will excuse me, I hope, any authors who may read this,

if I say that often the born writer has a disinclination to activity.
The very passion for putting pen on paper often precludes the
width of experience that gives the pen something to say. I think
this writer would have written well if she had never left her
native Buffalo. But perhaps fortunately, the Coatsworths were
born travelers. Part of their family live in Pasadena, and the
journey to the Pacific coast, with stops in the Indian country by
the way, became a regular event. Europe was taken for granted;
of course, one knew England and the Scotch lowlands where one's
ancestors had lived. After college, the Orient, China, Japan, the
Philippines. Later, a year along the shores of the Mediterranean;
again, Morocco, and later on Denmark, Iceland, Copán and
Guatemala. If Mrs. Coatsworth, sister Margaret, and Elizabeth
are gone for a few weeks, nowadays, it is not to rest from housekeeping in some hotel—they are motoring over the Gaspé Penin-
sula, or exploring a little known part of Florida. And I think the
Bestons' wedding journey was spent walking through Devon and
Cornwall. I know that if ever I travel anywhere, E. C. can say,
"Get the room in the tower of the old Sultan's palace, and lean
out when the muezzin calls under your window," or "Walk in
Watkins Glen at twilight," or "Don't miss the kakemonos in the
Freer collection."

At first, this resulted in a great deal of writing, both poetry and
prose, which was impressionistic, occasionally precious or studious,
often truly lyric, always keen in observation. Later, the depth of
the feeling grew, longer stories developed, a richer sense of character evolved. The wonder was always in the amount of her output.
Travel and friends take time and energy; even keeping a good
travel notebook is, as many of you know, a real task. But from the
first, E. C. not only wrote but was published prolifically, especially
in the field of poetry. The children's books began accidentally,
the accident being her happening to read Henry Beston's book

about the Navajos in the Little Library, *The Sons of Kai*. Roused to try her own hand, she tossed off *The Cat and the Captain,* that gay, amusing New England tale with its verses, the chants of the old black cook. It was a tremendous success, and is still selling. So was *The Boy with the Parrot,* the realistic tale of a modern Indian boy in Guatemala, one of the few stories available with a fine true background of South America, and a hint of its mysterious Indian past. *Toutou in Bondage* fell rather flat, in spite of its centering on the adventures of a small dog and an Arab master, its romantic desert background, its thrilling picture of the marketplace at Marrakesh. Neither did *The Sun's Diary* find a wide audience, and strangely, too, for so many people treasured its wealth of quotations and charmingly practical ideas carrying one round the year. I think there never has been an anthology or "almanac" I have enjoyed so much or used so often.

The climax of her popularity came with *The Cat Who Went to Heaven.* The author has told herself how she thought of this story of a small cat and a poor artist, why she wove the Buddhist animal stories into a story of a great painting, how swiftly she wrote it in California, years after her actual visit to the Orient. Its unusual quality appealed to the reviewers at once, it was reprinted within a month of publication, and the following year won the Newbery Medal. Then followed more Oriental stories, in *Cricket and the Emperor's Son,* and the beautiful fairy story, called *Knock at the Door.*

I think another climax, or height, in her writing comes with *Away Goes Sally.* Here, as in the famous "Cat," the weaving of story and poems seems perfect, the combination of meticulous detail of old ways of living with vigorous character and story interest, most complete. Bertha Mahony once said of it, "A book like this makes me 'go up' like the flame of a candle." Perhaps you cut out of the *New Yorker* and carried around in your pocket,

as I did, the poem "Swift things are beautiful," with the second
verse that makes a link to Sally's journey:

> And slow things are beautiful—
> The closing of day,
> The pause of the wave
> That curves downward to spray,
> The ember that crumbles,
> The opening flower,
> And the ox that moves on
> In the quiet of power.

Do you remember the final poem in *The Cat Who Went to
Heaven,* the eighth song of the housekeeper?

> This is too great a mystery
> For me to comprehend—
> The mercy of Buddha
> Has no end.
> This is too beautiful a thing
> To understand—
> His garments touch the furthest
> Grain of sand.

Do you remember the verses of fairy spells, as little Stephen
learned them, in *Knock at the Door?* In that book, too, is the
Christmas carol, ending

> Now by this candle
> I would light
> A fire in
> My heart tonight.

> Which, like a star,
> May shine above
> The cradle
> Of a newborn love.

Of course I must quote prose, too. Do you think a writer not a poet would have done so well this paragraph from *The Sun's Diary?*

> There is a place I know (says the sun) where I have seen ducks, ducklings, turtles, trout, catfish with whiskers like ugly mandarins, and young lavender eels, all crowd together in the water under a willow tree for crumbs. The ducks kick the turtles out of the way, the catfish bite the ducks' toes, the trout whisks a crumb away before the others see, the little eels try to take the food out of the turtles' horny beaks. There they all are in the water under the green willow tree.

This fall, came an adventurous American story from Miss Coatsworth, *The Golden Horseshoe,* set in old Virginia, full of drama and stirring in its picture of a romantic period. Some day you must have a selection of her poems for boys and girls, besides more of her adult poems. Some day she will surprise you, perhaps, with the sort of storytelling she gives her own Meg and Puss, and with a novel that is quite different from any of these present books. Anything is possible for a poet with the energy, imagination, and deep interest in people that belong to the unique temperament of Elizabeth Coatsworth. But if she wrote not another word, she would have made, today, a major contribution to American children's literature.

Dorothy Lathrop: Artist and Author

From The Library Journal, *June 15, 1938.*

When was it that most of us heard of Dorothy Lathrop? Was it in 1919, when she illustrated *The Three Mulla-Mulgars?* Here we saw what seemed the work of a mature artist in color and line, the interpretation of a highly imaginative and atmospheric tale about very real creatures. Writing in *The Three Owls* in 1927, Miss Moore said:

> It is an amazing piece of work for a young artist to have achieved, and will stand, in its black and white at least, as one of the notable achievements in illustration of this decade.

In 1919, this then little-known artist lived, as she still does, in Albany. In modest, fearful, gradual descents upon the city, through the usual visits to editors' desks and showing of her work, swiftly she became one of the most sought-after illustrators in America. It may have been for two reasons: one, the consistent hard work that is always a necessary adjunct to genius, and two, a very persistent idea of the sort of thing she wanted to do.

At home, she had an unusual background of artistic achievement daily before her in the work of her mother, a distinguished painter in oils. Dorothy and her sister Gertrude built a studio some distance from the house, which is in a suburb, surrounded by trees and garden, grass and shrubs. Gertrude, whose fame as a sculptor grew rapidly, kept her half of it alive with animal models. Dorothy's half of it had a greater variety, perhaps, of creatures, animal and human, and she worked chiefly in pen and ink, water color, and wood block. There was a family interest in dogs and other pets—an occasional rabbit, flying squirrel, lamb, frog—and, of course, in growing plants. The three artists were always very busy, and it was a happy chance that before Mrs. Lathrop's death, not only had they all been shown at the Academy, but a joint show of all their work was held at a New York gallery. It was opened by, or at least attended by, their Albany neighbor, now the President's wife [Eleanor Roosevelt].

How many beautiful books for children have come from that studio among the trees! I think first of the pictures for George Macdonald's books, because they represent her own choice to do tales long loved and reread. Out of a childhood generous in books, it was Macdonald who appealed to her most, the strength and moral beauty of his ideas, and the fineness of his prose, the kind of fantasy rooted in reality which has always appealed to her most. I had never heard of *The Light Princess* until she proposed doing it for the Little Library. I hope it is still used for that "middling" age of girl who is always thinking of a prince, whether in fairy-tale guise or not. Miss Moore said that these pictures "reveal a capacity for identification with childish wonder and experience." Bertha Mahony, in *Realms of Gold,* quotes George Macdonald's son as saying that his father's books for children are appeals "to the IMAGINATIVE seeing of a truth rather than a claim for its passive acceptance on the score of authority." I think it is this spiritual independence in Macdonald, as well as his adventurous fancy and deep feeling, that have appealed to the special imagination of Miss Lathrop.

There is not room here to discuss all of her books, but we must surely stop to give tribute to her share in *Hitty: Her First Hundred Years*. She and Miss Field bought the famous doll together, and I well remember their excitement as the earliest pages of text and pictures were created. As always, this artist was meticulous about all details of bookmaking, the old-fashioned cloth copied for the binding, the color work, hand-lettering, type, etc. Of course the pictures beautifully fitted each phase of Hitty's dramatic career. And the book was chosen as one of the fifty best books by the Graphic Arts Committee.

Soon after this began Dorothy Lathrop's own adventures in writing. She first told me the plan for a wonderful picture book; it drew on most of her favorite subjects—the small creatures of field and woods, the fairies, and the circus. She suggested writing a slight text to accompany the pictures. The pictures came, but I waited and worried about the text—until at last it arrived. It was exactly the right interpretation, the rich reflection of her stored-up wealth of watching out of doors with artist's eyes; it had a grace of style shaped by continuous good reading. This was *The Fairy Circus*.

What a variety of ideas have flowed from her pen and brush since then, in word and in picture. And a variety of treatment of black and white has come, too. *Who Goes There?* showed a great stride ahead, and used a technique further perfected in *Animals of the Bible*.

How can one put into words the peculiar personal quality of an artist's work? At first, one could identify Miss Lathrop by those evanescent fairies which caused so much discussion. You probably have heard her defend them: "But a FAIRY wouldn't have a fat jolly round body, would it?" Lately, however, she has become most famous for her animals, was chosen by Mr. Mukerji to illustrate his last book, created her own *Bouncing Betsy,* was chosen by Helen Fish to do this medal-winning book. What extraordinary patience she has to watch animals, and what an eye to catch those particular motions that are individual to each. Her sense of design has matured, with each book there are bolder attempts at dramatic placing of the subject, a fresh rhythmic interest in use of wing or hoof, leaping arc of back or tiny footprint. The power to evoke a magic atmosphere is still with her, but the variety of moods in her pictures has increased. Because she sensed this power to evoke moods with simple symbols, Sara Teasdale chose her to illustrate that beautiful selection of her poems for young people, called *Stars To-Night.*

But to define her work, one can only note carefulness and delicacy, eerieness and firm reality, a persistent effort to say each thing beautifully. She has a gentle humor which might better be called joyousness. Of course the jewel-like radiance of her color work is the despair of engravers, but it has been at least approached in some plates, and we must hope for more color from her.

For Dorothy Lathrop as artist, her future is assured. Whatever she may offer us will come in books that are to be treasured. But what will she give us in words? Will she experiment here, too? She is an artist first, a busy one, and very modest about her writing. But anyone who knows her letters, all her books, her paper on animals as models, and her talk, knows that she has much more to say in writing. Meanwhile, we are grateful for the lovely words and ideas in *The Fairy Circus, The Lost Merry-Go-Round, Who Goes There?, The Snail Who Ran,* and *Bouncing Betsy.*

I shall end with a page of her prose. This I choose specially for you, Dorothy Lathrop, and I copy it sending you thanks for the lovely originals on my walls, the woodcut of the frog that

THE famous doll "Hitty," and also the book "Hitty," are the joint property of the author, Rachel Field and the artist, Dorothy Lathrop. Hitty as a book, its size, shape, binding, color of paper, all are due to Miss Lathrop's taste and care. No small part of Hitty's fame is owing to the rare pictures Miss Lathrop drew, with Hitty posing for her, hour after hour, month after month, in her studio. But there are models, much harder to paint or draw, studied by this artist even longer than she studied Hitty. Those are the real creatures of woods and meadows, the elusive toad and frog, caterpillars, butterflies, the friendly squirrel, her own pet turtles, the wee eft, the firefly. For years she has treasured a secret plan to weave them into a fairy tale, and at last we have a book entirely her own, one of the most beautiful gift books of the year.

The Fairy Circus

Written and Illustrated by
DOROTHY P. LATHROP

Cloth, 9½ x 8 in., $3.50

Once the real circus was set up in a meadow. When the big tent went up, it caught some fairies in one far corner, so the fairies saw the circus. At once they wanted a circus of their own. When they went back to their own woods, they planned it all out—turtles for elephants, mice for horses, squirrels for lions, fireflies to light it all and to make the hoops of fire, spiders to weave the trapezes and tight ropes—and many other wonders.

What a circus they had! Of course they did many things strangely, and you who know the real circus will laugh at their tricks! But think—some of the things they could do much better than mortals. We want you to be surprised, so guess these for yourself, until you open the book.

What astonishing, beautiful, real and magical pictures! You will look at them for hours, and every time find something new. There is the big color spread of the circus procession, an endless delight; there is the marvelous color picture of the great diving act before the fairy queen; altogether, twenty big pictures.

But the story! You never read anything like it. These fairies poke fun at the ones in books—you'll see why. The ring-master of their circus listened carefully to the real one, and his announcements are awfully funny, full of those grand words that the circus loves. Beside such a laughing page, comes one so beautiful—when the tight rope fairy jumps over the moon, when the evening primrose opens—that you will look at the real world quite differently, after you've read it.

OTHER BOOKS ILLUSTRATED BY DOROTHY LATHROP

HITTY: HER FIRST HUNDRED YEARS. *By* Rachel Field. $2.50

STARS TO-NIGHT: POEMS FOR BOYS AND GIRLS. *By* Sara Teasdale. $2.00

THE SNOW IMAGE. *By* Nathaniel Hawthorne. (*The Little Library*) $1.00

THE LIGHT PRINCESS. *By* George MacDonald. (*The Little Library*) $1.00

THE PRINCESS AND CURDIE. *By* George MacDonald. (*Macmillan Children's Classics*) $1.00

16

🐾 *"FAIRIES* and Elves! The Roman Standing Race! See where they come, foam-flecked and furious!" Four powerful mice careened into the arena with two fairies standing astride them, a foot on each. One of the many exciting moments in Dorothy Lathrop's beautiful new picture book, "The Fairy Circus."

🐾 *DOROTHY LATHROP,* the artist who really knows both fairies and the real circus, who can draw squirrels as lions, and turtles trying to be elephants, and who paints butterflies so that they shine on the page.

makes little children laugh, the valentine of the gay lamb that makes older children sigh with joy, the special portrait of Hitty all my own, and that tiny woodcut of newts and efts. But also as I write I remember our evening in the country when you found me my first evening primrose. And my only message to you, of congratulation and hope, is to keep on saying what you see and feel in word or picture, whichever says it best for you. Here's your fairy tight-rope dancer poised on a cobweb, the dark night behind her glowing with fireflies, and you say:

> She stepped out on a thread almost invisible, she danced, twirled, and pirouetted, all, it seemed, on empty air. The evening primroses quivered. It may not have been her steps on the taut cobweb that shook them. The flowers open just so. The swelling bud quivers. A petal stirs and snaps open. The flower rests. Then shivers again. Another petal springs backward. The third and the fourth, too, with living movements, and the flower lies open and fragrant and still.
>
> All the buds were quivering open. Their perfume lay on the moonlight.

Gertrude Stein for Children

A review of The World Is Round *by Gertrude Stein
(published by William R. Scott, Inc.), in*
The Horn Book Magazine, *September, 1939.*

Here is a new book that is a new kind of book, and I like it very much. It is rather a job to tell you why, because it has to be read aloud. You and I should be taking turns, chapter by chapter, laughing and seizing the book from each other. For of course it is fun to find out how well one reads it. Inevitably one wants to see how much better one does the next bit, in spite of the lack of punctuation; how, in fact, one produces punctuation oneself with so little trouble.

But I must not talk about style before I tell you why you will like Rose.

> I am Rose my eyes are blue
> I am Rose and who are you
> I am Rose and when I sing
> I am Rose like anything.

For me, that verse is enough. And you, too, perhaps, can easily remember—or have you never lost it?—that peculiar, frightening sense of being yourself, and, at times, of being almost too much yourself. "The World Is Round," says the title, yes, that-is another appalling fact, the refrain of this book. Also the sun, moon, and alas, even the stars we once thought five-pointed, are round, and keep going round and round. Where do *I* come in? Please make someone stop it all and listen to *me*.

Taking this so obvious and simple a spiritual sensation, Miss Stein has explored it, tenderly, gaily, in her usual rhythmic flow of words. The story is subtle; to some it will seem no story at all, to others a thoughtful and entirely new exploration of the moods of childhood. Here is the child's quick apperception, his vivid sensation, his playing with words and ideas, then tossing them away forever. As for the story, Rose's part is clear. She tries to find the something that is not going round, that is always there. So at last she climbs a mountain, all alone—except, for comfort, she takes her blue chair. Willie's part is not quite so clear, but he will seem funnier to children—drowning (or almost), buying a lion, going to save Rose, and in a postscript, marrying Rose! But to an adult it does become clear, the difference between them, and Willie's sense of his apartness from Rose, yet his likeness to her.

I see I am becoming complicated, so I shall begin again, for the book page by page is ridiculously simple. Rose, we learn, had a very usual home and two dogs. She sang to herself a great deal, and it made her cry. (Her dog, Love, cried, too, when she did.) Willie, too, had a sense of himself as unique, and he too sang of it, but it didn't make him cry, it made him more excited.

> My name is Willie I am not like Rose
> I would be Willie whatever arose
> I would be Willie if Henry was my name
> I would be Willie always Willie just the same.

Well, Rose went away to school near the mountains (and all

the time the world was going round). And Willie went to stay in the country, and sang of the lizard that lost its tail, and the "frogs and pigeons, butter and crackers, flowers and windows."

"It was time Willie did something, why not when the world was all so full anywhere." So he went to a place where they sold wild animals and chose a lion which he wanted to give to Rose. After several chapters of one sentence each, recapitulating facts about this lion, there comes a floating-off-the-page picture of noise with a drum in the middle. That was when Rose, listening to the band at the door, knew that there was a lion, but it was not a real lion. This idea made Willie laugh very much and—"Billie the lion never was anywhere. The end of Billie the lion."

Now comes Rose on her trip. Before she went, she sang: "Dear mountain, tall mountain real mountain blue mountain yes mountain, high mountain all mountain my mountain. I will with my chair come climbing and once there mountain once there I will be thinking, mountain so high, who cares for the sky yes mountain no mountain yes mountain no mountain yes I will be there."

So—she goes. And there is a night of fear, but not half so fearsome as the woods in the Snow White movie. And was she lost? "She never had been lost and so how could she be found even if everything did go around and around."

Is it all utter nonsense? Well, lots of it is purposely playful, so that the author catches herself up with a "well, anyway!" For some children it will actually ring true to their half-spoken inner feelings. For some older ones Miss Stein's real meaning, that it is all imaginary, will be clear. For some adults it will carry a deep nostalgia for the dreams and fears and never-told impressions of childhood, and the sorrowful moments of consciously growing older. For others, it will be too much of a shock; they will recognize the line by line landmarks of sensation, but will be impatient of so much "stream of consciousness."

Because Miss Stein has such a personal conception of style, still others will be "put off." For me, this is the first time that her style has spoken truly and artistically as perfectly fitted to her thought.

But mountains yes Rose did think about mountains and about blue when it was on the mountains and feathers when clouds like feathers were on the mountains and birds when one little bird and two little birds and three and four and six and seven and ten and seventeen and thirty or forty little birds all came flying and a big bird came flying and the little birds came flying and they flew higher than the big bird and they came down and one and then two and then five and then fifty of them came picking down on the head of the big bird and slowly the big bird came falling down between the mountain and the little birds all went home again. Little birds do go home again after they have scared off the big bird.

For me, the whole is an unforgettable creative experience. It may be too esoteric to have a fair chance with the average child. But it is so new in its pattern, so interesting in its word rhythms, so "different" in its humor, that the person of any age who reads it gives several necessary jolts to his literary taste. Only a true artist could have written so charming a book as *The World Is Round*.

The publishers have tried it out on many children, all of whom were "surprised and attentive." The response was perhaps most intelligent and cordial in girls of about twelve to fourteen. But with such a style, it is true, as it has been true with so many modern artists working for children, that the actual age limit cannot be guessed and should not be defined. There may be some psychologically minded who do not believe at all in fantasy or in the encouragement of a child's own increased self-analysis. One could assure them that such books have not any other effect than the deepening of their poetic consciousness. And, in this material age, such books come seldom in the course of their reading.

The most acutely honest comment the publishers received came from a boy of twelve: "It is more relaxing than anything I ever heard of." Another said, "It is much more *human* than most books." Another, "The use of words has you laughing till your sides ache." A thirteen-year-old girl said, "I think Rose and Willie are wonderful. I like people who really feel things inside, and I adore the way they express themselves in their wonderful songs." Another girl the same age: "The story is simple and dreamy. You can forget yourself and live in a separate world while you are reading it." A younger child writes, "I love the new style writing because it is the way I, or any other child, would think and write." Of course there also were children who thought Rose, Willie, and Miss Stein were just "dumb."

The book is printed in large blue type on pink paper. Clement Hurd has done modern, flowing, symbolic pictures. His clever use of white is nicely balanced by large white numbers for each chapter. The whole make-up suits the material very well.

For a postscript may I add that it is no world-shaking matter to be for or against this book. But to those who honestly enjoy it, let me say it should be used, none too solemnly, with the most varied sorts of children. We don't want them all to write like Miss Stein! We do want to jog them out of the horribly ordinary prose that engulfs them. In the big inclusive volumes of Mother Goose we used to find strong rhythms and endless variety of word patterns, but our modern, emasculated, carefully selected and word-counted material has lost that strong tang. Miss Stein is not tops even in her own field; she cannot touch the Joyce of *Ulysses,* for instance, or Virginia Woolf. But she is one freeing agent who was peculiarly fitted to do her good piece for modern children.

Rachel's Gifts

From The Horn Book Magazine, *July, 1942.*

She was one of my very first authors, when I was a new young publisher, and soon I found out that she had much more of a "publishing sense" than I had. Her wide range of friendships lay mostly among people who wrote or drew or acted or sold books. Ideas of what *they* might do with their talents, and suggestions about their work, both to them and to publishers, were quite as much a part of her talk as her own work. She enjoyed all the aspects of bookmaking and bookselling, and had hundreds of friends in both fields.

As to her writing, I think other writers should know how hard she worked at it. She liked both pen and pencil but thought best at the typewriter, and rewrote and corrected at the same battered old machine. She wore out work chairs and tables and bit off all her fingernails. First Spriggin, then Trotty, her Scotch terriers, watched and listened to the noisy labor, interrupted faithfully to give them their proper walks. How often, if I wanted to see her, she would say, "Well, I'll just stop long enough to walk Trotty over."

Ideas for stories or poems she never lacked, but some innate taste or honesty made her able to choose, among those many ideas, the ones exactly suited to her special kind of ability. Twice, at most, in my judgment, did she stray without her own range. No one could have failed to find in her manuscripts something worth saying, being said very clearly, in a sort of inevitable personal style. No one needed to edit, except for the mere mechanics. Sometimes a troubled Rachel would come in with a plot or a chapter that was not going well. She would leave with a heart-felt thank you, but she had only thought it through for herself aloud. Never was an author who needed less help, or who took more joy and pains over the physical bookmaking, once the writing was done. It was she who brought Elizabeth MacKinstry and Dorothy Lathrop to my desk first, to work with her. Some of us treasure copies of *Taxis and Toadstools* hand-colored by her. She begged to be allowed to hand-color a whole edition of a book with her own pictures! She was very modest about her own cut-outs and pictures, did them "just for fun," moaned over people and their arms and legs, pored over Kate Greenaway and Lovat Fraser, but dashed off her own attempts in profusion so that the best could be chosen.

Her main work, that very hard work of writing, supplemented by various other jobs, earned her, laboriously and slowly at first, so many good things. "The Playhouse," in Maine, bought with returns from her first book of plays, led to all her Maine poems and stories. And how much fun she earned, too! Her journeys; the car she so loved to drive; the parties with her own grand cooking; always the theater; and her few particular treasures, chiefly books. We had one specially gay trip together, with Hitty and Spriggin, to Boston. Macmillan sent us in a drawing room, for Spriggin's sake, and put us up at the Ritz, and it was all very gala. She had to make a tremendous speech, didn't like that very much, but before long I think she didn't mind her "lectures," because of the people afterward; for she seldom tired of people, whether she

WE are lucky, in America today, to have several famous authors writing chiefly about American things, people, places, giving us an ever richer sense of our own present and past. Of these, Rachel Field is among the most beloved by boys and girls. When she took a tiny quill pen and guided the little, old, wooden hand of "Hitty", to write of "Her First Hundred Years", Miss Field produced a book already called a classic. As the Newbery Medal book for 1930, it achieved even greater fame, and took its author on a tour of America which won her thousands more friends and readers. They are going to find her at her best in another New England story, "Calico Bush."

Hitty: Her First Hundred Years

By RACHEL FIELD

Illustrated by DOROTHY LATHROP. *Cloth, square 8vo., $2.50*

Awarded the John Newbery Medal in 1930, at the A. L. A. convention in Los Angeles, to which Miss Field and Hitty flew in a T.A.T. plane, and where they were greeted by plane and by radio, by library, state and city officials.

From an open letter, written by Hitty to The Three Owls: "It is not everyone who has lived for more than a hundred years and seen the world from a whaling vessel and the Portland-to-Boston stagecoach. Besides, I have had more broadening literary opportunities than most. Was it not my privilege to have Mr. Whittier write a poem about me, and was I not picked up by the very gifted right hand of Mr. Charles Dickens? Not that I am boasting of these experiences; I only mention them by way of proving that my background is genuine. It seems to me that dolls and books have one very important trait in common: we never change our expressions. Even when I was undergoing my most harrowing experiences, I kept my cheerful smile and tranquil brow."

The Pointed People

Illustrated with cutouts by the author. $1.25

Delightful poems about children's every-day interests, many set among the pointed pines of Maine. Miss Field's first book.

Little Dog Toby

Illustrated in line and color by the author. The Little Library. $1.00

Story of a little dog of the Punch and Judy shows in Victorian England.

Calico Bush

By RACHEL FIELD

Illustrated by ALLEN LEWIS. *Cloth, 7 x 8½ in., $2.50. A Junior Literary Guild Book, December 1931. Published in November*

This is a New England story, set in the Maine country, which Miss Field knows so well, and bringing New England history and legend and Maine background more realistically to the page than any of her writing except her fine adult poems. We meet Marguerite Ledoux, a French girl "bound out" to the Sargent family, moving with them by a long sea journey from Marblehead up to Mount Desert. There they are real pioneers, with friendly and hostile Indians, with the wool shearing, the spinning and weaving, the hard-won crops. Legend and ballad have their share in the plot, and so does the quilt-making. A New England quilt pattern bears the name "the delectable mountains"; that praise seemed to Miss Field particularly to apply to Mount Desert, so it is used on the jacket and binding of the book.

As for the title, that will be explained when you read the ballad an old settler sings to the young French girl; and you can find the calico bush yourself, if you go to Maine. The reality and romance of this story, its poetic approach and fine plot, all make it appeal to somewhat older girls than the average reader of Hitty. All the adults who are Hitty's admirers will enjoy this tale of the "bound-out girl" of long ago.

The White Cat

French Fairy Tales, edited. Illustrated by ELIZABETH MACKINSTRY. *$3.50*

Miss Field has also illustrated for us, this year, Margery Bianco's new book, described on page 20.

14

🖙 *HERE* you see Marguerite Ledoux, the bound-out girl of Miss Field's new story, on her journey up the coast, to help start a pioneer home in Maine.

🖙 *MISS STEPHANIE BENÊT,* aged 7, one of the youngest readers who is enthusiastic about "Hitty." Her father and mother read most of it aloud to her.

15

liked them or not. We mustn't forget that trip to California when Mr. Brett, Jr., felt that Rachel *and* Hitty should go by plane to receive the Medal, and they had a welcome in the air from the Mayor of Los Angeles. Yes, Rachel had a lot of fun out of her work. When she and Dorothy were planning about Hitty, not a word written nor picture yet drawn, and Rachel had the outrageous idea of taking *bids* from publishers for it, she said that without doubt it would win the Newbery Medal, be on the Graphic Arts list of fifty books, and be a best seller. It did all three, though Dorothy and I only laughed at her then.

I want to tell writers a little of how hard she worked, and how she slowly improved her own strength and talent, as the list of her books so dramatically shows. But I also want to tell the *Horn Book* family how she made time to work at doing very special things for the people she cared for. Her gifts, for instance, were always different from anyone else's, and I can best illustrate by my own, many of them right here in my little children's book room. Here is the little old hooked rug she made for my wedding present, with a horse in the middle, supposed to look like my husband's favorite steed. Here are many quaint old children's books she picked up for me for Christmas surprises. From Maine would come a pot of her own wild strawberry jam, and with it this sea gull, beautifully soft and real, carved by an old captain. The children love this tiny Austrian merry-go-round, with its wee wooden people. My first music box came from her, with a painting of her own pasted on top, a valentine. How she loved old valentines and old dolls, and music boxes, and old clocks, and even funny old savings banks.

And dogs! How excited she was when I acquired my Mr. Nathaniel Winkle! What serious talks we had as to who was the best "vet" in New York. Whenever Rachel came, Mr. Winkle lost some of his tremendous dignity to show his love for her, a rare demonstration. Here is a small dachshund she gave me, made by a famous sculptor most perfectly out of delicately cut tin. Rachel's beloved Spriggin still lives on my wall in one of Dorothy Lathrop's first woodcuts, and she is buried in the garden of Rachel's dear friend, Helen Fish. Trotty was given her for solace by Pamela Bianco.

The perfect tribute to her music-box mania was paid by Priscilla Crane, who hired one of the few remaining New York street-organ-grinders to play outside the church door after Rachel's wedding.

Once when I was in the hospital for six months, many people were extra kind and clever at amusing me, but Rachel was at the very top of the list. There was a marvelous day when she brought Katherine Seymour to do her puppet shows for me. There was that miraculous tiny Christmas tree, about ten inches high (Alice Dalgliesh made me one, too), hung with minute gifts. Most thoughtful of all were the books she brought. There were not many good paper-bound books then, easy to hold for one who could not lift the head. So Rachel chose many Haldeman-Julius five-cent books and rebound them in gay bits of flowered paper and extra-illustrated them herself. Here are *Aucassin and Nicolette,* Andersen's *Fairy Tales,* in two books, *Irish Folk Songs and Tales, Old English Ballads.* Beside them on this shelf of little books is *The Seaman's Own Alphabet,* a picture book made for my first trip abroad. And here is her own most favorite book of all, given me on one of my few bad days, Herrick's *Selected Poems from the Hesperides.* In front it says, under a little sketch of clouds and stars, "Rachel Field, Her Book." Then—"Not after April 1st, 1932; it now belongs to Louise." On the title page is a spray of three blue harebells. All through are pasted in tiny paintings of flowers, and here a mushroom. I mean, of course, a toadstool.

That reminds me of the green felt belt she made me, all decorated with little felt toadstools. After she married Arthur Pederson, moved to California, and acquired Hannah, there was of course a change in my gifts and hers. The mail was full of pictures of

Hannah, and reports of her. But my last Christmas gift from her—found for Rachel by Arthur in San Francisco—was a handkerchief bordered with tiny wild strawberries. Still an unmistakable Rachel-gift, in spite of pressure of home and baby and the hard work finishing the new novel.

By now you see why one's own gifts to Rachel always seemed very inadequate and unimaginative. And I am only one of a host of friends who could write such lists. As if her books, with their special illustrated messages in front, were not gifts enough!

To take time and trouble for her friends, that was very important. Also, to be extra friendly to odd or lonely people, to draw them to her rooms to meet her other friends. This extraordinary warmth of heart, and fiery partisanship of all those she adopted into her life, is what many of us will remember longest. How did she have time for so many people, so many things done with her own hands, *and* her writing? (I remember her saying that her careful bookbinding was no trouble at all, because the chief part was to SIT HARD on them while she typed.) And Time haunted her, too. Like many poetic people, she felt Time as a physical presence, felt "him" sometimes for or against her, tried to cheat him by toying with astrology, wrote many poems about him. For all her home-making, housekeeping, practical qualities, there was a "sixth sense" about her, which she would have liked to cultivate more, had she believed in it more.

I wonder if I know why she was a very good writer for children. In the years when I knew her, she did not see much of children, she had few theories about them, she never tried things out on them. But her kind of acute attention to the visual details of the outer world was like that of an alert child. This and her special loves in books, as you see in my little booklist, and her love of the drama, all made her a good storyteller, and tended to a directness and simplicity of style that was inevitably appealing to children.

If she had had any theory about it, it would have been spoiled. She had a very vivid and accurate and long memory. It was not accidental that she did not write of her own childhood, for she remembered much of it very exactly. But she used it all as approaches to stories. And they are all good stories. *Hitty* is perhaps the best, as a unique piece of Americana. *Hepatica Hawks* and *Calico Bush* are written with more emotion than *Hitty*, and each touches on feelings not frequently dealt with in books for girls. Are the children today missing that darling story of "The Elfin Pup" in *Eliza and the Elves?* And will *Little Dog Toby*, with its sights and smells of old London, be forgotten? No, the verses will be read and said and sung, and the stories pored over, and sometimes acted out, and essays about "My Favorite Author" will be written about her for many years to come.

Caring enough for the toadstool, the wild strawberry, the old toy; caring enough for all one's host of friends; this capacity to care so much, this kind of generous giving of oneself to the world— this is the source of all the memories that make writing, and brings the rich return that was Rachel's happiness.

Tribute to an Artist-Wanderer, Thomas Handforth

From The Horn Book Magazine, *Handforth Edition, October, 1950.*

In the late twenties and early thirties, a happy brew was stirring in the children's book field; much of its spice and a good deal of the steam of the cooking came from the number of artists from all over the world who contributed to its bookmaking. The artists as well as the books came here from foreign lands; and our own artists traveled freely, too, to far places. One of the most intelligent of the American wanderers was Thomas Handforth, a young man beset with rather unusual ideas about proving the bases of his style through living in the lands where various styles originated. His wanderings brought us children's books from Morocco, Mexico, China, India. But the bulk of his work was in a great number of etchings, lithographs, and paintings. This is a well-deserved tribute, but it is much more than that: through faithful description of the progressive thinking of its subject, it points toward future thinking about the meeting of art cultures of different civilizations.

My first meeting with this young artist was in Morocco, through my old friend, Elizabeth Coatsworth. She had been there, and on her return had written *Toutou in Bondage,* a merry story of a stolen dog who finally chose the master who gave him work and fun instead of the mistress who gave him dull comfort. She had suggested an artist known to her through his agent in Hingham, an artist who was most luckily in Morocco. Now my husband and I were on our way to that exciting country. Before we left, some of the pictures arrived, and the book was published in that fall of 1929, the first book of Thomas Handforth.

We met Tom in Rabat, where he had settled down for a while, and made many Arab friends. One young Arab noble had begged him at a party to exchange clothes, so that he could "feel" how it was to wear American trousers. He had gone off for a week with Tom's best suit, leaving this fair-haired, blue-eyed American to go about in flowing Arab robes and headbands. Of course, one in such a costume made a fine guide to Rabat. Only he could have led us to that gay graveyard overlooking the ocean, where parties gather at sunset time. Later we bought Tom's fine etching which preserves that scene, "Graveyard Chess," a delicate summary of a whole civilization. We wandered, too, in the noisy marketplace, past the *souks,* into the fine French colonial museum, and lingered near the doors of the forbidden mosques. We had mint tea with sugared gazelle-horn cakes, looking out toward the famous pirate island.

But Tom's favorite city, and Miss Coatsworth's, and ours too in turn, was Marrakesh. Wilder, more truly Arab than the seaports, a crossroads for distant desert tribes, its primitive beauty has a dramatic setting against the long line of snow-capped Atlas Mountains. As much of all this as possible, especially of Marrakesh, Tom put into the pictures for *Toutou.* His work for this book is in a style well known in his etchings of this period. He used a delicate, nervous, exotic pattern, but also plenty of emphasis of story details for the action that brings the story to the eye of a child. The book struck a fresh note, both French and Arab in its undertones, sophisticated, gay, decorative, subtle, alive yet also a bit decadent. As a good, thinking artist, Tom could not have lived with that style for too long.

This unusual book was a bit too special. Morocco could not win many hearts, even when there was a little dog for hero. Marrakesh was waiting for Mr. Churchill to add to its fame by painting there. The book was one to be proud of, but it has been out of print for some years. Today, it looks as fresh and distinguished as it did in 1929. Perhaps it will be the French in Morocco who will give it another lease of life, for it catches all the charm of the old Arab ways as only one who lived there could see them. There is predominating humor, besides loving appreciation. The decorative approach never hides the fundamental good drawing.

Next, from Mexico came his drawings for Susan Smith's *Tranquilina's Paradise* (Minton, Balch) in 1930; then *Mei Li* in 1938 and *Faraway Meadow* (both Doubleday) from India in 1939. The last two had his own stories. In 1944, he illustrated *The Dragon and the Eagle* by Delia Goetz, happily lending his more humorous memories of his beloved China to a booklet of the Foreign Policy Association. Memories of China again brought charm and authenticity to Margery Evernden's *Secret of the Porcelain Fish* (Random, 1947). This lovely book and *Mei Li* alone are still in print.

For, as his Caldecott Medal book, *Mei Li*, so well proved, it was China that gave him his deepest inspiration. Best known of all his books, most appealing to children, still deservedly alive and popular, *Mei Li* shows him at his full strength as an artist. On every bold, big page it proves him akin to those great Chinese artists of old. Here he is saying something about that dream of uniting the arts of East and West. Such an inspiration could not have come from the static art of the Arab. Nor would he have found it in China had he not lived there and loved it as a home.

How easily he could have gone on, doing other picture-story

books in this same adapted Chinese style, bringing us other aspects of China. In fact, from the piles of drawings, prints, photographs he left, much more is available for books. But war drove him home to America, and he was diverted to painting for a while and to that extraordinary work with mentally retarded boys of which you will read here. One night he brought to dinner at our apartment in New York a huge case of the paintings these boys had done with him. It was a startling, moving experience to see these paintings, and to hear him tell which sorts of mental states produced them. It was a bitter disappointment to him that, after all the time he spent explaining them to art people and to medical men, they had no public showing during his lifetime. That showing was arranged by his friends after his death. But the work has not yet had the impact on both the art and medical worlds that he had hoped for.

Let me end on a gayer note. All of Tom's friends must have shared with me those extraordinary Christmas cards of his. With finical care and obvious gay delight, he would put together odd bits of Oriental papers, gilt laces, pictures, cutting, pasting, redesigning, until each of us had an individual treasure to bring his greetings. I look from one of these shining on my desk, to the wall where has hung for so many years one of his brush drawings of a Chinese mother and child, a portrait strong, simple, dignified, a noble tribute to a Chinese friend.

I wish he could have fulfilled further both these aspects of his bright promise. But he left more in accomplished work—etchings, lithographs, paintings—than many a one who lived much longer. These works will live, as will at least one of his books. So will that special intelligence that made him an artist-wanderer-thinker, and endeared him to Arabs, Mexicans, Chinese, Indians, and to us many lucky Americans who called him friend and miss his presence.

Helen Sewell, 1896-1956, the Development of a Great Illustrator

From The Horn Book Magazine, *October, 1957.*

You climbed a long flight of creaky stairs to find Helen Sewell at her bright open door. Within, high white walls, a few oil paintings by her friends, flowers, and books made it a place of light and color. A door opened on the little room she called her studio, where shelves were neatly stacked with materials for her work and her drawing board stood ready. Over twenty-five years ago I had first come to this old house in the East Thirties in New York, when Helen had one big room, with a leafy balcony.

On a special day last year, we sat with big sheets of brown paper spread about. These were her latest paintings, bold designs done in one color with a broad brush. They were astounding experiments in rhythmic form, each more surprising and exciting than the one before. They were a climax in her work. All her life, in her books and in her painting, she had been searching for the style that best expressed her inner self. An artist friend said, "She had to find the artistic truth for her, and now she has found it." In this new way she now would go on to paint and draw more surely and happily than ever before.

Ever since she was eight years old, Helen had found drawing and painting her pleasure and necessity. When much older she found that her painting kept hand and arm and mind ready for new, freer rhythms when she returned to the small compass of a book page. The development of her techniques was matched by imaginative progress, for she was a great reader; her thoughts about art, art criticism, and the philosophy of art grew with the years, as did her understanding of many loved authors she reread. Our talk led her to find the manuscript of a recent speech by her philosopher friend "Susie" Langer. Certain chapters in Mrs. Langer's highly successful *Philosophy in a New Key* and in her later books, she had discussed with Helen while writing them. Helen urged me to read an English book in which she was absorbed, *On Growth and Form,* by D'Arcy W. Thompson. She said, "This is giving me a plan for an exciting book, a picture book that will explain form to children in a new way."

Always when with Helen, one was stirred by fresh ideas. She was a quiet, shy person, deeply modest about her own art, but in such talks one felt the special inner serenity and wisdom that made her so important to all her friends.

Her importance as an illustrator is obvious. It becomes exciting when one gathers most of the seventy books she made and considers them by years. They show a range of style, mastery of different techniques, and capacity for understanding different authors, that are unmatched by any illustrator today. Her books of the twenties and thirties look fresh and "modern" still in the fifties. Every style is based on sound training in traditional art and design, and long practice.

The eight-year-old who was determined to be an artist was born at Mare Island Navy Yard, California, on June 27, 1896; went around the world before she was six; then lived for two years on Guam where her father, Commander William E. Sewell, U.S.N., was Governor. She writes, "I remember Guam only too well, a

wild place full of earthquakes and typhoons and lizards." The
three little Sewell girls, wearing the ruffles of the nineties, were
photographed there, in a tiny barouche drawn by two ponies.
Helen has said that the influence of the tropics dominated her art
work for years. Surely the greatest influence of all was her young
mother, who was a talented artist.

But Helen seldom spoke of her mother, for shortly after they all
returned to America, to Portsmouth Navy Yard, New Hampshire,
both parents and one sister died in a tragic accident which she
could not bear to talk about. Then Helen and Marjorie went to
live with a beloved aunt and uncle in Brooklyn, New York. There
Helen attended Packer Institute, and, at twelve, was the youngest
art student at Pratt Institute. She and Marjorie were led to Pratt
by its Saturday morning art classes for children. She knew that
"Navy children must earn their living when they grew up," and
decided to earn hers as an artist. Meanwhile, she was happy in the
large family of cousins, many of them younger than she. It meant
that she often cared for children, knew them well, and kept vivid
impressions of them. She says it led naturally to her wanting to
make books for them.

Later, she studied painting with Charles Hawthorne and at
Archipenko's Art School in New York. She began to earn her living
by going every day to the Norcross office to make Christmas cards.
I have kept some that are exquisite designs, suggestive of medieval
illumination. They added greatly to the Norcross reputation and
her first book was published by Norcross in 1923, the handsomely
printed, colorful *Cruise of the Little Dipper,* with text by Susanne
K. Langer.

A Vassar classmate sent Helen to me at Macmillan's just when
I had at hand a poetry manuscript by Mary Britton Miller. She
made *Menagerie* (1928) a handsome book, its creatures drawn in
a bold, crisp style. Then in 1929 she made of Miriam Clark Potter's

Sally Gabble and the Fairies one of the gayest of the Little Library books; in the same year she did wonderfully amusing pictures for *Mr. Hermit Crab,* a fairy tale by an English child, Mimpsy Rhys.

Her next book, *A B C for Every Day* (1930), was all her own. It took a small boy and girl from "Awake" to "Zip into Bed." The amusing words were chosen by her small niece, Pat, and a neighbor boy, who were her models. The big figures of the children were done in brush, in bold strokes of gray, with red and blue cleverly alternating. Intelligent parents welcomed it with joy. Dr. John Finley chose it for "Bompa's Book of the Moon Club" for his grandchildren, and the Child Study Association gave it a prepublication party.

Helen's sister, Marjorie Cautley, had become a distinguished landscape architect. After a trip to Scandinavia, she wrote *Building a House in Sweden,* which Helen made into a striking two-color picture book (1931), using a strong line style for the realistic sketches and giving it a truly Swedish feeling. It was a forward-looking book; we even agreed to introduce children to bits of the language of that country, a device very popular today.

It was an exciting day for me when Helen brought in the plan for *A Head for Happy* (1931). This story was to be told in pictures, with only a few captions lettered in by the artist. The plot was about three little sisters who made a big doll for a brother and went around the world searching for a proper head for him. It had all happened to the Sewell sisters shown in their charming Victorian dresses; and the family treasured the real Happy for years. Her early style here was at its best. Very strong outlines are formed by exaggerated shading at the edges. Broad white highlights within the forms and white where the forms break, as at the knees or elbows of a child, give the effect of light playing through the picture. The varied rhythmic patterns for waves, whether calm or stormy, for smoke, for curly hair, all are both "patterned" and real, very modern as symbols but very clear to a child's eyes. All is done with boldness, freshness, and gaiety. There is humor in the story-telling of each picture, also in many details. The sharp black and white is enhanced by the soft blue borders. Though long out of print, this distinguished book is widely treasured, listed, and re-membered. In it we find among the children's toys a paint box.

Twenty-five years later Helen told me: "Some of my early books remind me too much of my Christmas card style. They look old-fashioned, as perhaps they should, for their stories. But 'Happy' was more my kind of thing. It was really a step toward what I am trying to do in the fifties."

We see further developments in 1932 in the first of Mrs. Wilder's Little House books and in Helen's amusing *Words to the Wise*, but chiefly in Langston Hughes's poems, *The Dream Keeper*. There is increasing use of black on white, as in a dark woodcut, a skill which came to its height in the wonderfully humorous pictures for the Irish stories of Máirín Cregan, *Old John* (1936). In so many pic-tures, she showed with her pen the skill of a wood-block maker and the feeling of a sculptor. I think her final style bears out this tendency to think as a sculptor but she never admitted to me any interest to do sculpture. In all these early books we see often her very fine pen treatment combined with strong outline and the in-creasing use of dots rather than crosshatching, which led to the style of her Bible. We also feel her greater sympathy for poetry and imaginative writing than for realism. *The Dream Keeper* has lived on, with a ninth edition in 1954. It is a prophetic book, with a mix-ture of styles, some symbolic, some done with a strong poetic realism. Both would appeal to the teen-agers for whom the poems were intended.

From her ninth year on through all her life, a second home to Helen was Fo'castle Farm at Burnt Hills, New York, where lived her aunt and uncle Claude Bailey, a retired Lieutenant Commander in the Navy. They also had a cottage on Lake George, near that of her grandfather, Admiral John W. Moore, where many cousins gathered in summer. She knew all this beautiful country well, before the days of automobiles. Here, her uncle says, he watched her "read more and more widely and think profoundly as she matured." He shared books with her on archaeology and anthropology, philosophy and religion. He says, "She was one of the most satisfying intellectual companions I have ever known." At Fo'castle Farm still stands a ship sign she carved. In the Burnt Hills Episcopal Church is the stained-glass window she designed in memory of the beloved aunt who had helped to bring her up, Emily Moore Bailey, who was also an artist.

The barns and all the creatures of this farm are exactly shown and truly named in *Blue Barns* which I published in 1933. The exact realism is made lovely by her mastery of form and design and by the many tones of her lithographic crayon. The amusing, gentle, true story she wrote is just the right length for the picture-book listener. The book delighted critics and children both. It has had a postwar edition in England and a seventeenth American printing in 1957. The farm, the funny gander, the wild geese calling have a timeless appeal.

Here was a highly popular style and limitless farm subject matter. But Helen never used either again. It soon became clear to her editors that she never wanted to repeat herself.

In 1933, I had begun a fairy-tale picture book series, one of which was Elizabeth MacKinstry's brilliant treatment of *Aladdin*. Helen's *Cinderella* was a great contrast, its large pages delicate in flat colors, the Perrault period costumes modernized, and the borders of flowers stylized. Each pair of pages makes a clear tableau, easy for small children to interpret, even without the very simple text which Helen herself devised. In the same year she illustrated Elizabeth Coatsworth's *Away Goes Sally,* the now famous story of the little house on sleigh runners. To match its old New England feeling, she used a brand new style, a technique like that of engraving, rich with dots and crosshatching, delicate in detail but strong in overall effect. Once again, her treatment of every detail of the bookmaking was superb, especially the snowy end papers. In somewhat the same style, she did four later companion volumes to this first Sally story.

But all the while she had been putting long hours on what may well prove to be her most famous book, for in this same year Grace Allen (now Mrs. Hogarth of London) produced *A First Bible* (Oxford). This fourth book of Helen's in 1934 still stands out with distinguished beauty among the many Bibles illustrated for children. The black and white pictures glow with varied light effect achieved by painstaking pen stippling. The simplified, strong figures are superbly drawn and speak to a child as very real people. The subjects chosen are dramatic and make each story memorable. The book has a timeless dignity; it often becomes a long-treasured family possession. It was greeted with truly understanding praise. Both English and American editions sell on and on. Oxford made an eighth edition in 1955.

This work was done with a fine pen, all the shading of draperies and molding of faces done in stipple. Each fraction of a picture meant hundreds of dots of the pen. The whole took infinite patience, following many trials on tracing paper to get the overall design right. This same technique she used later in *Pride and Prejudice* for the Limited Editions Club (1940). They wrote of it with amazement, calling it an imitation of nineteenth century engravings. I doubt that Helen imitated any bygone skill and consider this a development of the feeling for form shown in all her earlier work, a reaching toward sculptural wholeness on a flat surface.

Within another year, Helen illustrated *A Round of Carols* (Oxford, 1935), one of the loveliest song books ever offered small children. The costumes and decorations are medieval, happily simplified. The style is bold, with soft outlines, and handsome, rich use of two colors. Where the Bible pictures are dramatic, awesome, or mystical, these are gay and tender. This rare book was selected as one of the Fifty Books of the Year by the American Institute of Graphic Arts.

Between 1935 and 1943, Helen made five gay, small picture-stories about real children, for beginning readers. Each of her texts has clarity of action, brevity and humor on the level of five- to seven-year-olds. The pictures are done in a skillful free line, with increasingly clever use of flat color. In *Ming and Mehitable* (Macmillan, 1936), she remembered a little dog given her on Guam by a Japanese sailor. *Peggy and the Pony* (Oxford, 1936) reflected a journey taken with her sister Marjorie and her niece Pat to England and France.

Long loved, both here and in England, is *Ten Saints* by Eleanor Farjeon (Oxford, 1936). The full-page color plates suggest stained-glass windows with their strong outlines and fine use of flat colors. They are as varied in feeling as the saints themselves; their subjects sometimes are touched with humor, sometimes gravely heroic, always childlike in concept. For a new edition in 1951, Helen redrew the basic plates, the first plates having been destroyed by government order in the war to conserve metal, a fate that befell many books.

In 1942 came another high point in her work, with *A Book of Myths: Selections from Bulfinch's Age of Fable*, published by Doris Patee who had succeeded me at Macmillan's in 1934. Bulfinch had been a favorite of Helen's youth. She found that many growing children liked his clear, brief stories as an introduction to the longer epics. Her style here was completely new. It probably developed from the Greek vase figures but is very modern. The eight pages in two colors are intellectually fascinating, fresh and varied in concept and design. The twenty-four line cuts are in a delicate, single outline style, yet very bold and sure as to form. The wonderful figure drawings have a modern French feeling. The effect of the whole is heroic and poetic, with an airy, sunny, magical atmosphere. It is an outstanding book of our time.

Of Helen's books for May Massee at Viking, I must mention the beautifully printed story of the child Jesus, *Once There Was a Little Boy,* by Dorothy Kunhardt (1946). The color pages match the text perfectly in realism, simplicity, and tenderness. Their appeal to the five- or six-year-old who listens to the words will continue to give the book a long life.

In her imaginative books, Helen was inclined to draw mostly from memory, perhaps after study at the Metropolitan Museum, or in her art books. In her "real" books, she occasionally felt the need of a model, and so began the increasing group of children who came to the studio, successors to all the cousins and the niece, now grown up. I heard much about one "Doodle" who came there when she did the Wilder books and loved them as much as Helen did. *Three Tall Tales* (Macmillan, 1947) is dedicated to the eleven boys and one girl whose discussions of books, pictures, and "the comics" led her to make her own "comic" book. The three amusing stories were told her by Eleska, that gifted artist who gave us our first good cloth books. Eleska had traveled far in Asia and had entrancing sketchbooks of her journeys. The children really did help with the text; also they were very insistent on certain comic-book techniques, such as the balloons of talk inside the pictures. So here is such a comic book as you will never see on newsstands, truly funny and truly artistic. The style makes frequent use of blocks of pure color without outline. It keeps the free pen outline of some older styles but looks toward new methods.

In 1948 Helen made a beautiful cut-out book, *The Golden*

Christmas Manger (Simon and Schuster). The style was traditional, using many colors and gold, a Renaissance nativity effect. The cut-outs were carefully designed in big, simple forms easy for a child to cut. The book can be set up as a crèche, with the several acts of the Christmas story. I was very proud to have this distinguished, lone "toy book" of Helen's dedicated to me. She hoped to do a "Noah's Ark" to follow it but it never did get done. Nor did she make funny pictures for my Bowker Lecture, "Books in Search of Children," which she had in its modest New York Public Library edition. She wanted to get it printed alluringly in a cheap book "so that millions of parents will read it."

We had collaborated on something very different. Doris Patee suggested that Helen should illustrate my story *The Brave Bantam* (Macmillan, 1946). She came to the country where, during the war, we were truly farming, to meet my heroine. In the big chicken yard she sketched the hundreds of Leghorns and one family of Bantams. She said she must refresh her memories of Chinese scroll painting. "They're the ones who know how to paint birds and fowl and I must get a feeling of their style in this book." When she brought a layout to show me, she had done over the sketches hastily, with a broad pen, in swiftly dashing lines, almost a calligraphic style. It was all so gay and free, so artistically right, that I urged her not to touch these drawings again. The result is illustration that is among her best work.

A sympathetic collaborator turned up when Helen and I both felt inadequate to make a story for older children from material she had long treasured. She had clippings, letters, and a diary that told of a group of Russian orphans adopted by a U.S. Army colonel after the First World War. Alf Evers wrote *The Colonel's Squad* (Macmillan, 1952) ever so well, and here we saw for the first time another new style, with heavy outline and simplified, very modern forms.

From 1948 to 1951 she had been developing this style, with marvelous humor, in those first three wonderful *Azor* books, for Eunice Blake at Oxford. Then came the more surprising *Grimm's Fairy Tales* (Oxford, 1954) done in collaboration with Madeleine Gekiere. They had worked together to gay effect before, making a colorful book of *Mrs. McThing,* the popular play by Mary Chase. They collaborated in a way new for an artist team, each doing separate parts of a scene, or facing pictures that belonged together. In the *Grimm,* Miss Gekiere made the delicate, fairy parts of a scene, Helen the more "real" parts or people. It was an astounding tour de force in bookmaking. Its wide praise from reviewers I think surprised the publishers who, while greatly admiring the art, had begun to think of the book more as for adults than as a fulfillment of a long-ago contract with Helen for a children's book. However, one of the best reviews was written by a child in *Junior Reviewers.* I feel sure that, in recent years, Miss Gekiere, a neighbor artist and devoted friend, encouraged Helen to "find herself" in her art as her old teacher Archipenko had done.

But she had more than one "modern" style to offer. Very appealing is her work for Alf Evers' *In the Beginning* (Macmillan, 1954), a new telling of the story of Genesis for small children. Here are big, simple forms, bold and pure, a further development of her use of flat color. She used it in still another way, in her exciting pictures for *The Three Kings of Saba* (1955), made for Eunice Blake at Lippincott. Helen had discovered, in *Marco Polo,* a little known, dramatic, legendary telling of the story of the Magi, which Mr. Evers retold in a fine style for any age to enjoy. The flat color is placed in blocks, on or within bold forms defined with a fine pen line. The modernized medieval effect is completely new and has great power. The pictures flow on as if in a play, with the three kings strongly characterized. It would make a splendid TV Christmas drama or could be read aloud with accompanying tableaux.

Another surprise in her style, one that is a climax of all her color work, came in the pictures for Alice Dalgliesh's *The Thanksgiving Story* (Scribner, 1954), which has proved a juvenile best seller. This was far and away the most distinguished artwork for children of that year. A bold choice of varied forms contains each picture, within which figures and objects are placed in rhythm to fit that form. All is connected by the lovely succession of colors, rich yet cool, carrying us through the New England year. The pictures add to the able text, which is so simple and direct for younger children, an aura of mood and a hint of legend.

Equally exciting is her work for *Poems by Emily Dickinson* (Limited Editions Club, 1952). Here the feeling for new forms seen in the boldly simple, gay *Azor* pictures and the strong, heavy shapes in the *Grimm*, reached a very special, very individual, completely adult expression. And here all her interpretive powers were truly tested. Louis Untermeyer, editor of the book, wrote:

> These drawings excite me more than I believed a drawing could excite these ancient eyes. . . . They never are mere decorations or "illustrations." On the contrary, they are amazing creations which are translations of one art in terms of another. They go below the surface of the lines (as the poet did) and reveal implications which are provocative, frequently teasing, and sometimes terrifying. They bring out dimensions which even admirers of Emily Dickinson frequently ignore; they add new emphasis to the tart humor, the wit and whimsicality, as well as the pure suggestive power of the poetry. The accent is New England—with universal overtones—and the artist's use of the half-archaic, half-stylistic method is everywhere justified. . . . Miss Sewell indicates the poet's astonishing range, from badinage, to brilliant mockery, and to breath-taking leaps of the imagination. . . . The poet has found her true visual interpreter.

Helen's last book was also for the Limited Editions Club, again a Jane Austen, *Sense and Sensibility* (1957). Here is the same "witty, ironic, penetrating power" that made her *Pride and Prejudice* such a contrast to earlier illustrated editions, but she met the different mood of this book by using a style more like that of the *Emily Dickinson.* In sending me the book, she wrote, "I simply had to work out a new style for it. I wanted it to be just as 'appealing' as the other Jane Austen work, but still new. It had to be NEW."

One can hope that, with increasing interest in the graphic arts, in high schools as well as in colleges, these three adult books of Helen's, along with the *Grimm, Mrs. McThing, The Three Kings of Saba,* and the *Bulfinch,* will be treasured and shown to young artists. In the Youth Rooms of public libraries, they will lure modern teen-agers and stimulate them to new understanding of the texts.

Actually, Helen Sewell's last work for a book came about in a surprisingly happy way during her last illness. Scribner's used some of the new paintings described at the opening of this article, on the jacket of *Problems of Art* by Susanne K. Langer (1957), author of Helen's first book, *The Cruise of the Little Dipper.* It is dedicated "To my lifelong Socratic teacher in the arts, Helen Sewell." Much that Mrs. Langer has written of the necessity for new art forms, of "the genesis of artistic import," is borne out in the development of this artist who never stopped "growing" in hand or mind.

Nowadays, artists are more and more studied and judged from the sketches or drawings which are their "quickest" work, often the surest test of their skill. Most of Helen's sketches were destroyed by her, except those in the layout dummies she made for publishers. But these last "designs," the "fast work" shown on the Langer jacket, are sketches in the sense that they were never re-touched. They are the "bones" of future work. They can be compared to many sketches in current books of "master drawings" in which we find artists reaching, as she did, toward fundamental forms. Hers are something truly new. They combine the solidity of boxlike forms with imposed angles in most original suggestions of structural pattern.

At the opening of this piece, I referred to this latest style as if it were the one which gave Helen final satisfaction. Actually, I now feel sure that she was thinking toward still another style. However much one admires this latest work, one must admit that its impact often is tragic, even when it is humorous. It suggests to me a special creative acceptance of a personal pattern reaching deeply into the rationalizing of art and nature, into that dark subconscious strength we must all call upon when facing the inevitable. But I am sure that Helen's last reading impressed on her the variability of nature and its changes in pattern and form. I am sure, too, that that tragic sense of life had been conquered by her humor and her philosophy. Her love of beauty in all forms would have kept her searching on for new ways to express it.

In a survey of the seventy books, one must realize how much planning went on in her mind as well as at the drawing board. She prepared dummies, or advance layouts, for each picture book with meticulous care. Imaginative understanding of the texts takes time and makes the record of her work, against each year, even more astounding. One must remember, too, that some books, like her beautiful reader for Heath in 1951, *Secrets and Surprises,* took a solid year to finish.

So it is not surprising that she was not well known personally to so wide a circle of book people in New York as she deserved. Nor was she publicized to a wide public, for her modesty cheated her out of many of the usual forms of publicity. Understanding reviews and letters were her greatest reward. But she did have honors, too, such as being commissioned to do a Children's Book Week poster and having all her recent books featured in *The New York Times* lists of ten best-illustrated children's books of the year. Seven of her books for Macmillan have had either English, Irish, Swedish, Danish, Norwegian, or Finnish editions.

No one who knew her could doubt that Helen had a happy life, or that she faced the challenge of each new book with delight. She had her special circle of interesting, devoted friends and was absorbed in her big, far-scattered family. The qualities that made her friendship treasurable were the same that made her such a sympathetic interpreter of diverse writers. The central tragedy of her early childhood, the later loss of her sister, her growing deafness, the pressure of necessary hard work did not make her withdraw from life. Instead, they expanded a spirit already generous and tender, stretched her imagination further, and intensified the drive toward artistic expression. You feel all this even in so simple a picture as one of little Azor—he strikes you with a zest as bracing as the sea wind.

It is cheering to realize that, like all truly creative people, Helen made time, or took time, for experiments that were her kind of fun, that released new skills as the painting did. Here I have an etching she made long ago, deeply bitten, printed by herself in brown ink, a dark caricature of a subway scene. A charming small etching of the farmhouse at Burnt Hills is among the many Christmas cards she made for the Baileys. One year she did a number of humorous small drawings for *The New Yorker*. Many friends must treasure other things which are the happy overflow of her genius.

On the other hand, looking backward, one is sorrowful that so much energy went into book work that proved ephemeral. Every book that was Helen's own idea deserves to live long; many of the others are truly distinguished. But in the years through the Second World War, the return on all her books was so small that she had to do some happen-chance books to live. An artist cannot wait to be sure a manuscript offered is "great"; she must be glad her work is wanted at all. The plan of an author sharing royalties with an artist was not in effect in Helen's early years; children's book sales then were much smaller than now and artists were paid much less. I only wish that some wise Maecenas might have helped her so that more of her time could have gone to her painting or to the sculpture I always felt she should have done. But her heart was wholly in her bookmaking.

The special qualities of this artist one would say were: originality, integrity, cultured intelligence, boldness and strength of style, a high sense of humor, a deep sense of the poetic. Her books bring children both beauty and fun, but also lead their eyes on into the world of adult art of which they are a part. In them one meets a personality with inflexible high standards, a mind always searching to express itself in art more clearly; a person outwardly very gentle and physically fragile, but inwardly ever so strong, wise, and fearless.

Helen's wish was "to be well again just long enough to do some of the new painting I have in my head, and to make a few more books." One, she had told me with glowing eyes, was to be a selection from the poems and prose of John Donne. At the end, she was valiant and calm, dreaming of her new work.

Margaret Wise Brown, "Laureate of the Nursery"

From The Horn Book Magazine, *June, 1958. Based on a speech opening the Margaret Wise Brown Collection in the Westerly (Rhode Island) Public Library.*

What do writers care most about? My answer would be two simple things: first, that they continue to feel a joy in the act of writing; second, that their work be published so that possibly it may live. Margaret Wise Brown was one whose joy in writing was most obvious to all who knew her. She wanted her books published even more than most writers because she conceived them as picture books and couldn't wait to see the picture part completed. She had that satisfaction to a remarkable degree, with the added joy of huge sales which told her she had delighted many children.

Her success was almost fantastic. To date, about one hundred books by her have been published, with total sales probably over fifteen million. She collaborated on, or contributed to, a dozen more books, including some school primers. She wrote a children's page for *Good Housekeeping* and helped make several Victrola records. She was given an illustrated write-up in *Life,* for which she and the interviewer concocted a rather fantastic picture of herself. Probably humor or fantasy is all one can use who is asked to explain what drives one to publish from four to eight books a year, when it is not financial need. Her inner ambition was to write adult poetry, of which she left a great hoard, all unpublished. More or less secretly, she kept trying to be a painter. She was adult and sophisticated in many ways, yet she never lost the special sensory acuteness of childhood nor a present sense of the real and the dream worlds of her childhood.

How can I describe this engaging friend, to make her come alive to you? She was medium tall, slim, with flying flaxen hair, and never a hat upon it. I saw her most often in winter, in a worn old fur coat, holding the leash of one or both of her big Kerry Blue dogs. Her pale face had a golden glow to match her hair. Her large, light blue-green eyes were quiet, watchful, often lit with fun; when she talked they became most luminous and expressive. She had an odd, gentle, high-pitched voice; she talked slowly, often hesitantly, hinting at a complex emotional make-up.

Margaret Wise Brown was born in Brooklyn, New York, on May 23, 1910. Her father, Robert Bruce Brown, was a prosperous manufacturer. Both he and her mother came from Kirkwood, Missouri, where his father had been a governor and a United States Senator. Early in her childhood they moved to Whitestone Landing on Long Island where she had the freedom of woods and beaches. She had many pet animals: the thirty-odd rabbits and "one dog of my own plus six borrowed dogs" foretold the many animal heroes of her books. Her brother being a bit too old and her sister a bit too young for close companionship perhaps bred an independence in play and friendships. Very early she showed that special love for and need of privacy that never left her.

She attended Dana Hall, in Wellesley, Massachusetts, after spending two years at school in Switzerland where, she insisted, she learned "French *and Scotch*." She went to Hollins College, Virginia, where she won her Bachelor of Arts degree in 1932. At school and college she was chiefly interested in experimental writing and in reading "new" writers. After college she took a short story course at Columbia but said she gave it up because she "couldn't think up any plots." That she was more a poet than a storyteller is obvious in most of her children's books.

Chance suddenly led her into a field of writing she had never considered. She heard of a truly experimental writing group, a class conducted by Lucy Sprague Mitchell at the Bank Street School, then called "The Bureau for Educational Experiment." Her very first work there made her happy. She said, "Experimenting in writing for children is so much less *precious* than doing it for grownups."

The brilliant Mrs. Mitchell who ruled over "69 Bank Street" was the sort of creative person who analyzed writers shrewdly and helped many besides Brownie to find themselves. I often visited her writing classes to criticize or to advise about publication. After one of them Mrs. Mitchell said to me, "That Brownie bears watching. She is a poet, and really knows small children."

At Bank Street, Brownie could tell stories to various age groups of children. She could watch them through those windows at which they cannot see you looking in. She was put on the school's publication staff, and helped through the press Mrs. Mitchell's second *Here and Now Story Book* to which both she and I contributed, and in meetings about it we became friends. She took down stories told by children at the Little Red Schoolhouse and said they were "a revelation of spontaneity, of imagination and of language." So she studied lower age levels "to find how and when this creative vitality started." She found that Mrs. Mitchell had already studied the same problem and written upon it.

Soon she met young William Scott and his partner John McCullough, who were starting a new firm to publish new kinds of books for the "neglected" nursery-age child, the age of their own children.

She was their first official editor, and author of their first book *Bumblebugs and Elephants* (1937). Printed on stiff cardboard, its "big and little" creatures still delight the very youngest. A bit before that, Harper published *When the Wind Blew*, a fantasy based on a story by Chekhov. Then in 1938, Dutton issued *The Fish with the Deep Sea Smile*, and Scott, *The Little Fireman*. Altogether, she had seven books in those first two years and was well started on her extraordinary career.

In 1939 came Brownie's and Scott's first big sales success, *The Noisy Book*. We met the little dog Muffin, with his bandaged eyes, guessing at city things about him by their sounds. A child must guess, as Muffin does, before you turn the page. Thousands of parents found out how their youngest children were all attention for a book they had to talk back to. The brilliant flat-colored modern art by Leonard Weisgard fascinated them. So a series was started which now has seven titles, all nursery classics. Harper published the last three and have now taken over also the first four. When interviewed about them, Brownie once said that they were intended "to make children give honest sensory responses, not take them from a page without thinking."

Brownie's greatest editorial excitement, while still an editor for William Scott, was in persuading Gertrude Stein to write a children's book for them. She loved to tell about the day the manuscript arrived, how she and Mr. Scott and Mr. McCullough gathered at her apartment that evening, forgetting dinner, to read it aloud. A huge birthday cake in the shape of a ship stood there, intended for a friend. They sat up most of the night, reading and rereading *The World Is Round, or Rose Is a Rose* (Scott, 1939) and gradually ate up the cake. The book caused a tremendous stir; some adults were "against" it, but lots of children loved it and saw the fun of the style. I wrote a vigorous bit of praise for it in *The Horn Book*, included in this book (page 85).

With four books a year, and half a dozen more contracted for, Brownie left her editorial job. During the war, I once met her for lunch at the Museum of Modern Art where she introduced me to that great Mexican artist, Orozco. I told her I was against her using pseudonyms—"Golden MacDonald" and "Juniper Sage"— that they didn't hide her real name from anyone. She gleefully announced a third one, "Timothy Hay," but *he* had only one book, *Horses*. She claimed that each name had a different personality, and publishers didn't like having so many books a year under one name. Probably I told her that success was ruining her.

Be that as it may, "Golden MacDonald" wrote some of Brownie's best books for Margaret Lesser at Doubleday. What child could resist *Red Light, Green Light* (1944)? What adult could fail to buy *Little Lost Lamb* (1945) for which Leonard Weisgard created that appealing small shepherd and of course a *black* lamb? Then in 1946 he illustrated *The Little Island*, which won him the Caldecott Medal, and of which more later. Whatever the "alias" used on them, these books surely will live as Brownie's.

As "Juniper Sage" she collaborated with Edith Thacher Hurd, a friend of the Bank Street days, on that startling book *The Man in the Manhole: and the Fix-it Men,* illustrated by Bill Ballantine (Scott, 1946). A new edition has appeared recently, taking children again under city streets to see the mysteries that bring them light, heat, and water. Brownie and Mrs. Hurd also did together the Little Golden Books about firemen, miners, policemen, etc., bringing those heroes to the level of very small children, weaving facts into brief, amusing stories.

Brownie's first Simon and Schuster book was a "big" one, *The Golden Egg Book* (1947), with truly gorgeous color by Leonard Weisgard. It was the essence of spring and a most welcome new version of the Easter bunny idea. It was a great success, and of course they offered her further contracts. This got her into trouble with her other publishers. Simon and Schuster's children's books were sweeping the country, and other countries, too. Publishers of the "regular" trade editions were apprehensive and wanted to keep their authors to themselves. But Brownie would sign no contract restricting her output, and she won. As a matter of fact, she had books with nine publishers by 1952.

Well I remember the day when she received her first huge check from S. & S., huge because they paid in advance on the printing of the first edition, which might be 50,000 to 75,000. She was dazed, and decided to spend it at once before it proved untrue. New cars were hard to get that year so she took her one remaining Kerry Blue on a plane to Florida where she had heard there were lots of new cars. "I'm going to buy a big station wagon," she said. "A dog like a Kerry isn't comfortable in a little car." It was the same spirit in which, ten years before, she had taken her first advance royalty check from Dutton straight to the steamship office to buy passage to Ireland.

Her eighteen titles with Simon and Schuster have sold, up to this writing (February, 1958), almost twelve million copies. The best seller is *Five Little Firemen*, over two million. All have had foreign editions, mostly in European countries, some in the Argentine and Australia. The delightful *Color Kittens* wins with nine foreign editions. Brownie's editors here were Georges Duplaix, Dorothy Bennett, and Lucille Ogle.

My own firm favorite of these books is *Mister Dog*, "the dog who belonged to himself." He is named Crispin's Crispian, after Brownie's big black poodle who succeeded the Kerry Blues. What a lovably ragged, characterful person Garth Williams made of him! He appears again in *The Sailor Dog*, a fine story told her by the eight-year-old neighbor, Austin Clarke, whom she credits as collaborator. Dog lovers of all ages chuckle at the details in *Mister Dog* and at the very essence of dogginess in this lovable book. The touch of genius is in creating a small boy who also "belongs to himself," as all little boys realize they do, while they laugh at the pretend boy who lived with a dog.

Brownie could write anywhere and on any old scrap of paper, in an airplane, in the station wagon in front of her grocer's. But of course her homes were important to her books. When I first knew her, she lived in an apartment on West Tenth Street, a conventional, well-kept home, with lovely old furniture, many books, unusual paintings. There was nonsense around, too, possibly gifts from members of her "Bird Brain Club" which held Christmas at any time of the year they wished.

Later she bought an old house on the Maine island called Vinal Haven, twelve miles out to sea from Rockland. There she had spent several summers in childhood. She named it "The Only House," because it was the last of a group built long ago by granite cutters. In its attic studio, she told me, she felt as if living in treetops, wonderfully alone with the sounds of the sea, "wanting to think hard but happy just in being." The magic of the place, its dramatic changes with mists and tides, seeped into her. No words or ideas about it seemed worthy of it; she waited and waited. "Suddenly I had the thought that it is such a relief, when we are adults with the bewilderingly gigantic world around us, to remember that we knew, as children, that the world is as big as the part of it we really know."

So she slowly wrote and rewrote *The Little Island,* with its kitten who learns that the island is both part of the great world and a world of its own. Mr. Weisgard came to the attic studio to make the pictures, and later wrote of it all vividly for *Junior Wings:* about the window opening on a sheer twenty-foot drop to the sea; apple blossoms in another window; bees and bats coming in and out; the odor of fish chowder rising from the kitchen. Together they made an outstanding book, which Doubleday gave very fine color printing. It captures the magic of all islands.

Now let us put the pail of clams we have just dug, some flowers, a big basket of books, and the dog, into the station wagon and head for New York. We go home to "Cobble Court," way up on York Avenue. We ring the bell of a shabby old brick house, go through its dark hall, and out onto a sunny courtyard, neatly set about with clipped trees in tubs and perhaps potted daisies or chrysanthemums. There stands a tiny old white gingerbread house, a storybook house, built in 1810, miraculously left among factories and skyscraping apartments, and still heated only by wood fires.

In the hall hang Brownie's big brass beagle-horn and velvet beagling cap. There are fur rugs, a big fur-covered chair, and in the bedroom a fur rug on the bed. You go upstairs for the living-dining room and galley-size kitchen. Here sun pours in over plants in bloom and a row of big shells. A typewriter looks incongruous, and you note with surprise that Brownie knows how to use it. On an outer balcony you see piles of oil paintings, "all beginnings," says Brownie, "no good, but I can't stop doing them." She tells of an illustrator, whose work she criticized severely, who said, "You're really a frustrated painter."

One day she showed me her "Diary," kept in an old book with a worn Florentine leather cover. "What's in it," she said, "isn't facts of my life, but other matters. Dreams—I have wonderful dreams—and I put down interesting colors, and faces, and places. A few stories—here are some told me by children at a school in Harlem. Maybe I'll use them some day, but not as they are here, the children wouldn't like that. They want words better arranged than their own, and a few gorgeous big grownup words to bite on. Most children are so wonderful. After being with them I decide that almost no stories they have are good enough for them. I mean, of course, very small children. One can keep trying new ways to release their own feelings and imaginings."

It is odd to think that I jotted down these words in 1946, meaning to write a *Horn Book* piece about Brownie. Little did

I know that soon I would be reviewing her books each season. How difficult it is to choose a few more to mention here! First I turn with satisfaction to the Harper books, where her first editor (1937) was Louise Raymond. Ursula Nordstrom, her assistant, was soon to be head of the department. Harper has published thirty-two of Brownie's books, more than any other publisher, proving Miss Nordstrom's very special understanding of, and friendship for, this unique writer.

The Runaway Bunny (Harper, 1942), with its beautiful pictures in five colors by Clement Hurd, is a treasure for young mothers to read aloud and for young eyes to look at over and over. Brownie said she was "using the repeated cadences of an old French love song, transferred to the real world of a small child." It has sold on and on. Less popular, but still being reprinted, is *The House of a Hundred Windows* (Harper, 1945), introducing fifteen modern paintings to children. Each was a window in a magical house where lived only a cat. At the end, "It was up to the cat!"—whether or not he would go out the door and never return, a mind-stretching question. The talented young architect De Veyrac created this house and helped make the book one of rare distinction.

And oh! the fun I had with *The Little Fur Family* (Harper, 1946). Do you remember it, all bound in rabbit skin, in a little box with a hole to show that little fur stomach? That box alone made a kindergarten class roll on the floor with laughter. I had to read it to them over and over, and pass it around for loving pats, and for squeals of joy at Garth Williams' entrancing, tiny pictures. After over 100,000 were sold, and it had appeared "in fur" in three other countries, it turned out that rabbit skins were sadly prone to worms and moths. So a new edition appeared in more normal book format.

Of thirty-eight illustrators of her work, Mr. Weisgard has been her most frequent collaborator, with twenty-two titles. His are the books with the most varied styles and moods—he can be funny, real, magical; he can evoke beautiful places, create appealing children and creatures; he used a striking poster style in *The Noisy Books* and a brilliant, Dali-like exactness in *The Important Book*. Clement Hurd, with his power to make the present world both real and touched with magic, and his special understanding of small children, comes next with ten titles. Garth Williams, in nine books, brings to life unforgettable creatures, expressive, wonderfully funny and appealing, always real animals. All three artists were superbly able to fulfill Brownie's book plans and to supplement them with their own different sorts of imagination. But she was in a very real sense a collaborator with each artist, discussing her own layout, their sketches, and all details. When a picture was finished, sometimes she changed some words in the text to fit it better. She generally "pulled out" the best work of every artist. She was always eager for collaborators with "new" styles, such as Lucienne Bloch, Dahlov Ipcar, Symeon Shimin, E. Slobodkina, Marc Simont, Remy Charlip.

An artist whose work Brownie greatly admired and was proud to have illustrate her words was the French-Mexican Jean Charlot. He did *A Child's Goodnight Book* in 1943 and made a larger, revised version of it in 1950. With all his forceful strength and bold design, he still captured the humor and tenderness of the text and took the poetic suggestions a leap further. His handling of *Two Little Trains* (1949) is superb. In fact, all five of his books for Brownie's texts are masterpieces of modern children's bookmaking. All were published by her old friend William R. Scott, who since those early days has done twenty of her books. He has cleverly revived some of the first in new editions, such as *Willie's Adventures* and *Sneakers*.

Mr. Scott wrote in 1938: "The tremendous success of her books is due to a rare quality: sure emotional insight into the realities of a young child's world bounded by the here and now." With equal discernment, he wrote in 1955: "All her books have an elusive quality that was Margaret Wise Brown. . . . [They have] simplicity, directness, humor, unexpectedness, respect for the reader, and a sense of the importance of living."

In years to come, publishers will be able to rediscover and reissue books by Brownie for a most fortunate reason. They can turn to the permanent collection of her work at the Westerly (Rhode Island) Public Library. To date, they possess all but four of the ninety books of which she was author, the eleven which she adapted or edited, the seven story collections in which she appeared. They have some of the artist's originals and the author's book layouts; records, filmstrips, and much other fascinating material.

In the early days a publisher once asked Brownie, "Have you another manuscript you can show us?" She replied: "I have a big drawer full of them. I dream them up in twenty minutes, then polish some of them for a year." A person who is creative in this way (and I think most truly creative people are prolific) is not apt to be self-critical, that is, as to relative values of separate pieces of writing. Brownie believed in the criticism given her by children themselves. She would often try out manuscripts and finished books on children she knew in various homes and in schools. This way of testing books is far from infallible. But anyone who has seen small children make a beeline for her books knows that, with her, it worked.

I suspect that she enjoyed the wide arena of her publishing world in the same sporting spirit as that which took her off to hunt with the Buckram Beagles on Long Island. She enjoyed any contest of wits in a publisher's office, whether over binding or punctuation (her idea of this was, the less the better). She seemed shy in public but she was very curious about people and interested in editors she felt were truly creative. As to the business end of it all, she was far from reliable. She kept no proper record of her sales and royalties. I find a letter which tells me one firm paid her 40 per cent on a book! It is said that once she claimed she *couldn't* have to pay an income tax because that year she had spent more than she had earned. One list she sent me that I fully believed in is headed "Books Under Construction." Some of these you will see in 1958 and 1959.

To her host of friends, news of her death in France on November 13, 1952, was a terrible shock. She was extra happy that year, for she was planning to be married. How could she, the adventurous, strong one who could chop wood, ski, skate, do so many things well, just suddenly go, after a normal appendicitis operation? It couldn't be true. She had had fun in Paris, celebrating the appearance of *Mister Dog* in French. She was staying at the Château Barlow, near Eze, the magical little ancient castle town on its steep hill above the Grand Corniche. She died suddenly, in the hospital at Nice, thinking she was well and ready to go home.

Once she said to me, "In the back of my head, I keep busy; in the front of my head, I am slow and stupid." I love to think of her at Eze, seeping in impressions of that beautiful old world and the sea spread out below, wondering whether she would now, in a new life at home, turn at last to writing for adults. The last words should be her own:

> A book can make a child laugh or feel clear-and-happy-headed as he follows a simple rhythm to its logical end. It can jog him with the unexpected and comfort him with the familiar, lift him for a few minutes from his own problems of shoelaces that won't tie and busy parents and mysterious clock-time, into the world of a bug or a bear or a bee or a boy living in the timeless world of story. If I've been lucky, I hope I have written a book simple enough to come near to that timeless world.

Padraic Colum:
A Great Storyteller
of Today

From The Catholic Library World, *December, 1960, in
which The Catholic Library Association announced the
award to Padraic Colum of the 1961 Regina Medal for
his "continued distinguished contribution to
children's literature."*

A unique figure in the literary world today is that distinguished
Irishman Padraic Colum. He came here for a short visit in 1914,
but stayed on to make New York his home. The young Dublin
poet and playwright had known the exciting days of the beginning
of the Abbey Theatre; he had shared the opening turmoil of the
last phase of the Irish revolution. He was welcome here, first as a
lecturer, soon as a critic, dramatist, novelist, and especially as a
very popular reciter of his lyric poetry.

Now in his eightieth year, Colum has been honored by the
National Academies of both his countries, among many other
awards. He was chosen by Hawaii to go there to record its folklore.
He has edited two great anthologies of Irish literature, besides
writing more poetry, plays, fiction, essays, and biography. And,
along the way, he has created a rare shelf of books for children.

In all Colum's work, there stands out his love of literature and
learning for their own sake. He has served them wholeheartedly,
untouched by the increasingly commercial literary scene. To his

MAKING BOOKS FOR BOYS AND GIRLS

COLUM, PADRAIC. From a boy in the Irish country, Mr. Colum grew into a young poet and dramatist of the first group who formed the Abbey Theatre. His writing took him to England, then to America, which has been his home for some years now. He writes criticism, poetry, and fiction. His most important contribution to American children, and to the world's literature, is that, as a poet, as one who was trained at the hearth by the Irish story-tellers, he has retold the world's greatest myths and legends, fusing each into a new poetic whole for the children of this day to understand. His power to be true to the literary spirit of the original, yet to create a new literary whole, is unique among story tellers, and could be achieved only by a scholar and a poet.

DIX, BEULAH MARIE. While she was still an undergraduate of Wellesley, Beulah Dix's first historical fiction became a printed book. Her chief interest was in the period of civil war in England and colonizing in America. Her books in this field have become classic. Of recent years she has written chiefly for the movies, and lived in Hollywood. She is now Mrs. Flebbe and has a daughter twelve years old. We believe in her stirring plots, her historical accuracy, her sureness of choice among the kind of incident that holds young people's imaginations and recreates the past for them.

MEIGS, CORNELIA. A younger writer than Mrs. Flebbe, Miss Meigs' work has gone far in the parallel field of American history. She lives in Iowa, and is of an old New England family. Tales of east and west, of pioneers and of clipper ships have come down to her as a family possession. In both her modern fiction and her historical books, she makes use of this heritage in a striking way. Large families of nieces and nephews keep her close to young people's tastes. Her new books and her poetic plays more than fulfill the high promise of her first. "Master Simon's Garden" was a most unusual first book. Its blending of stirring incidents from three periods of American history, a poetic thoughtfulness about the spirit that was steeping the new land, is a rare contribution to the character building of American children.

TEASDALE, SARA. One of the most distinguished and also most popular of lyric poets. The genius which created such books as "Love Songs," "Rivers to the Sea," "Flame and Shadow," brought a special gift to the selection of the few greatest poems for children to know, in "Rainbow Gold." Sara Teasdale was born in St. Louis, has traveled widely, now is married and lives in New York City.

From the 1924 catalog of Macmillan Books for Boys and Girls

multitude of friends, here and in Dublin, his presence means a shared excitement about things of the mind.

For me, his editor in the twenties, he epitomized a genius as did no other living author I knew. His small, erect figure, his noble head with that huge brow, his voice with its pure "Dublin English" accent, were a revelation to one who knew only the "stage Irishman." He was impractical, forgetful, picturesque, excitable—the traditional poet; but he was also gentle and wise, and had always a commanding dignity.

Some sources of his many-sided genius lay in an early childhood spent at the country workhouse of which his father had charge. There he met the wandering casuals of Ireland's recent past, the surviving ballad-singers, tinkers, fiddlers, whose recitals delighted a small boy. As a schoolboy in Dublin, he still visited relations on farms where, around the peat fires, he heard tales from the last of the *shenachies,* or listened to their learned talk. From these oral storytellers he absorbed a wealth of epics and legends, and many a strange personal adventure besides.

This was reflected in his first book for children, the beautifully retold epic called *The King of Ireland's Son,* published when he first reached America. It was read by an appreciative fellow Irishman, an editor of school books at The Macmillan Company, who commissioned him to do a new telling of Homer for elementary grades. So *The Children's Homer* appeared in 1918, and was a great success. It has lived on to this day, in a trade edition, with a special rediscovery in the fifties, when Lionel Trilling wrote of reading it and *The Golden Fleece* aloud to his children.

Thus began Colum's writing for young readers and for storytellers, of which there are twenty titles to date. They have followed two main lines: the retold epics, Greek, Norse, Welsh (the King Arthur stories of *The Mabinogion*) and Irish, and the shorter books reweaving legends into tales of wonder and magic. He has also retold stories heard in his childhood, as in *The Big Tree of Bunlahy,* and has invented his own fantasies, as in *Where the Wind Never Blew.* He introduced and edited several classics for children; and also brought his learning to a great book of world mythology, which recently has had a paper-book edition. Some of these children's books have fascinating postscripts or notes at the end, relating their sources to world literature and history, as in *The Legend of St. Columba.*

Colum's prose style for children has a special, lively, personal flavor. He says that he learned from the traveling bards of his boyhood "how to keep the living speech, the flow, the stylization, the fantasy." When he so naturally weaves poetry into it, the repeated verses follow the "rests" of the old *shenachies.* There is a strength and a variety to the rhythm which make it wonderful to read aloud.

Each hero he presents with great sympathy has a buoyant courage which uplifts us. Moreover, his tales let children enter the adult world; they stretch young minds toward "deeds and wonders" of their own. They encourage children to read things whole, not cut up into bits, and to appreciate legend as a continuing part of life.

Through the years, Colum has often written on the importance of cultivating the imagination. In an essay in *The Fountain of Youth: Stories to Be Told,* he says: "Some day there may be written above all places of education, 'Imagination is the beginning of creation. You imagine what you desire; you will what you imagine; and at last you create what you will.'"

All his own writing has the power to turn our imaginings away from the trivial; to lead us with its beauty, humor, and excitement toward new understanding of the human mind and heart. For children, he has been a modern *shenachie,* "a cell through which the past flows to inform the future."

Boris Artzybasheff
(1899-1965)

From The Horn Book Magazine, *April, 1966.*

It is a well-known story: how the young Russian who had left school to fight with the White Army escaped the Reds to take ship on the Baltic, landed on Ellis Island with a few cents in Turkish money, endured several years of odd jobs, despair, near starvation. The chance to do murals for a new Russian Tea Room led to his first book, *Verotchka's Tales,* for Dutton, in 1922.

In the next ten years, before he was thirty-three, Artzybasheff illustrated about twenty books, and was famous. By the sixties, the total is about fifty. Several had texts by himself; many had limited editions. But gradually he had left the book world for still greater fame with *Time* and *Life,* and was doing his unique machine pictures for advertising.

In the twenties, his style was new to our eyes, with its bold use of black, the imaginative devices for decoration, the patterns with Oriental overtones. In his second book (1926), a peasant pattern in purple and a masterly color portrait made Martineau's *Feats on the Fjord* look surprisingly modern, in the early Macmillan Classics series. It was as truly Norwegian in feeling as his next book was truly Indian. Mukerji's *Gay-Neck* (Dutton, 1927) still stands out as one of the best-designed Newbery Medal books. One critic said of it: "Even the initials and tailpieces—elephants, monkeys, strange birds—are little masterpieces."

His collaboration with Padraic Colum began in 1925, for *The Forge in the Forest*. These legends of fire, water, earth, and air, inspired double pages of brilliant, flat colors, and an all-over design which won it high praise. Equally dramatic was his plan for a book of Colum's poems, *Creatures*, which had a limited edition, signed by them both. For Colum, too, he illustrated the big book *Orpheus: Myths of the World*, recently done as a paperback. Sent to Morocco to do a travel book, he wrote his own wryly humorous fable, *Poor Shaydullah* (1931), distilling the Moslem attitude toward God, whom he pictured as looking like G. B. Shaw. Had it come after the Second World War, some soldiers would have recognized his typical Arab beggar.

Of his other books for me, *The Fairy Shoemaker* (1927), though out of print, is still famous, often pictured in histories of illustrating. For these four magical poems, he invented a new way of cutting through to white on a surface of black veneer. Lynd Ward said it was "The most enchanting and perfectly made picture book of many years, by a book-artist and book-craftsman!" A. C. M. said, in *The Three Owls*, "Such a book is a living contribution to the appreciation of good art." Colum wrote, in *The Horn Book*, "What he has as an illustrator, is, first of all, integral design; what he does comes out of a clear, single conception. The picture of the child in bed is masterly. It is not fairy-like, in the conventional way—it is too powerful for that—but it suggests an escape into vision, an escape that is not for a child only."

This book came to be at a time when Boris was very broke. He begged me to let him do "any little job for that Little Library." To get him the full payment allowed, I chose some magical poems myself, finding that he laughed at the mad old King in that favorite of children, Allingham's "Up the Airy Mountain." When his first pictures came in it was obviously foolish to make them into a little dollar book on cheap paper, so I devised the larger format, expecting to put it into the Little Library later. But it was still selling well when I retired in 1934.

In 1929, came a stunning, over-size book for Knopf, *Three and the Moon,* French legends retold by Jacques Dorey, where his elaborate use of odd, brilliant flat colors, his bold adaptations of medieval concepts, outdid any previous work. A limited edition on vellum paper was signed by the artist. Its success led Knopf to an unprecedented offer of a contract to work for that firm alone, which he declined.

One day he told me he saw no book existing which told boys what he had longed to know about machinery when he was a boy. So he designed and started that remarkable big book, *What Makes the Wheels Go Round,* with its dramatic cross-sections in color of a dynamo, a dam, a Diesel railroad engine, etc. The research was stupendous, and an engineer friend had to complete it. In 1933, it was one of my proudest productions, but engineers appreciated it more than children's librarians or booksellers, who failed to show it to those boys like Boris who would have loved it. There still is no book at all like it. Here was the first evidence of that love of the machine which later brought him such fame. The Massachusetts Institute of Technology, fifteen years later, bought what he called an anthropomorphized depiction of a B-29 radar set.

He is quoted as saying, "I would rather watch a thousand-ton dredge dig a canal than see it done by a thousand slaves. *I like machines.*" Mr. Auer, the publisher of *Time,* says, "By a glimpse of a locomotive walking on crutches, or a truck holding its head, he showed us his belief that machines have souls."

Most of his books for Viking are still in print, the icy-blue realism of Hall's life of Nansen, the powerful, witty woodcuts in his *Aesop,* and *The Seven Simeons* (1937), which had new plates made in 1961. For this Russian tale, which he retold himself, he used a new style, never imitated, as was much of his other book work. Here one is entranced by the maze of delicate unending lines, almost calligraphic, printed in several colors, magically combining into people and action clear to a child's eye.

In 1940, he spoke before the Trade Book Clinic of the American Institute of Graphic Arts, which had put most of his books among the annual Fifty Best. These witty, sardonic remarks were preserved in a booklet by the A.I.G.A. entitled *Let George Do It.* "George" of the title is George Macy, of the Heritage Press, for which Boris had illustrated a Balzac. Among other authors he illustrated were Margery Bianco, Tagore, Alfred Kreymborg, Edmund Wilson.

From 1934 on, his book work decreased, as he was given commissions by *Fortune* and *Life.* These led to the world-famous portrait-covers for *Time,* of which he made 219 between 1941 and his sudden death in 1965. They were a roster of the great of that era; Mr. Auer paid them tribute in a moving editorial, keenly analyzing his genius, and the often fantastic interpretations of history that he devised as backgrounds to his portraits. These will be long remembered, but his bookmaking alone will keep his name alive. In his books for children, he offered them his best, trusting their intelligence; each was more inventive, each technique and style completely his own.

Some of his later work is collected in a rare picture book he called *As I See* (Dodd Mead, 1954), with a few paragraphs of his philosophy of life, tersely put. Here is the famous Christmas card of the mechanized man and woman of the future. Here are nightmarish "escapades," monstrous satires made, as Mr. Auer says, "because he was on the side of Man." Here his imagination and techniques go far beyond any of his former work. The editor says, "One may call Artzybasheff *the* depicter of his era, as were Hogarth, Goya, and Daumier of theirs." These pages, ironic, beautiful, often terrifying, have a power indescribable in words.

The poverty-stricken young exile had attained a success beyond his dreams. He achieved a home of his own as comfortable as that of his childhood. With his spirited, pretty wife, Betty, he had first a house in New York, then a country place in Old Lyme, Connecticut. In his loneliness after her death, he worked even harder, relaxing with a new hobby, photography. He was seldom seen at the clubs which had so proudly voted him a member, the Century Association and the Grolier Club. He was an honorary member of the Royal Society of Arts, London.

The power and hard-wrought perfection of his work contrasted with the gentle charm of his presence, his quiet voice with its musical Oriental tone. The handsome early publicity pictures we used were very serious; later ones have caught the smile that was truly B. A., wise, mischievous, and kind. In the fall of 1965, *Time* held a comprehensive exhibit of his work; it includes many originals loaned by private collectors, museums, and such places as the Computation Laboratory, at Harvard, the British Interplanetary Society, the Aluminum Company of America.

There was no other graphic artist in our time to compare with him. Among the great, he was unique in having brought new beauty to bookmaking and also showing us ourselves and our machines in peerless satire.*

* See pages 50–51 for Artzybasheff's comments as a juror at the first show of children's books of the American Institute of Graphic Arts.

Of Children and Books

The Giant in Children

Originally published by The Atlantic Monthly,
Boston, Massachusetts, 1927. *Reprinted
with permission.*

Children—catapults of energy, dynamos of ideas, summer suns of
affection, lonesome dark dreamers. Children—flaunting borrowed
plumage, desperately flying ancient flags, laboring herculean-wise
at nothing. Singing, grimacing, wide-mouthed, informative, earthy,
ethereal, combustible, secretive, acrobatic.

Let me remind you of that boy of ten who turns a handspring
and comes up quoting the book of Job, with astonishment at himself for having shaken it out. And of the girl of twelve who read
Dante's *Inferno* in the Doré edition, hanging over the edge of her
cot, the huge book on the floor, shielding a candle so that the long
weeks of midnight revel be not discovered. That Scout of fifteen
whose energy and persistence in photographing stars have made
a university contribution. The lad of six who picks out all the
makes of automobiles on the avenue. The girl of eleven who begs
to be taken to Faust, and upon questioning reveals a five-year
admiration of the plot and of the protagonist. The boy of twelve

ON
CHOOSING
A NEW BOOK

"Child, since you ask it, fruit's in my basket,
Fairy fruit in my green, green basket:
Apples to keep you fair, plums to make you sweet,
And a little silver sickle pear to give you dancing feet.
What do you choose, child? Which shall it be?"
— *Rachel Field.*

Here are the new books, ready to march into the new catalogue, and trying to get into orderly groups for your ease and pleasure. They make a gay procession, with bright jackets and endpapers, hinting at wonders within, and bright bindings strong enough for small people to handle with strenuous friendliness. Here's a bird's-eye view of the parade.

Fairy tales come first. MacDonald's princess, she who was Curdie's friend in "The Princess and the Goblin" and "The Light Princess" tossed in the air, may take the lead, to assure them of our equal affection. With them is the

FAIRY TALES

"King of the Golden River," Ruskin's tale of the good brother and the bad "black brothers" who were turned into stones. Another irresistible folk lore tale is Henry Beston's "The Sons of Kai: the Story the Indian Told." A part of this real American magic, yet something quite new and different, is the reindeer story by Mr. Burgess. It is written particularly for the reindeer who are coming from the real Kringle Valley in Alaska to bring Christmas to many American children this year, and it creates a new Christmas legend. Along comes another animal story, "The Tale of the Good Cat Jupie." Neely McCoy's friend, James Stephens, kept insisting solemnly that children should know how truly good her cat was; so here he is. Who is this with wild elf-locks? It is Eliza, the child the elves wanted—and got! Her stories, verses, *AND* pictures are called, of course, "Eliza and the Elves."

The pines of Maine loom as background for this part of the procession; glaciers of the Arctic and tornados of the Southwest linger in their wake; they are travel books as well as fairy tales. A boy to be envied is leading them, a

TRAVEL AND HISTORY

small brown boy with a large red monkey on his shoulder, painted by Helen Damrosch Tee-Van, under brilliant tropical foliage. In "Red Howling Monkey" he has many adventures in the jungle. Then comes a fourteen-year-old explorer, Kennett Rawson, telling his own tale of ships and men in "A Boy's-Eye View of the Arctic." Stefansson has abridged his classic, "My Life with

2

the Eskimos," for older boys and girls. One of the merriest travellers of all, Washington Irving, brings on king and priest, soldier and troubadour, in the new edition of "The Alhambra."

Persian crafts are to be traced in the ruins of that Moorish palace, but the new tales of the Shah Nameh are a far cry, in time and place, from the legends told to Irving. "The Epic of Kings," as Wilfred Jones presents it, is a book

HISTORY IN FICTION

of deserts and plains, tiled palaces, dreams and battles that made ancient history. Robber barons from the middle ages in Germany, fresh from the battle at the ford, parade under the title "The Dove in the Eagle's Nest." "The Gauntlet of Dunmore" catches the eye at first glance. For all its brevity, it gives a fine full picture of a medieval boy's life and training for knighthood. Shifting to an American setting, comes another historic character, the magnificent McGillivray, that "White Leader" of the Indians whose adoption of a pioneer boy was one link in the breaking chain of downfall to his dreams of an American empire.

Is it fair to make these real characters walk apart from the adventurers of romance? The young men who take that heroic raft journey in "The Mountain of Jade," the strange company who journeyed to the mysterious Casa Bianca for

ADVENTURES

"Snake Gold," the gentleman highwayman called "The Scamp"—all these are as real as any one out of history. Nor are the men the only adventurers. Here is "Toto," in the black apron of a French working girl; "Mary and Marcia," working like Trojans through a New England vacation; and "Brenda," who stayed at home when the other girls went to college.

Will Pinocchio arrive again safely? We save him a place to jump into at the last minute. There was many a month and many an accident before he was bound in strong American covers last year. Let us hope, my dear children, that the weather in Florence will be propitious and the waves on the Atlantic very kind to the second edition. A ship that passes will be carrying back to Assisi Michael Williams' story of "Little Brother Francis."

There is a noise of hammering at the end! Charlie is busy in "The Surprise House" he fixed for his mother. The children who have been using "Your Workshop" since spring are now such good carpenters that they are the envy

THINGS TO DO

of their elders. "Playing with Clay" suggests Christmas gifts for the very young potter. "First Lessons in Nature Study" gives you lots to do on your walks and in your own garden. Last of all, with the roll of a hoop, the clamor at a snow fort, the laughter of "Mrs. Maginty," comes "Games for Every Day."

Now read the pages that follow and look at the pictures, then go to your bookshop with the list under your arm. When you see the books themselves, who knows what may happen? The most matter-of-fact grown-up realist may

LOOK AT THEM ALL

succumb to the wiles of "Eliza"; the shyest dreamer may leap to the saddle for the honor of Dunmore; and our red howling monkey, with parrots and jaguars in his path, may march into first grades that were never taken to a zoo, and never knew how much they wanted to sail for South America. Choose for yourself!

who listens to James Stephens' sophisticated nonsense about the value of poetry, chuckles and remarks at intervals, "Gee, that was a wisecrack!"

Now the word "childish" means "that ought to have outgrown something, or to have been outgrown." And "childlike enthusiasm . . . is only that of a man who has not let his heart grow hard." (See *The Oxford Book of Modern English Usage.*) It is impossible to define child. Any certainty of that word as implying a mental state is shaken by the army and other intelligence tests and the records of circulation of daily papers of every sort. For all our valiant new psychology, we are still so far in the dark that our only honest recourse is to try to treat each new person as a person, the hardest effort in the world, even in adult relations. But we do know that there is, not hidden but obvious in this turbulent estate, some treasurable quality which the greatest sages keep to the end. To foster it, we try to offer it nothing which it will have to outgrow.

Therefore, no "childish" books. No so-called child to be insulted by having such "dusty fodder offered him for food" as no so-called adult could respect. But you grownups make yourselves such stupid books: their print is small, their looks are drab, their spirit is not often that of play, their stores of knowledge (until very recently) have been presented with so little ease and gaiety, and they are so obsessed with what you call love, a matter on which we could give you more happy advice than you suspect. So there has come to be a classification, a specializing, which is both good and bad, in the field of children's reading. In a big publishing house, a big bookshop, a big library, it is inevitable. But the perfect library still is the book-lined room at home, with hearth and apple, big chair and long vista out of a well-loved window, and a sense of countless treasures free to be chosen. The perfect bookshop still is where one person offers with excitement the few books he knows are real and fine, to people who respect him because they trust his knowledge. And the perfect kind of publishing—Oh, well! In the midst of my "fall list," I confess to a dream of a long year by the sea, spent in writing some Songs of Innocence, illustrating them, printing them on hand-made paper, coloring and binding the edition by hand, and delivering them on foot to my private list of booklovers, blowing loudly as I march on my occarina or my Chinese flute.

This specialization, so far as I know, is due to (1) the long pull in the library field for specially trained children's librarians culminating in the dignity of university extension courses in this work; (2) the establishing of this separate department at Macmillan's; (3) the founding of Children's Book Week. Its disadvantages are numerous—overproduction by the publisher and the author; overinvestment by the bookseller relative to the ability of his staff; overexaggeration of the "appeal to the child" versus the literary content; and overwhelming statistics tending to discourage the essential spirit of the creative reader of whatever age.

One of the most honest of these attempts to collect statistics was the "favorite book" voting contest conducted by the *Youth's Companion* recently. Granted anyone's ability at any moment to put down honestly a single favorite book, and taking the most uninteresting part of the returns, i.e. the top fifteen titles for boys and for girls, these are the results:

You agree that this is a "low" literary return. There is more of the vital stuff of literature on the boys' list than on the girls'—see their 4 and 11. The boys' 1, 2, and 10 are the only titles also on the girls' list. In my opinion, a boy gets more out of his 7, 8, 9, 11, 15 than a girl out of her 3, 4, 5, 6, and 13. Perhaps the girls' interest in travel weighs even with the boys' interest in out of doors. Perhaps the Tom Swift books outweigh the Bobbsey Twins (I prefer them myself). There is greater range and individuality in the boys' voting.

One notes the frank indifference to literary value, the lack of

BOYS—553 VOTES   GIRLS—862 VOTES

BOYS

Age	Vote
6	5
7	9
8	30
9	23
10	90
11	111
12	202
13	83
Total	553

Books
1. Treasure Island—65
2. Tom Sawyer—44
3. Robinson Crusoe—42
4. Robin Hood—37 (ed.)
5. Tom Swift Series—32
6. Swiss Family Robinson—28
7. Doctor Dolittle's Books—24
8. Call of the Wild—22
9. Huckleberry Finn—20
10. Hans Brinker or the Silver Skates—16
11. King Arthur and His Knights—14
12. School Books—14
13. Two Little Savages—13
14. Lad, A Dog—12
15. Penrod—12

GIRLS

Age	Vote
6	4
7	9
8	31
9	79
10	146
11	206
12	273
13	114
Total	862

Books
1. Little Women—187
2. Heidi—121
3. Black Beauty—82
4. Pollyanna—74
5. Bobbsey Twin Series—70
6. Beautiful Joe—37
7. Five Little Pepper Series—37
8. Treasure Island—37
9. Hans Brinker or the Silver Skates—33
10. Tom Sawyer—33
11. Laddie—31
12. The Secret Garden—28
13. Girl of the Limberlost—27
14. Little Men—26
15. Twin Series (Lucy Fitch Perkins)—26

fairy tales, and the conservative staying appeal of the misnamed "children's classics."

Chiefly, this proves what we have been giving them. Would you consider a child deprived of his birthright to "childish" things if he had none of these, ever, but instead such a list as this: the Odyssey, the Iliad, the Norse myths, the Bible; fun from Lear and Carroll, and the *Just So Stories;* history from Plutarch, Parkman, Prescott, and Green or Macaulay; adventure from Melville, Masefield, Conrad, Kipling; poetry and romance from Andersen, Hudson, James Stephens, De la Mare, Kenneth Grahame, and the *Oxford Book of English Verse;* science from Lagerlöf, Fabre, lives of Curie, Pupin, Steinmetz, etc. The child in your house may spurn every one of these and yet in his twenties have a fine discrimination in his reading. Taste does not come from without, nor can it be forced. But with so many great books, and so little time in one earthly span, and so many boys and girls who do love such books as this second list, why not try?

There are many different tastes and needs which the publisher and bookseller must answer. People in the South and West tell me that we in the East have no conception of the rural child problem. Library people say there is so little information written simply and stirringly for the adult whose university is the library. Progressive school people who are using fewer text books are inspiring us to present original source material with type and pictures suitable for boys and girls. And with the subtly shifting tastes of each new decade, new rhythms in pictures, new appreciation of colors, slowly force out the old picture books and inspire the new artist to try his hand at the old themes.

There is room for it all, but it is hard to say that the new thing has a fair chance. So many of you grownups stand between me and the children. You have your notions about size and thickness, and number of colors on a jacket, and this style being "too foreign" and that set of names being too long. You're too scared of everything, from prices (look what you get in a two-dollar children's book as compared with a two-fifty novel) to expressing yourselves. Give yourselves some noisy fun, once in a while, by running back to the children's counter (alas, it's always way back, or up, or down) and reading to the gang that perhaps you had sense enough to invite in on their way home from school, your favorite uproarious passage about Hercules and the robbers, from *The Golden Fleece*. If Princeton Prep. boys have read that book through in one night and come back with several places marked as "good laughs" you can risk your dignity on it.

Then, you can try the children's rental library. It is being tried and it seems to work, so far as effecting further sales goes, much the same as the adult rental library. In theory, it would create more sales, the child being wiser in longing to cling to his treasures, and to reread his favorites. The library cards show which these are for a start. The library children's room is your town's best bookshop in its field. It practices the art of display and publicity, from each item of which, including its storytelling hour, the sensible bookshop reaps definite profit. I have never seen library or bookshop which to my mind had enough signs. We talk about "merchandising," yet we put books in piles and rows, and leave them to speak for themselves. They can, on one round table holding six books. In greater quantities, one must help the eager, puzzled, but perhaps single-track-minded person to realize that there's many another kind of book besides this on the most familiar counter. And don't let parents come back to the same sign. If they keep no neat check lists of their own on the variety of their children's interests, remember the color of their coat tails and push them about under your brightly lettered cards for science, travel, handicraft, music, biography, for boys and girls.

Of course it is a temptation for me to confess that I am still searching for good books under all these headings. At the conference on children's reading, recently held at Vassar College, we asked each publisher to send his twelve best books. What came was entirely imaginative literature. They were rightly most proud of the purely creative thing, as opposed to the bread-and-butter books. My poor mind was really bent upon urging a certain librarian to talk more about her children and Shakespeare, and upon modestly inserting my success when teaching English, with Keats, Shelley, Housman, Masefield, in the fifth grade, and upon bringing out the mother who did the Greek epics, with maps and costumes, with boys of eight. But I found myself talking about my "Work and Play Books" for small children, showing slides of *The Boys' Own Book of Great Inventions,* and of *Politics,* and recommending Hawksworth's *Story of a Pebble, Tracks, Trains and Engines,* Hyde's *Modern Biography,* Patch's *First Lessons in Nature Study,* Tee-Van's *Red Howling Monkey,* Deming's *Indian Child Life,* Lamprey's *In the Days of the Guild,* Stefansson's *My Life with the Eskimo,* Nance's *Sailing Ship Models,* Quennell's *Everyday Things in England,* etc., Elizabeth Watson's *Bread,* etc. etc. etc.

Imagination is not rooted very deep in make-believe. How often I have been irritated by having a kindly but casual person lump all of Mr. Colum's work as "fairy tales." His dedication of *The Children's Homer* answers them: "For Hughie and Peter: this telling of the world's greatest story, because their imaginations rise to deeds and wonders." A youngster needs the strong stimulus of mythical figures, striding about a simpler earth with grandeur, and he must see beside them the small plain men of our day in whose minds this grandeur speaks, however differently.

It is justification for all this separate attention to children's reading if we can help round out the yearly book giving in families in this way. Librarian, bookseller, publisher—all are eager to make such suggestions. There are sequences in reading, very simple to plan, which may by happy accident mean more than several terms' school work. Conversely, it is to the inspired teacher that I look most eagerly for new bread-and-butter books. Good teachers are too busy teaching and too humble about each step of their experiments to be frequent authors. Another of my forlorn hopes in this field is the advertising man: he has the quality of expert presentation, witness the clarity and actual poetic charm of Gaylord Johnson's *The Star People* and *The Sky Movies*. Are there more like him? And lawyers should try their barrister powers more frequently on children: when William Bowen did it, his power over complicated plot and neat wit gave us *The Old Tobacco Shop*. Here you have a slight hint of one publisher's conceit that great writing is a byproduct of life. It is not only Yeats, hunting the bird calls at dawn on that isle of Innisfree, who makes literature, but also Melville before the mast, and also Dr. Bowman, writing *The World That Was* as he collects dimes in Pittsburgh to build the skyscraper university.

When the states begin to spend more money on books outside school books, for the public schools; when children themselves are allowed freer access to the new books; when the special children's bookshop or book department becomes a local focus of interest; when club programs, college conferences, lectures, radio, best book of the year displays, etc., have created a buying public which chooses a book with honest regard to content and format; then—well, by then we may be making something very different from these books of today.

Today we have some refreshing experiments in this field, which have already justified their existence in spite of all the hindrances sorrowfully listed above. Jennie Hall's *Buried Cities,* shrugged at by the bookshops, had the vitality in it of a lady who actually had dug up bones and crowns of ancient kings—and it lives on successfully without a peep of its Pompeian jacket on a counter. Margery Clark's *Poppy Seed Cakes* has reached the children themselves with the Petershams' vigorous line and clear flat colors. The "big" Pinocchio bought in Italy in fear and trembling is in its second large edition. Such purely artistic, rather aloof and exquisite books as *The Velveteen Rabbit* with Nicholson's pictures and *The Little Wooden Doll* with Pamela Bianco's pictures have justified themselves. The Edy LeGrand *Grands Voyageurs Français,* and the German toy book, *Our Little Doll's House,* have had new editions due to the American market. One never can tell, one has to dare, to keep on searching for the writer and artist who put the greatest ideas into the simplest, most beautiful, most vigorous form, in a style both competent and accurate and stirring, able to speak to the childlike spirit in anyone.

To trust this power of childhood—that is our challenge. Our foreign-born children are our strongest allies. They are not yet bit by the bug of journalism, nor snared by the scraps on the radio, nor spoiled by great rich rows of carefully graded selections. They are close to the rhythm of long oral cadences in old tongues; they can still be concentrated and passionate and satiric. Our children are like them before the neat suburb, the automobile Sunday, and the leveling weight of proper primers and schedules have touched them. I believe in the open-minded good taste of the child left free to choose, and in its upward discipline, granted the stimulus of books gay to see, happy to hold, a bit wild, a lot funny, and very honest.

Books Before Five

From The Horn Book Magazine, *September, 1941.*

It was surprising to me, when I first began to work with the New York Kindergarten Association, to find that teachers who spend day after day with small children (mostly pre-kindergarten) complained loudly about picture books. "How very few," they said, "either in picture or word content, really suit children before five." So we held some interesting conferences, which led me to watch and listen with new eyes and ears, and finally to draw up a list.

In an age of mechanics, radio, comics, cheap magazines, movies, the nursery is affected as well as the child who runs about in the street. For babies, as well as for big brothers of six to eight, new moods and tempers condition the responses. The nursery school teacher must adjust herself, not only to exiled children from war-torn countries, but to native-born children from bookless homes who are wise in peculiar new ways. On all very small children the great outer world has pressed itself more closely. Their attention is more difficult to hold, their emotions are more diffused. And all these small people are potential readers of our public libraries, soon to be citizens whose choice of adult reading will depend on the start they are given when very young. For this start they need new material, new approaches to a new world.

Yet for them all there are age-old keys still the same: rhythm and laughter, the sense of climax, the magic of words. Nursery observation has chiefly proved how very slowly true appreciation develops, and how important is the opening of the gates of "here and now." Nursery school practice uses a great variety of book and picture material as tools—it relegates the book *per se* to a less important place than it has in the home.

In my little book room at home, the majority of children "before five," if left alone, simply slam over the pages of one book after another. They shout or sing if some single picture catches the eye. They look up away from the books for something active to happen in the room. Suppose I gather them on the sofa and read, showing them the pictures slowly: then the brighter ones respond, but half still squirm and shout in irrepressible spirits about nothing at all. But if I have found a very good story, and *tell* it, stopping frequently with a question or a chance for imitation, the audience is absorbed. *That* is the story they want again next time. Meanwhile, of course, an unusual child may have crept off alone with a book she loves, to apply her more mature powers of eye and mind, murmuring her own tale to herself as she fingers the lines of the pictures lovingly.

Babies, we know, can be as different at two as their parents are at thirty. The home can treat them as individuals, and so can some schools. But in a group, the material and the methods must differ from those at home. At school, being so very imitative, they frequently seem either brighter or duller than they really are. Only the home can have the greatest pleasure of discovering books. The school experiments more widely and has general purposes in mind, so sometimes it discovers things the parent would not be apt to find out. The school does not impose traditional likes, as a parent does. Some mothers, who leave everything to school or nurse, are startled when they do "read aloud" at the response or lack of it, and draw unfortunate conclusions. They *could* have the same fun the school has, with experiment in storytelling. But parents still are apt to push small children too fast in language process and picture appreciation because these are easier skills for them to share than the subtler growths the nursery school is watching.

The very first stories come at two and three years old. No one who has not worked daily with children will believe how simple they should be. To say that two hundred words is long enough puts it too easily. The point is, much more, the utter simplicity of word and content. In these first experiments in attention, as opposed to songs and nonsense verse, there should be a delicate balance of reality—something that could happen to you—and of nonsense and action. Little that is ideal has been written for such use. Therefore mothers and teachers make it up, build up from what is going on about them. Many schools say, wait till the book means more; use these informal casual personal tales; save Peter Rabbit until it is honestly understood and enjoyed. Others begin very early with traditional stories. The poems and songs, of course, continue.

At three and four years old, attention has grown in power, and we meet more sharply the problem of style. Simplicity does not mean brevity and easy words only. The body which has been developing an exciting lot of varied responses, the mind which has heard songs and poetry, quickly feel the wet blanket of dull prose. In books purposely written for small children, how little text is good! Then there is the matter of the "comeback," the question or pause for answer or imitation that lets the small child actively enter the story, as he longs to do. Shall it be put in print, as part of the rhythmic pattern, or left to the ingenuity of the adult reader or teller? We know how the really good story has to be told over and over—how it is chanted with the book upside down. It ought to be very good!

Then, toward five, horizons have widened, someone not yourself can be your hero; you may have played in groups or alone, but your interests are many. Very few writers have shown the power to draw upon and unfold further the many things a small child can as yet express only with action, gesture, or sound. But toward five, one can sit more quietly, one can listen longer. One still longs to share in the story—but wonder can put one off in a dream, the slow thought can be kept and brought forth in a question at the end. As a boy, one is seriously interested in men at work, and in many practical affairs!

We have gathered a few criteria for style for these years: rhythm, repetition, brevity, sensory range, "comeback." As to content, we all agree on those elements of "just like me," of humor, the love of bump and fall and grimace that mark this primitive age, and we are apt to differ only on the fantastic. Here indeed is a snag. For what is imagination, in these young years? Is it not imagination to play you yourself are a train or an auto or a plane? Is it very different to imagine you are Peter Rabbit or Snow White? Wasn't Snow White a little girl just like you? It is surely impossible to keep to the tangible world too closely. The favorite old folk tales do keep to reality, and most of them could happen on the farm next door, or to people in your house, or to the frog in your pond. So when the nursery schools say, "content for the play world must be built from the real world," we need not worry that imagination is being dampened. We cannot guess the limits of reality to the child, any more than we can always understand why he laughs. When expression itself is a very laughable matter, exactly what does seem "real"?

In a brilliant paper reprinted in the November, 1940, *Horn*

Book, Mary Edmonds railed against the dull book with a thesis, the story written to order. She pointed out, with excellent examples, the difference between literature and the ordinary, purposeful, realistic story. She was speaking mostly for older children, but I chuckled when she gave a horrible example from the Charlie books. How many thousands of those we sold, and how well I remember the very literary parent who wrote me in a rage after two months of being asked for Charlie every night. My only answer to Miss Edmonds on behalf of Charlie, and also of the many recent books I list about animals, trains, machines, etc., is that babies do like them and want them at certain stages just as the lover of Shakespeare also reads detective stories. The point is to see that the stages pass. "Content" has to touch many sides of life that the very best writers still have not put into fine, poetic words, either for the youngest or for older ones.

There are many other problems too long for this paper to enter. Why not ABCs? Because reading no longer is taught that way. But when Wanda Gág uses the ABC for a perfect nursery tale of a bunny, when Françoise uses it for one-minute stories, when Helen Sewell uses it for a babies' dawn to dark of everyday, it is irresistible, whether the letters are to be learned or not. When one thinks how early those giants of the nineteenth century read not only English but Latin and Greek, one doesn't worry too much about an accidental learning of ABCs.

The whole field is so experimental that no rules as to size, colors, kind of artwork, can be applied. The taste and wisdom of the adult buyer still turn to traditional material, but the growing number of nursery schools will stand by the experiment. In spite of Mrs. Mitchell's pointing the way in her two Here and Now books, so much is still untold and unsung. But very few publishers or authors seem to know babies, or be willing to take the time for trying out material on them.

As to lists and recommendations, very few are based on experience. Those published annually by the Child Study Association result from trial of the books in the homes of a committee of fifteen mothers. A list published at 69 Bank Street, New York City, grows out of the experience of Miss Stanton and the teachers at the Harriett Johnson Nursery School. Miss Ruth Andrus of the New York State Education Board publishes a nursery reading list. All these people were consulted in making my list, as well as the very helpful teachers of the New York Kindergarten Association, who checked many titles for me, and whose checking proved how much different neighborhoods in our great city varied in their interests and in the racial groups of underprivileged children. Any list as short as this becomes arbitrary in its omissions. It is much more a school than a home list.

The intelligent young mother, however, will be ready to learn from the nursery school, and will find out the fun of sharing both play and language growth on a realistic age level. She will find that one child is overstimulated at school and needs a different balance at home. For another, school may not find the key, and only Mother's experiments unlock attention and imaginative response. But she must realize that these early steps are important—that it does count enormously to *tell* stories, each year a bit longer; to read poems, each year with more variety; to have the child treasure lovely books. With a little investigation, she will soon see how one writer speaks of "here and now" very dully, and another so well that it is the beginning of literature.

Mother or teacher, she will be amused at discovering the stories a child likes, those she does not, and why. As the child's sensitiveness and appreciation grow, she will know that the audience for good books has a new recruit. Perhaps her own awareness of the child's world will have been so refreshed and reshaped that she will turn her own hand to a good new nursery poem or story.

BOOKS BEFORE FIVE—A SELECTED LIST

I. For Mothers to Begin On

HERE AND NOW STORY BOOK, *Lucy Sprague Mitchell*

ANOTHER HERE AND NOW STORY BOOK, *Lucy Sprague Mitchell*

The two indispensables, for use from 2 to 6. I like the second better for homes, the first for schools, but both are full of useful instruction, suggestion, reports of real children, and very fine verses and stories. Humorous, too. Proved by many years of use with children of each age. Include many kinds of story and verse.

STORIES TO BEGIN ON, *Rhoda Bacmeister. Photographs by Tom Maley*

Not thrilling, but pleasant and useful, for 3 to 6. Both prose and verse about familiar experiences.

PLAYS AND TOYS IN NURSERY YEARS, *Beatrix Tudor-Hart*

This excellent small book briefly summarizes the best English nursery school practice, mostly parallel to our own in theory. Wonderful photographs. Book list for America, grouped by subject, not age, made by Child Study Association, but many best for 5 and 6 or over. Their play material list very important, with notes where to buy.

THE JINGLE BOOK, *Mary Dana*

Perfect choice of seven very first songs, on rough cloth with gay pictures. Only the tune is given.

RING-A-ROUND, *Mildred Harrington*

The 260 pages of this anthology are worth the price. Many old familiar friendly poems children love at over 4. The editor made it up from a nursery scrapbook, tested in several homes. You must have enough poetry about!

SUNG UNDER THE SILVER UMBRELLA, *Association for Childhood Education*

A dozen or more fine verses here for 3s, those on the rare subjects of mittens, mufflers, etc. The rest to be tried between 4 and 6. The other A. C. E. books definitely for 6 to 8 year use.

PEACOCK PIE, *Walter de la Mare*

The most truly poetic and beautiful child verse ever written. Wonderful variety of rhythm and rhyme. For sound, try some on 3 and 4. Much of it best saved till after 6.

MOTHER GOOSE: THE TENGGREN EDITION

You like these pictures or else you think they're "too Hollywood." Good to have the music, if you haven't it elsewhere—136 pp.

MOTHER GOOSE: THE WALTER FOLKARD EDITION
Smaller edition, Children's Classic Series

This is the "student's" edition, the biggest collection of all, from which the others are chosen. Pictures banal, but great range of text fascinating. Fine for many later ages.

RING-O'ROSES, *Leslie Brooke*

The loveliest pictures of all, with a small selection of favorite verses; pictures can be used at about 4.

II. For Two to Three Year Olds

A B C FOR EVERYDAY, *Helen Sewell*

Use as recognition book. Good active words.

THE GAY A B C, *Françoise*

Tiny stories, some few finely rhythmic. For 2 and 3.

THE 1, 2, 3, PICTURE BOOK

Colors a bit garish, but idea good.

CLOTH BOOK NO. 1, *by "Eleska"*

This refugee artist's attempt has given us the best of the cloth books. She is now revising it for a second edition.

CLOTH BOOKS 1, 2, 3, AND 4

Nos. 1 and 3 by Leonard Weisgard are the best, of very familiar objects.

CLOTH BOOK, "OUR DAY," *Mary Dana*

A very usable kind of cloth, but pictures very experimental.

BABY'S DAY, *M. Sutton. Illustrated by Pelagie Doane*

Very simple verse for 2 or under. Not enough variety of rhythm. Too many pictures on some pages. A good attempt at true nursery subjects.

PAT THE BUNNY, *Dorothy Kunhardt*

Most interesting and successful book of last year for babies to play with. Good psychology in use of first sensory experiences.

MOTHER GOOSE, *Illustrated by Pelagie Doane*

These gay simple pictures might be country babies in Austria or your own baby dressed up gaily. Very charming. A good selection for babies themselves.

THE FIRST PICTURE BOOK, *Mary Steichen*

THE SECOND PICTURE BOOK, *Mary Steichen*

No words—just the photographs. No one has done much better as to content, even in the new color books. For 16 months to 30 months old.

FROM THE TEN CENT STORE BOOKS. *Use for pictures only:*

ANIMAL FRIENDS, HORSES ON FARMER BROWN'S FARM, COWS ON FARMER BROWN'S FARM

DUCKY DOODLES, LITTLE MOTHERS, BIG ANIMALS, BABY'S FIRST BOOK

Stories and verses from both of Mrs. Mitchell's HERE AND NOW *books, listed above.*

III. For Three to Four Year Olds

THE CITY NOISY BOOK

THE COUNTRY NOISY BOOK

THE SEASHORE NOISY BOOK, *Margaret Wise Brown.*
Illustrated by L. Weisgard

Perfect in every point—fun, story progress, sensory exploration, "comeback," rhythm. Starred on all lists. Every child will welcome the little dog, Muffin, some at 2 years.

THE LITTLE FIREMAN, *Margaret Wise Brown.*
Illustrated by Slobodkina

Story has good guessing quality, good response. Pictures very modern, gay, flat and toylike. Some like it best for over 4.

THREE LITTLE KITTENS, *Illustrated by Kurt Wiese*
Illustrated by Terry Brice

ASK MR. BEAR!, *Marjorie Flack*

Good story pattern for 3s, good simple pictures of familiar animals. *The Story About Ping* by the same author, very good, but its text better for 5s.

THE ABC BUNNY, *Wanda Gág*

These fine black and white pictures often liked at 3, to make up their own stories. Beautiful and interesting. Use with text and verses later on.

PANORAMA—TOWN, *Clement Hurd*

PANORAMA—COUNTRY, *Clement Hurd*

These two gay strips of pictures can lie flat on the floor, or be tacked on the wall. Short story at the back, but better to make up your own. Splendid for home or school.

THE LITTLE FAMILY, *Lois Lenski*

> Style is dull, yet many children love its "just like me" quality. For many children, better at 4. One of the few good "little" books.

THE LITTLE AUTO, *Lois Lenski*

> There is no logic to Mr. Small's being small, but children don't mind that, they love him. The text has not a good style, but the children talk at once themselves about the auto. Other books in this series better for 5 and over—all very popular.

SALLY AND HER FRIENDS, *Lena Towsley*

PEGGY AND PETER, *Lena Towsley*

> Photograph books proving that one publisher knew what his children liked. Text flat, but 3 year olds will make up their own stories, noises, chants for the familiar happenings.

I KNOW A SURPRISE, *Dorothy Baruch*

LUCKY LITTLE LENA, *Marjorie Flack*

WAIT FOR WILLIAM, *Marjorie Flack*

WILLIAM AND HIS KITTEN, *Marjorie Flack*

THE BOBBIE AND DONNIE BOOKS, *Esther Brann*

CINDER, AND THE FUNNY NOISE, *Romney Gay*

FROM THE TEN CENT STORE BOOKS, *stories to be adapted:*

> THE THREE BEARS, THE THREE LITTLE PIGS, THE GINGERBREAD MAN, THE LITTLE RED HEN
>
> LET'S PLAY STORE, LET'S PLAY TRAIN, LET'S PLAY POSTMAN, BUTTERCUP FARM, BOOK OF AIRPLANES, BOOK OF AUTOMOBILES, BOOK OF TRAINS, BOOK OF SHIPS, A GOOD LITTLE GOOSE, A KIND LITTLE KITTEN

IV. For Four to Five Year Olds

PELLE'S NEW SUIT, *Elsa Beskow*

A lovely simple story of sheep and wool, with beautiful childish pictures.

THERE WAS TAMMIE, *Dorothy and Marguerite Bryan*

Doggy homes will welcome this and its successor, *Tammie and That Puppy*. Story pattern good.

THE LITTLE WOODEN FARMER, *Alice Dalgliesh*

Excellent book for play with toys. The second story not so good, about a zoo.

THE CHOOSING BOOK, *Alice Dalgliesh*

A small book with questions that make it into a simple game.

TIMOTHY TURTLE, *Alice V. Davis. Illustrated by Guy B. Wiser*

A truly wonderful picture story about familiar small creatures in the country. Attention span may be a little long for younger listeners, but pictures are so good they will tide them over.

ANGUS AND THE DUCKS, *Marjorie Flack*

Angus slowly learns things about dog behavior, and continues in *Angus and the Cat*. *Angus Lost* and *Topsy* are equally good. Clever relation of words to pictures, fine simplicity of both.

MILLIONS OF CATS, *Wanda Gág*

Deservedly famous. Some children like it better later. Must be in the home.

COCK-A-DOODLE-DOO!, *Berta and Elmer Hader*

You can adapt text to the noisy, simple recognition for which this age likes farm pictures. These artists' *Farmer in the Dell* is good for 6 and over.

OVER IN THE MEADOW, *J. A. Hartell*

This lovely old nursery song is a soothing answer to an over-excited child, delightful for all children. Fairly good large pictures of baby creatures familiar to country children.

THE RACE, *Clement Hurd*

A wonderful idea, and fine big color pictures. Words don't match the text for detail, and story has poor rhythm and no comeback, but children like the idea and fix up the story themselves. Good first transportation pictures.

BABAR, *Jean de Brunhoff*

Better saved till 6, but if given in nursery use the pictures for your own storytelling, much shorter and simpler than present text. Let the 4s and 5s make up their own stories. All the Babar pictures delight small children.

MR. BRADLEY'S CAR, *Caroline Leach. Illustrated by Angela*

Another auto story, and a funny one, is a blessing. Pattern good.

BLUE BARNS, *Helen Sewell*

Charming big pictures and simple story of a big white goose. Story to be adapted according to ages.

A LITTLE WHITE TEDDY BEAR (*etc.*), *Dorothy Sherrill*

Became very popular in days when less was available. Amusing idea. Material suitable for 3s, interest span better for 4s.

CAPS FOR SALE, *Esphyr Slobodkina*

Very funny story from a famous old tale of a cap-peddler and the monkeys. The 5s love to act it out—full of gestures and noises.

LITTLE BLACK SAMBO, *Helen Bannerman*

ALL ABOUT COPY KITTEN, *Helen and Alf Evers*

JUNKET IS NICE, *Dorothy Kunhardt*

SNIPP, SNAPP, SNURR, *Maj Lindman*

THE LITTLE ENGINE THAT COULD, *Watty Piper*

PETER RABBIT, *Beatrix Potter*

I GO ATRAVELLING; I LIVE IN A CITY (*Verses*), *James S. Tippett*

Use in adapted form, stories from the following information series:

HAPPY HOUR BOOKS
THE POSTMAN, THE FIREMAN, THE POLICEMAN, THE STORE-
KEEPER, *etc.*

In City and Country Series: STORY OF CORN, STORY OF WHEAT,
MILK FOR THE CITY, FUN ON THE FARM, *etc.*

Scribner's Science Readers: POLICEMAN, FIREMAN, AIRPLANE, *etc.*

Cooperative Teachers' Publications: TABBY AND THE FIRE BOAT,
THE TUG BOAT, FIRE, FIRE!, A STORY OF MILK.

Stories from many sources, some adapted, as: EPAMINONDAS, SLEEP-
ING PRINCESS, CINDERELLA, SHOEMAKER AND THE ELVES, BILLY
ROBTAIL, THE OLD WOMAN AND THE CROOKED SIXPENCE.

V. Books Best Kept till Five or Six, but Possible for the
Bright Child Earlier

JOHNNY CROW'S GARDEN, *Leslie Brooke*

A ROUNDABOUT TURN, *R. H. Charles.*
Illustrated by Leslie Brooke

ANIMALS EVERYWHERE, *Ingri and Edgar Parin d'Aulaire*

FAVORITE POEMS BY EUGENE FIELD.
Illustrated by Malthe Haselriis

LITTLE ONES, *Dorothy Kunhardt*

THE SECOND PICTURE BOOK OF ANIMALS

WHEN WE WERE VERY YOUNG, NOW WE ARE SIX, WINNIE-THE-POOH,
A. A. Milne

BENJAMIN BUNNY, SQUIRREL NUTKIN, MRS. TIGGY-WINKLE, THE
TALE OF TWO BAD MICE, *Beatrix Potter*

SHADOW AND THE STOCKING, *James S. Tippett*

THE TASHA TUDOR "CALICO" BOOKS

A TALE FOR EASTER, *Tasha Tudor (New, younger than the text of
the little books)*

THE FISH WITH THE DEEP SEA SMILE, *Margaret Wise Brown*

THE LITTLE CHILDREN'S BIBLE

Brief selections from the King James version, arranged in an interesting order, by the Syndics of the Cambridge Press. Far and
away the best for first home use, does all the brain work for
Mother, and lures her to read on regularly. Follow up with the
Older Children's Bible, longer and more selections. Both of these
should be in every home.

Thinking About Children's Classics

From The Packet (*D. C. Heath,* Fall, 1955). *Reprinted by the Christian Home and School Society and by a number of Parent-Teacher Associations and libraries.*

The perennial question arriving at a book reviewer's desk is: "What are the *best* books, the ones my child must not miss?" Or, it may be: "What are the *necessary* books for beginning our home library, while our children are growing up?" Or, more starkly put: "Send me a list of the *real* children's classics."

Each answer hurts this reviewer's conscience. One should know the child, his past reading, the home and its present books, before sending any list. One is apt to fall back on the lists of others, such as Anne Carroll Moore's *Seven Stories High* (Compton), *Too Good to Miss* by May Hill Arbuthnot and others (Western Reserve Press), and Virginia Haviland's new one, *Let's Read Together* (Campbell and Hall, Boston). Notice that they all avoid the word "classic." One's own list keeps growing and changing, and never is ready to print.

The changes in concept of the "classic" for children have been fascinating to follow during thirty years of interest in this field. Children themselves, of course, do not like the word, and today it is fading in importance. Moreover, few adults agree on its meaning. To the purist, classics are the great works of our literary inheritance, many of them not written for children, but not to be missed by them, and preferably introduced, perhaps in cut or simplified form, before they reach high school age. To the less exacting, any book that lives on and is widely loved through several generations becomes a classic. For many, there is a definite corpus of children's literature, juvenile books that are specially well written as well as adopted (or adapted) adult classics, all of them books that should count in a child's memory.

For many years, at The Macmillan Company, I was responsible for a set of children's classics. They are now, necessarily, being revised, with new type and format more appealing for this era. Such sets begin, naturally, with material whose copyrights and plates of early editions belong to each publisher. They continue (or new ones originate) with out-of-copyright material, thus creating many rival editions of older books at a wide range of price. In my day, the Macmillan set, with Mother Goose, the Bible, Homer, Grimm, a poetry anthology, etc., could be considered the basis of a child's library. Today, with so many competing sets, parents are very much at sea in choosing the best edition of any special old favorite, from the Bible to *Little Women* or *Treasure Island*. Many questions come to my desk on this matter.

In reissuing the obvious favorites into sets of children's classics, the publishers face the problem of great shifts in reading ability, as they reconsider the length and difficulty of the older books, and also of changes in the educational pattern that do not create a background of interest in many titles once popular. Another factor in book-buying and in children's advance into adult reading is the lack of space for (and money for!) the old-fashioned home library, which used to contain several generations' favorite books, often in sets. So the growing child, whose ability to read well suddenly bursts upon him, does not roam among adult books at will, making his own discoveries. Nor does he often hear the older writers discussed by his parents, who themselves are not rereading them. Nor does the average child nowadays have much money to spend on books to keep and reread on his own bookshelf. Perhaps the great number and variety of books freely available to children in school and public libraries, and the colorful fairs and exhibits devised in so many places, do offer a great stimulus to reading and book purchase. In spite of the emphasis given specially good books by medals and other awards, the enormous annual output is overwhelming to both parent and child, as they meet it in bookshops and in book fairs, where what is new and what is most popular naturally are emphasized.

One needs to remember all this in wondering as to "what is a classic" and "what are the basic books." In spite of television and comic books, children are reading more than ever, in America, and more children are reading for pleasure than ever before. Are most of them reading "classics"?

In my children's book room, in our country home, a place for neighborhood borrowing and book discussions and discoveries (I have learned to say quickly that it is not a bookshop or a public library, just my own book collection), the very arrangement and popularity of the shelves speak eloquently of the changes in children's reading.

As you enter, the first shelves you meet contain, from floor to ceiling: The Bible, and other books on religion; Homer, Aesop, and classic myths; epics and legends from Norse countries; King Arthur, Robin Hood, and English legends and fairy tales; Irish and Welsh story cycles and tales; the famous tales of other European countries, Grimm, Perrault, Don Quixote; epics and legends from Asia and Africa; and—a big *and*—the Shakespeare shelf.

Since the last war, these have been the shelves least used,

except by the occasional ambitious teacher or storyteller, the high school student who rushes over "because we haven't a Shakespeare," and some church school teachers. Now I am busy making these shelves over, adding books *about* these books: photograph books of some of the countries; new and old archaeology books; the Quennells' *Everyday Things In* — books; the beautiful French book *King René's Book of Tourneys,* from my art books, and so on. The Shakespeare shelf would take pages to describe, with its Van Doren and Margaret Webster, its priceless Hodges' *Shakespeare and the Players,* its picture books, songbooks, and fiction about the period.

Here, surely, are the true "classics," the core of real literature we want our children to know. It may or may not be important, before some of them leave school for good or go to specialized schools at high school age, for them to "taste" the great classics. But even in a journalistic, atomic age, the range of reference of poets, magazine writers, newspapermen still includes such heroes as Hercules, Odysseus, Ajax, Pegasus, Jason; Noah, Moses, David, Joseph, Amos; Thor and Sigurd and Balder and the Knights of the Round Table; the heroic speeches of Henry the Fifth and the magical words and songs of Ariel; the rare rhythms of speech as well as the heroes of the old Irish epics; stories of saints who belong to all the world. The briefer, the funnier folk legends happily persist in anthologies and in school readers. The stories of the older long classics do not. Gone are Roland, Sohrab, the strange heroes of the Kalevala, the old retelling of Chaucer, and many others— gone, at least, from current storytelling and from the general reading of those under fourteen.

What has lapsed from use here are the "big" books, the "long" books, the ones a growing child used to lose himself in for a whole month at a time. Some books of fairy tales and of legends go on and on. If a child today starts on a single-minded pursuit of magical stories, all the Lang "color" books, with their small type, appeal after, rather than before, modern fairy tales. Favorite fairy tales are more apt to be loved in the large-type, separate picture books than in the big collections. Such "hard" books of the twenties as Firdusi's *Epic of Kings,* May NcNeer and Lynd Ward's beautiful and exciting telling of a Japanese epic in *Prince Bantam,* are long since out of print. The big Pyle books of King Arthur and Robin Hood are seldom embarked upon. The King Arthur most used is the easy-reading one by MacLeod, not the Pyle or the Lanier; the "small" Robin Hood by Pyle, recently offered in a trade edition, is the one children know best from its school use. The really "easy" telling of Homer by A. J. Church, still a fine read-aloud introduction, no longer appeals to younger children; the beautifully done Colum *Children's Homer* is in type now too small for under fourteen, and "looks" too long. Such fine books as Ryder's *Gold's Gloom* (from the Panchatantra), Deutsch's *Heroes of the Kalevala* (still in print), long or short versions of *Don Quixote,* have quietly faded away, along with big collections of *Arabian Nights* stories; also complete editions of *Pilgrim's Progress,* though Robert Lawson's cleverly selected and illustrated short one is still in print.

Meanwhile, postwar publishing has approached these classics in some interesting new ways. We have Olivia Coolidge's retelling of the classic myths, giving them a setting in time and place; also her fine book *The Trojan War.* Last year's *The Rise of the Thunderer* by Tom Galt was a fresh, very interesting introduction to Greek myths which may make its way, to be read aloud, or to be used by storytellers. His new *The Adventures of Rama,* for teen-agers, should be noted as a fresh approach to Indian classics. Ansley's *The Good Ways* is a fine brief introduction to world religions, for over twelve.

Recent books in this field have tended more to new collections of legends from countries not represented before, such as *Which Was*

Witch? from Korea, *Tales of Faraway Folk* from Central Asia, *The Dancing Kettle* from Japan, *Anansi, the Spider Man* from Jamaica, all for readers under twelve. The handsome, interesting Courlander books, *Kantchil's Lime Pit* (Indonesia) and *The Fire on the Mountain* (Ethiopia), are for older readers.

My shelf of American tall tales and legends grows apace, and naturally the favorite folk heroes are Davy Crockett, Pecos Bill, Old Stormalong, Paul Bunyan, all of whom do lift the imagination beyond the comic-book mood, and answer the growing boy's love of adult heroes and fantastic achievement. At the same time, they give him a vital sense of America's past and of purely American humor. American legend and folksong have found a central place in children's reading, tying into the covered wagon, and other pioneer stories, also the cowboy stories. They could lead to certain outstanding biographies; they could even lead back to the folk heroes of older classics, but generally do not.

It is possibly inevitable that the "classics" for children, chosen from great world literature, are the least part of their classics reading today. It is true that when Chapman's Homer burst upon Keats's mind, he was not a child. When T. E. Lawrence made his vigorous new translation, his impulse went back to a boyhood of classical education, but his full appreciation came when he was grown and had seen war himself. The superb satiric prose of Swift is beyond most children's appreciation, however much they are amused by cut versions of Gulliver. But if they fail to be introduced to these great books before they leave junior high school, and meet them only as required reading in versions sometimes antipathetic, they miss them altogether. No more does an adult settle down to several years' reading of Dr. Eliot's Five-Foot Shelf, so satirized in Mr. Marquand's latest, nor does a growing child explore such a set.

When Colum dedicated his *Children's Homer* to two small boys "so that their imaginations might rise to great deeds and wonders," he knew well the difference between the concepts of human nature in epics and in the familiar fun of short legends. It is the difference between such a modern "folk" concept as Superman and the stories of Moses and of Joseph in the Bible; between our own Davy Crockett and Prometheus; a difference of concept of the hero in relation to the world's slowly changing ideas of true heroism and supernatural powers. Of course there is also a difference in use of words. If a growing child never meets such beauty and nobility of phrase as in some of the great classics whose stories he definitely enjoys, he has no standard of comparison in style. It is, moreover, not only a matter of meeting great English style, but of meeting ideas bigger than the easy, familiar, funny ones, a matter of feeling and atmosphere, a matter of thinking about a larger world with imaginative understanding. It is the reading that takes a child beyond the facts of beginning history and geography, beyond the humanly illuminating fun of folklore.

Let us walk on around my book room. Following the section of great books, comes a section of poetry. We shall pass it, for the moment, to look over a section where we find many of today's generally accepted children's classics, among them the modern imaginative books that began with *Alice* and *The Wind in the Willows*. Here are two truly "great" books, most happily met when nearer twelve than when very young, yet in some families shared and quoted so that the youngest know them before they can read. This also is true of Andersen's tales: the short easy ones delighting small children, and the collections better appreciated later. Here are *Doctor Dolittle, Pinocchio, Mary Poppins, Charlotte's Web, Homer Price, Ferdinand,* and *Rabbit Hill.* Of course they are "necessary"! So are such rare ones as *Poor Cecco, The Great Geppy, The Twenty-one Balloons, Rootabaga Stories,* and *The Cat Who Went to Heaven.* Has C. S. Lewis taken the place, in the more literate homes, of George Macdonald? Are the *Jungle Books* still loved as once they were? Or have shorter, funnier animal stories taken their place?

Here are the shelves where many parents who visit me linger longest. "My child seems to have missed this!" "I wonder if I could read this aloud: it surely is needed, in the midst of all these fact books." Many have been steadily popular with children, but the shift in taste is obvious, with *Gulliver's Travels* and *The Rose and the Ring* giving way to *Mr. Popper's Penguins* and *Honk, the Moose.* Recent years have given us delightful new imaginative writing, from the picture book fun of Dr. Seuss to the more poetic imaginings of Harry Behn, from the modern setting of Edward Eager's *Half Magic* to the Old World background of Benary-Isbert's *The Wicked Enchantment.*

When one comes to the section of "true" stories, the shifts both in taste and ability to read again are obvious. Here many old favorites linger on, whether in classics sets or not, that one would happily see replaced. No one surely can call "necessary" today *Black Beauty* or the splendid old *Bob, Son of Battle,* or such strange survivals as *Tom Brown's School Days, The Story of a Bad Boy, The Secret Garden,* and *Little Lord Fauntleroy.* Are *Five Little Peppers and How They Grew, Rebecca of Sunnybrook Farm,* and *Anne of Green Gables* classics or not? We are on firmer ground with *Tom Sawyer, Huck Finn, Little Women,* the series of Little House Books with their wide age range, *Treasure Island, Hitty, Caddie Woodlawn, Johnny Tremain.* I would add *Away Goes Sally, Calico Bush, Tree of Freedom, Big Tiger and Christian.* I would consider Masefield's *Jim Davis,* Meigs's *Master Simon's Garden* and *Clearing Weather,* Pyle's *Men of Iron.* Two former favorites, *Two Years Before the Mast* and *Kidnapped* appeal now only to high school grades, where they are often on required reading lists.

It is difficult here to choose both for literary value and for

importance of content. The one obviously popular theme is a
varied interpretation of American background, and at least a
dozen fine books interpret it with characters worth meeting plus
the adventure and excitement children want. Which are important
as literature? It is to be noted how many of the "classic" imaginative books are by English authors, and how few English books
have survived among the true stories.

We have no time to go into the classics on the picture book
shelves, but I will give you a quick visit to one shelf in my room
where I keep picture books "for every age." Many superb picture
books should be shown boys and girls far beyond the "picture
book" age, and they greatly appreciate them, whether or not they
are would-be artists. This shelf has certain favorites of mine from
the work of William Nicholson, Claud Lovat Fraser, Edward
Ardizzone, Rex Whistler, L. Leslie Brooke, Randolph Caldecott,
Elizabeth MacKinstry, Helen Sewell, Boris Artzybasheff, Jean
Charlot, Ludwig Bemelmans, Lucienne Bloch. From Europe are
"Uncle Hansi," Elsa Eisgruber, and others; such fine ones as the
Czechoslovak books of the twenties; also some modern Mexican
and Spanish books. Among special treasures I count Pamela
Bianco's *Flora*. Work by such artists stimulates eyes brought up on
photographic magazines, on repetitive, pretty work that is "good"
but average; and on clever modern art, whose basis is caricature.
Such a collection does interest all ages. Many teen-agers and adults,
in my little book room, have met for the first time some of these
artists; have compared Pyle and Crane to Dürer, laughed at Caldecott's skill, wondered at Jean Charlot's power, and at the changing,
beautiful styles of Lynd Ward.

We have no space to discuss the many poetry anthologies at
different age levels. Our classics list surely would include, besides
anthologies, books like Sandburg's *Early Moon*, Teasdale's *Stars
To-Night*, the Benéts' *Book of Americans*, De la Mare's *Peacock*

Pie, Welles's *Skipping Along Alone,* besides Edward Lear, Hilaire Belloc, Milne. A fine new anthology for high schools is *Imagination's Other Place: Poems of Science and Mathematics* compiled by Helen Plotz. But alas! Poetry, like Shakespeare and art, demands a separate article.

Are there "classics" among nonfiction books? This answer is long overdue. The first Newbery Medal was given to Van Loon's *Story of Mankind,* recently brought up to date and reissued. It is hard today to find anyone under fourteen to read it, but it is an outstanding contribution, a reasonable, lively interpretation of world history. The James Daugherty biographies of our pioneers, Gray's *Penn,* Eaton's *Leader by Destiny* (Washington), Sandburg's *Abe Lincoln Grows Up,* are truly distinguished and not to be missed. So is the Newbery Medal life of Louisa M. Alcott by Meigs. Katherine Shippen's *Men, Microscopes and Living Things* is outstanding. Perhaps Clark's *In My Mother's House* and Holling's *Paddle-to-the-Sea* belong among the informational classics too, though they are thought of as picture books. Do Bischof's *Atoms at Work* and Hyde's *Atoms Today and Tomorrow* belong here? What about the fine books "for Sam" done by Maxwell Reed? Genevieve Foster's remarkable cross sections of history, *Augustus Caesar's World, George Washington's World, Abraham Lincoln's World,* are superb introductions to history, perhaps for the "special" reader under fourteen, but surely to "use with" any beginnings of history.

The problem in creating "good" readers at an early age is that of leading from the easy works of both fact and fiction into books a child can bite into, which are longer and harder in the sense not necessarily of words but of content. When, as so often, a child plunges into one line of reading, the watchful librarian or parent or teacher can lead into many of the classics, can connect the fact books with the works of imagination, can help the one concentrating only on fairy tales, or horses, or outer space, to discover for himself the longer, more adult books, perhaps only by their unexpected proximity on the bookshelf. Here such a series as the Landmark Books are fine steppingstones into longer fact, fiction, epic, or biography. The point is that, besides what is easy and charming, gay and funny, cozy and familiar, children need to be led into what is stranger, more noble, more heroic, more brain-stretching, whether it is creative work of long ago or of today. Among the greater books there is plenty to match their dreams of conquering space, to illumine their sense of courage and their respect for hard work, and to warm their hearts with understanding of human beings.

Judging what is a classic, what is "not to be missed," is a matter which educators must share with parents and librarians. Changing methods of education have shifted the backgrounds of history and literature which used to be offered to children under fourteen. The tendency to use in readers what children already like best, what is easiest as a step toward books on their exact age level, has meant the elimination of much that still is recognized as "classic" in the library world. The concept of the hero, too, has changed, and though it always will be changing, children themselves are keen to grasp fundamental values, and know well the difference between the real hero and the comic-book hero. It is significant that in a recent voting contest in schools, the Gettysburg Address stands high as a favorite piece of literature along with Huck and Tom.

Such recent Newbery Medal choices as Krumgold's . . . *And Now Miguel*, and DeJong's *The Wheel on the School* contain realistic subject matter far from the usual run of current popular children's works. These two books are specially worthy because the implications of their childlike stories are in an adult world; because their range of characters broadens a child's concepts of human nature, good and ill; and because, in different ways, both touch the emotions deeply. Both have messages a child could turn back to, years later, to strengthen and broaden his own thinking and emotions. Miguel's religious discussion at the end may not appeal to many children, but to some it will be stimulating, for what a saint can do for you is a matter of wonder to many children besides Miguel. Both these books cross the age line of younger reading to that of the junior high school age, where they really would be most appreciated, even though they are about younger children. The Dutch background of the DeJong is far more illuminating for children of today than that of *Hans Brinker*. The scene of the Krumgold, with its references to Los Alamos and to modern war, has implications which the author made movingly clear in his speech accepting the medal. An adult who reads either book aloud would be as much moved as a child, though for different reasons.

We have a similar adult approach and stretching of the mind in such recent books as Ullman's *Banner in the Sky,* which, besides its mountain-climbing adventure, proposes fresh aspects of morals and heroism. In Lawson's *Mr. Revere and I* the swift and humorous survey of our Revolution demands wit and brains enough to appreciate its kindly satire. Another distinguished, unusual recent book that comes to mind is Baumann's *The Caves of the Great Hunters,* that absorbing introduction to new ideas about man's ancient art expression. In all of these recent books, one senses a creative approach to living, a writer who has something to say beyond his story, a style and a plot possibly conceived purposely on a child's level, but written as if this were the inevitable way to write of both people and setting. They certainly are books that both growing children around twelve and adults can enjoy together (possibly one test of a classic). They are far beyond many of the traditional classics in literary value. Which of them will be long and widely loved by many boys and girls, which will get into the

school readers, is hard to guess. It depends greatly on their enthusiastic introduction by adults, and their inclusion on school
lists at grade levels which catch *both* the bright child in lower
grades and the reader in higher grades who will more easily appreciate them. It depends on the making of more "family" reading
lists, and on urging parents to enjoy them and talk about them.
They are the sort of reading that prepares the mind for "long,
hard" books.

This discussion may not have clarified the answer to what is a
classic. It may, however, start some thinking as to what a growing
child "should not miss." A "classic" can be as simple as "The
Princess and the Pea," or *Ferdinand;* it can be as rich, long, and
epic in quality as Pyle's *King Arthur,* or as clear and obvious as the
masterly combination of Natty Bumpo stories in the recent new
edition of James Fenimore Cooper; it can be as gently touching as
Beatrix Potter's animal stories or as deeply moving as *Bambi* and
The Yearling. A classic can be puzzling as to its obvious age interest, and have defects of style, yet live and be loved for an inner
quality that overrides its difficulties. This quality may be sheer
fun or a deep spiritual revelation. In any case it will be a book that
stretches and opens both mind and heart.

Imagination's Other Place

A *review of* Imagination's Other Place: Poems of Science and Mathematics, *compiled by Helen Plotz (published by T. Y. Crowell, Inc.), in the* New York Herald Tribune Book Review, *November 13, 1955.*

There is a home in New York City whose two older children brought to the family discussions an increasing interest in various sciences, in the matter of science vs. religion, and in the relation of literature, especially poetry, to all these subjects. The talk was stimulated by a scientist father, and the mother, to keep up with them, read more and more science. Meantime, she was searching her literary memory for applicable poems, which finally she collected in the new anthology whose title is "Imagination's Other Place." Its subtitle is "Poems of Science and Mathematics," a true description, yet lacking something, as you will see.

For this reviewer, it is without doubt the most distinguished and stimulating book of the fall of 1955. Children's thinking today turns very early toward science. Even beginning readers want to know about the atom, and there are books to tell them about it. Their toys, from "space suits" to chemical sets, reflect their mood. By high school and college age, we have youth with a wider interest in science than ever before. But for the first time, to this reviewer's knowledge, the sciences have been connected with the

stream of world poetry, from the writing in Genesis and The Book
of Job to that of MacLeish and Ciardi. Mrs. Plotz shows that poets,
in looking at their world with precise observation plus individual
insight, have always offered special illumination as to many aspects
of science, at times reaching points of prophecy. They have
written not only about various sides of nature but about astronomy,
geography, mathematics, physics, chemistry, biology, and medicine.
Fortunately, Mrs. Plotz has added some poems about religion,
philosophy, and "learning" in general, to these chief subjects of
her search.

In brief introductions to the four sections of her book, the editor
connects the poetic expression of different eras with their progress
in science, suggests that we think of poetry in human terms, and
points out how often the language of poet and of scientist is alike.
These little essays are fine, clear thinking for youth reading alone.
They also offer ammunition for family discussions, and for teachers
of literature and science.

How right and inevitable is the opening verse from Blake:

> To see a world in a grain of sand,
> And Heaven in a wild flower,
> Hold Infinity in the palm of your hand,
> And Eternity in an hour.

Other significant short quotations, each fortunately set apart on
its page, include Claude Bragdon's

> The point, the line, the surface and sphere
> In seed, stem, leaf and fruit appear.

And here is Housman's—

> To think that two and two are four
> And neither five nor three,
> The heart of man has long been sore
> And long 'tis like to be.

Do you know David McCord's "Weather Words"?

> I know four winds with names like some strange tune:
> Chinook, sirocco, khamsin, and monsoon.
> Like water over pebbles in Lost Brook:
> Sirocco, monsoon, khamsin, and chinook.

It may be long ago when you read Traherne, Pope, Shelley, Tennyson; they will come to you with new meaning, in dramatic comparison with similar thoughts of poets long before and long after their time. Even more surprising are the portraits in poetry of various scientists, which include some recent tributes to Einstein.

There is a happy scattering of humorous verses. We met again with joy that "young lady named Bright who traveled much faster than light." Edna Millay's "Journal" shows her easy, mordant wit, as she peers into a microscope; we also meet her in her best sonnet, "Euclid Alone Has Looked on Beauty Bare."

"Speculation about man's place in the universe," the editor calls "These terrible questions . . . first raised in the Victorian era." These poems, some about religion, are a striking group, entitled simply "Both Man and Bird and Beast."

"What am I, Life? A thing of watery salt?" asks Masefield. "The force that through the green fuse drives the flower drives my green age," says Dylan Thomas.

In this group the anonymous "I saw a peacock with a fiery tail" is placed near Robert Frost on helium; Emily Dickinson on the angleworm is next to Tristram Coffin on the spider. Such arrangement is proof of anthological genius. We are grateful, too, for the accuracy which tells us that "I do not love thee, Dr. Fell," is Thomas Brown's translation of Martial, and for indexes by authors, by titles, and by first lines.

It is heartening to read in the acknowledgments that Mrs. Plotz made several of her most unusual discoveries in a magazine of the XYZ Club of Erasmus Hall High School (Brooklyn), published under the aegis of a mathematics teacher there. One imagines with what joy similar high school clubs will seize upon this book.

Besides its importance for older readers, the book is significant in relation to younger children's reading. No one knows just when the space enthusiast, the would-be atomic scientist, the collector of rocks or beetles, who may be anywhere from eleven to fifteen, will be stirred by such reading as this. The point in reading arrives differently for each child, when he turns against the "easy" poetry generally offered in elementary school, and is ready for that "other place" in imagining, a place where poetry interprets the modern, adult world. The young reader who "doesn't like poetry" seldom is shown that technical skill and scientific discovery have any relation to the thinking of the poets, or that the intuition of poet and of scientist may be alike.

What of the puzzling title chosen by Mrs. Plotz? It comes from the remarkable final poem by a young English poet, James Kirkup, "A Correct Compassion." He was among the tense crowd of spectators in the operating theater of the General Infirmary at Leeds, England, watching a surgeon perform a difficult heart operation. His exact report of the event, in this poem, includes minute surgical details, the comments of the surgeon, a description of the appearance of the human heart itself. To these facts observed he brings fresh poetic concepts, even when he speaks of the surgeon's tools. All is woven into the dramatic story of the saving of the patient's life. At the end

We find we breathe again, and hear the surgeon hum.
Outside, in the street, a car starts up. The heart regularly
Thunders . . .

. . . This is imagination's other place,
Where only necessary things are done, with the supreme and grave
Dexterity that ignores technique; with proper grace
Informing a correct compassion, that performs its love, and makes it
    live.

Often, on these pages, a poet has taken us to a "high, triumphant place," but none more clearly than Mr. Kirkup. The surgeon and some of the watchers were lifted to that place. It took the poet to put it down forever in memorable words. Is poetry important? Is it important that young people should "like" poetry? Share this book with them and you will know the answer.

Of Times and Trends

Books in Search of Children

The Tenth R. R. Bowker Memorial Lecture, delivered
at the New York Public Library, 1946. Published by
the New York Public Library, 1946. Reprinted in
Publishers' Weekly, January 19, 1946; in The
Bulletin of the New York Public Library,
Vol. 50, 1946; in Typophile Chap Books,
Vol. XVIII, 1948; and in Bowker Lectures
on Book Publishing (New York,
R. R. Bowker Co., 1957).

I. HISTORY

All our dignity, then, consists of thought. By it we must elevate
ourselves, and not by time and space which we cannot fill. Let
us endeavor then, to think well: that is the principle of morality.
By space the universe encompasses and swallows me up like an
atom; by thought I comprehend the world.

—Blaise Pascal, *Pensées* (1670), notably quoted by Rebecca West
in *The Thinking Reed* and by Norman Cousins in *Modern Man
Is Obsolete*

We meet today as adults whose minds are drawn with difficulty
from their chief concern. That is our adjustment to a world newly
conditioned to the atomic era. Nothing is more important for the
children than that each of us should grow ourselves new minds to
fit these new needs.

As we see the one world in this new light, we see its little
corner of the children's books lit up too. At such a moment, so

prescient, so adult in implication, we turn with wonder, relief, and joy to the children's books. It is as if we never had seen them before. The war, the atomic bomb, has not blown them away. No, some were even published abroad under the very noses of the temporary tyrants. Straight on through the years they have brought laughter, beauty, and a healthy release of tears and courage.

So we may now look back with a sort of extra curiosity at the history of this publishing of children's books.

We think back upon, as oddities, the early English *Babees' Book,* the sixteenth century Horn Books, the gloomy moral books of the seventeenth century, Comenius' grand *Orbis Pictus* of 1658 "to entice witty children." We smile at the grim New England Primer, and we thank John Locke for letting children read Aesop's *Fables* and *Reynard the Fox.* We treasure the little volumes of John Newbery, and we note the century that produced Rousseau, William Blake, Maria Edgeworth, Mrs. Ewing. We celebrate with the child of today the birthdays of Shakespeare and Andersen and Dickens. Some of the world's great books we forget are adult books because now they so firmly belong to the children.

Let us turn to America, in the year 1919, the year of the first Children's Book Week. It was instigated by the fairy-godfather of children's books, Mr. Melcher, and by Mr. Mathiews of the Boy Scouts who had begun his crusade for better books for boys. Its theme for 1919 was: "More Books in the Home." It was the first effort toward community cooperation to increase all children's use of books. It was accompanied by pressure from the *Publishers' Weekly* toward year-round selling of children's books.

Also in 1919, Mr. Brett at Macmillan's started a special department for the making of children's books. Today there are thirty-two such special departments, and forty-six publishers specializing in this field. The gross figures are interesting. From the United

States Biennial Census of Manufactures: In 1919, 24,435,000 juvenile books, including pamphlets. In 1939, 60,232,000. No comparable figure for the forties, but the WPB survey gives juvenile books sales in dollars in 1943 as $19,753,000. From the *Publishers' Weekly* records of juvenile new book titles, we have these figures: 1919, 433; 1938, the peak, 1,041; 1944, 645; in eleven months of 1945, 604. What does the decline in titles mean? Is it an omen?

Also in 1919 came Anne Carroll Moore's reviewing of children's books in the *Bookman,* and the publication of Clara Hunt's "What Shall We Read to the Children." In 1922, again the fairy-godfather acted, when Mr. Melcher instituted the annual award of the John Newbery Medal. In 1937 he followed it with the Caldecott Medal. In 1937 the *Herald Tribune* started, under Mrs. Becker, its spring book awards. Mr. Melcher knew there was no one "best" book! His awards focused a wider public interest on this field, and also focused the judges' thinking on the problem of merit, the eternal problem of what is a good book.

In 1916, Bertha Mahony had started the first "Bookshop for Boys and Girls" in Boston. Out of its lists and publications grew the first issue of *The Horn Book* in 1924, still the only magazine in the world about children's reading. In 1919, Marion Cutter opened her children's bookshop in New York.

Now we may ask of our little history, why did all this happen in 1919?

The last flowering of good writing for boys and girls had come after the 1880's. Then America, like England, felt the result of the industrial revolution. Freer printing, greater freedom of thought, wider public education brought more books. In America, in 1880, a young lady could write in her diary, "Even ladies and gentlemen seldom have the 3 R's." In 1850, reading here still consisted of moralistic, sentimental English books. But in another twenty-five years, America began the procession of such authors as Mark Twain, Stockton, James Otis, Howard Pyle, Eggleston, Kirk Monroe, James Baldwin, Daniel Beard, Louisa May Alcott, Frances Hodgson Burnett, Laura Richards, and Kate Douglas Wiggin. The *Youth's Companion* had started in 1827. Soon came *St. Nicholas*, under Mary Mapes Dodge, and *Harper's Round Table*. Out of the good editing of these magazines came more good books. So from 1880 to 1900 we had suddenly a wealth of good reading for young people.

After 1900, what happened? The landmarks changed. We had the Little Colonel series, the Wizard of Oz series, the Katy Did series, the spread and very slow decline of the Elsie books. We had *Rebecca of Sunnybrook Farm* and *Penrod*. Where were the top-flight writers? Why did they lie fallow?

In the years between, came the days of Caroline Hewins in Hartford, and the founding of the first training school for children's librarians at Pittsburgh. She gave us and they gave us the gradual revaluing of children's literature. It slowly sent forth trained librarians, it created more library schools, it opened school libraries. Bookshops and department stores began to have separate children's book sections, as under Mrs. Pleasants and Miss Torney at Brentano's and Veronica Hutchinson at Halle Brothers.

The year 1919, we cannot forget, marked a release from war. It brought a general increase in book production, a new prosperity, new techniques in printing, and the inspiration of many beautiful books from Europe. All this flowered into children's bookmaking of the twenties and thirties such as the world never before had seen.

So much for a thumb-nail history.

II. PERSONAL: PRO-BOOK VS. ANTI-BOOK

When I was as high as that
I saw a poet in his hat.
I think a poet must have smiled
At such a solemn-gazing child.
Now wasn't it a funny thing
To get a sight of J. M. Synge
And notice nothing but his hat?
Yet — life is often queer like that!
—L. A. G. Strong

For fifteen years I shared in that exciting bookmaking era of the twenties and thirties. The book was my happy concern, days and nights and holidays. Now, for twelve years I have lived in a different world. You who recently have known a period when almost any book you could put upon paper would sell, I think cannot take in the truth of my world where the book is not the one absorbing interest. Perhaps you will look for a moment at the world of the general public, where I wonder every day who buys all the books.

Quoting again my friend Mr. Melcher, I give you his report of a United States Army librarian who had charge of six hundred libraries in the Pacific Islands. He stated that of one hundred men on an island, 10 per cent would find books under whatever conditions, 10 per cent never would read, and the remaining 80 per cent were hopeful in spots, were worth trying to help find books, had had some sort of book contacts and could possibly be given more.

In my life of so-called leisure, I find his percentages about correct among civilians at home, both children and adults. The book world has much to do to convert that 80 per cent, to make even another 10 per cent of them good readers. In the higher brackets of earning, people seem to have no time for books; in the lower brackets, they cannot afford books. You know, I am sure, that over 80 per cent of Americans, before the war, earned under $2,000 a year. In one's leisure, one meets many more of this 80 per cent, and the Army librarian's 80 per cent, face to face.

For instance: I sat in with a United States Army committee for shaping the contents of primers to teach hundreds of thousands of illiterate soldiers how to read, before they were demobilized. They had discovered how to bring a grown man to a third-grade reading ability in six weeks. They were giving these men special news-papers and books in third-grade language. I pray that their work really does go on today. But it takes more than third-grade lan-guage to give us a book-reading man.

Again, I met the 80 per cent in the wards at Bellevue. If you figure that the gallant green ladies, with their book trucks, are filling those wards with book readers, you have another guess. Both there, and in my country hospital, I watched the adults take magazines, if anything, and the children take piles of comic books. The person with a real book, in a ward, is the great exception. And don't suppose that such a literate nurse's aide as I had any time to talk books!

What of Victory gardening, another wartime job I took seriously? The hardest toil of any, I assure you, that of raising food, can be lightened and illuminated by that wider knowledge of the whole cycle of plant life, by the story of soil conservation, by the real study of horticulture. It is all in good books, in great books. Well, the 80 per cent might read the gardening manuals, but the study of nature, in this larger relation to the world, in our schools, is pitifully neglected. Therefore, fewer and fewer children are grow-ing up to be horticulturists. Hope may spring from those noble

4H young people, whose weekly program on the air was one of the most heartening parts of the war.

Most of our city and suburban children have lost touch with those inexorable forces of nature that long ago gave us the very gods themselves. Perhaps, as Ella Young says, the gods of nature have withdrawn, to prepare for the gods of atomic energy. But isn't that, too, nature? In other words, to the 80 per cent the books have not carried yet their message about their very source of life. The imaginations of both city and country children are captured and standardized by mechanical things.

Another instance of the 80 per cent, the non-book people, is the way my many reading neighbors are willing to take both the world and books second-hand. Adults, as well as children, read *Life* and the *Reader's Digest,* and other digests. They think a news reel in the movies gives them the news. They think their minds are working when they are full of unrelated pictures, pictures, pictures, and compressed pellets of articles. In such minds, there is little room left for imagination. They think all is "known," but it is never known till it reaches the heart. This takes time and the act of thought, and this takes words, good words, all the words, not words selected, cut, and compressed. As John Bainbridge said in *The New Yorker,* "If literature can be condensed like milk, . . . there is a technical facility for doing it. . . . A skeleton is the original party in concentrated form, but with a little flesh on him he might be more fun to have around the house."

So much for 80 per cent of my neighbors! My leisure has also taken me afar, even to a writers' conference in the Rocky Mountains. I did not have to go there to meet a representative of the New York garment trade, for I did know trades union parents and their children as varied in their reading as any other social group. But he surprised me, in the shadow of the Rockies, attacking me in the halls of a great university, as well he had the right to do.

First he said I was for the "elite," the geniuses, in my ideas of children's reading, and he was for "the common man." I replied that that is the most hateful phrase invented in our era, much as I admire Mr. Wallace. Then he said, "In a way you agree with me. The world needs a return to medieval Judaism. To the New York City children I know, a comic book is A Book, their one book. They have no time to go to libraries, they are working. For them I want the classics put into the comic books."

Do not forget this friend of mine! In his way, he was speaking for the 80 per cent. I thought of him as I read of the boyhood of George Norris, fighting liberal, who had no books till after he was twelve years old, except the Bible, and never saw one children's book. I think of him when I see well-to-do mothers too lazy to read Anne Eaton, Ruth Sawyer, Anis Duff, Phyllis Fenner, *Realms of Gold,* the fine bookshelf waiting to help them give the best to their children. What is in such books is someone else's job! Or, let us ask our queer neighbor Mrs. Bechtel, to make us up a book list!

I have no time for more instances, but I assure you my outer world is not a book world. Often, however, I wonder whether the 10 per cent children and adults who do a great deal of pass-the-time reading, and those of the 80 per cent who read so many comic books, might not better spend this time, or most of it, in acquiring a real skill with their hands, or pursuing a real hobby, both of which, of course, could find inspiration in books. Some communities do see this question, and by intelligent group work, at last come round the circle and *back* to the good book, no *time* being left for the poor one. Reports of such experiments you find in *The Springfield Plan* and in *For Us the Living: An Approach to Civic Education* by John J. Mahoney.

My anti-book world is what, against his will, Mr. Brett allowed me to look at twenty-five years ago in transcontinental sales journeys. I met it, partly in bookshops and libraries, but mostly in state normal schools, in country parent-teachers' meetings, in merely looking out the train windows and talking to people on trains and in strange hotels, listening to congressmen milling around in the lobby. I made talks, not only to librarians but to Rotarians and Lions, and working girls' clubs and Y.M.C.A.s. I sat with children at movie matinees, in cities near and far. And believe me, there is an 80 per cent you can still convert to be pro-book.

This world I see as only one of seven parts of our subject today. The other six are: children, schools, authors and artists, libraries, and you, the publishers and the bookshops. The seven are inescapably parts of one whole. Will they ever pull together for the good of all children?

III. THE CHILDREN

If you will take any flower you please, and look it over, smell it and feel it and try to find out all its secrets—not of flower only, but of leaf, bud and stem as well, you will discover many wonderful things. This is how to make friends with plants, and very good friends you will find them to the end of your lives. I had got to know them as friends when a little child, long before I could find out what their names were.
—Gertrude Jekyll, *Memoirs of a Gardener*

When I was young
I had not given a penny for a song
Did not the poet sing it with such airs
That one believed he had a sword upstairs.
—W. B. Yeats, *Collected Poems*

Thank God there will always be new children, and more kinds of children than there are kinds of adults. It gives us more chances for more kinds of books to succeed with them. It gives us the new audience to give the old book new life.

The children's book editors know that it is wrong for anyone to generalize about American children. In getting book reports from them, in trying out manuscripts on them, editors have seen how utterly different two children in one family can be, two groups in one community, two reading groups in one library.

An interesting sort of article appeared in *Publishers' Weekly* for October 27, 1945, reporting in descriptive detail on publishers' children and the books they read. Here indeed was a group of children conditioned by overexposure to books and manuscripts. What wonderful individuality, what opposing tastes at the same ages! Two children at four love Black Sambo and the Three Bears, and a third turns them down because "I'm afraid. *I* don't want to be etten up. *Nobody* wants to be etten up."

One thing I notice about all these healthy, happy, well-read children is that they are able to read freely, evidently by about eight. In the hinterlands I inhabit, reading freely comes more slowly, generally only at nine or ten. Publishers should note that this leaves very few years before the adult book is required. I am hoping that army methods of teaching reading some day will be applied in schools. It is ridiculous to defer till so late acquiring an ability most children could acquire before six, as some do.

If I dared to generalize about children today, I would say that their temperament is very different from that of the twenties, so is their power of attention, and their taste. Too many books are both edited and packaged for the passé child of a protected nursery. I feel that the latent egotism and paganism with which we all begin our lives has had recently much less restraint. The freedom from any religious training which many more of them enjoy today, the hardening influences of the kinds of stories in comics and on radio, have given us a tough-minded, amoral, impatient lot of youngsters. Plenty of them still are sentimental—but it is a surface sentiment. So many, of all classes, have had much less normal home life since the war, that the way the war itself took hold of their imaginations was not healthy. We cannot talk here of the lost generation of children in Europe—among them many became heroic adults while still young. That happened in less degree to some American children, on whom extraordinary burdens rested, of extra work and shared adult emotion. Others led a seemingly normal life. But all were affected deeply by the atmosphere of war, as all have been affected by mechanization of life, and materialism.

It is odd that one of the best analyses of children's reading was written by a Frenchman, Paul Hazard, in *Books, Children and Men,* a most notable example of a bookman's and scholar's holiday. With a good deal of satire, he describes the overturn in the world when children, not adults, became the lords and masters; how they invaded the adult world and took to themselves part of its newspapers, demanded toys made from the newest inventions (no longer dolls and farmyards and rocking horses) and demanded of their books both accurate realism and above all *thrilling* adventure. "Talk all you want to," the father of a family says to Mr. Hazard, "of the time when children used to be oppressed by men; I am telling you the time will come when men will be oppressed by children."

He calls his chapters on the great overturn of the eighties, "Children Have Always Defended Themselves." I suggest to you today that in embracing the comic books, children have been defending themselves by thinking they entered there an adult world denied them in their children's books, besides defending themselves from their deferred skill in reading. And I suggest that the current passion for pop-up, push-out, pat, play-with books is the children's defense against homes where they haven't enough to *do* with their hands.

Please think of two small boys on my road in the country. They can "pat" real rabbits, cats and dogs, and ponies. One has trained a rooster to ride on the bars of his velocipede. One has a small tool chest beside his father's big tool chest. Both work with plants in greenhouse or potting shed. One, at the age of five, made me a miniature green dish garden for Christmas. One at six had charge of some pigeons and taught a tumbler to box with him and ride around on his head. Both have had *time* to look at a flower, and many other plants, as Miss Jekyll said she looked when young. In their play they are sharing adult occupations. They literally haven't time for stunt books, and are very indifferent to picture books. At eight, they were reading very poorly, and clamored to be read aloud to from "those good *long* books, not the thin ones." Also they search out *adult* reference books on airplanes, railroads, plants, and animals. Lucius Beebe's railroad books are their passion, no choo-choo picture books.

What I am watching now, as they go on to be nine and ten, is the inevitable clamor to go to the movies with the other children, the rising passion for radio serials, the borrowing of comic books at school, and less borrowing of real books from me. But I think their "foundations" may be firm, in having looked at a flower, patted real animals, and heard read aloud some good books.

What of city children who cannot have much of this? The sad fact is, they could have so much more, even in a city. The trouble with a small child's hobbies is that they are so much trouble for a parent. It is so much easier to give him a book, any book, to keep him quiet! There are many clever books about things to do that would explore and increase the skills of children. In general, they do not sell well to parents. The publishers cannot change the parents—but they could help to change the schools where such skills could be fostered.

Some of these parents believe in a kind of free reading that really ought to produce little geniuses. They believe in individualism to a startling extent, and are proud to have small children discuss great matters, to "express themselves" in almost any way. They now demand, too, that the children's books offer them democracy on a silver platter. As if democracy, or religion, or heroism, or any other great matter, could be put into a little pill or a little cake or even a little book, and taken as a dose! The children are too smart to read such books.

In all classes and races, some children are snobs. "Social Studies" have not eliminated them yet. Boasting about your family, your possessions, reflects their inner longing for security, their deep need for a hero of their own, their passion for excitement not answered by "nice" books. Of course it is answered by the comics, and the movies. Perhaps this cannot be changed; but the dreams might be channeled into other conceptions of their careers, other conceptions of patriotism. It is the whole force of their young, ardent, unexpressed feelings, blowing off in the general lack of enough to *do*. Books alone are not the answer, yet the good books, the best books, as opposed to mediocre stuff, could help.

What we must realize is that a child today is not a child in the sense of 1880 or of 1919. In 1946 they are conditioned by all that conditions adults, in radio, movie, magazines. They seldom like what we want them to like at the moment we offer it. One year, only books about horses or railroads, the next year, only fairy tales, the next year only love stories. Our job is to see that the books are there, and that they do meet the real powers of young emotions with good words. All the while, we must try harder to give them time and chance to gaze long at a flower, to gaze long even at a book.

IV. THE SCHOOLS

A book may have a real cultural value that at the time for a child is only an escape value . . .

To understand the literature of the present, one needs training in the literature of the past.

—Harvard University, Graduate School of Education. Committee on the Preparation of Teachers . . . *The Training of Secondary School Teachers, especially with reference to English* . . .

How healthy it would be for trade publishers if once a year they were forced to attend English classes in a variety of our public schools. In my county, our remarkable Children's Association undertook to combat juvenile delinquency by conquering the problem of what are now politely called "retarded readers." In sharing this campaign, I had to look at some of our elementary schools, and I briefly report to you, they need your help as citizens, and as hopeful booksellers. They need better teaching of English! That alone will create good readers.

In writing texts for remedial reading cases, I met in embryo the problem of reducing the good book to a graded-language level. I met the debate only touched upon in *The Horn Book*, "Can our children read?" The question is not only, *can* they read, but *what* can they read, and do they understand it? How do you know what they get from all this free reading, unless you know the quality of their school reading?

Why did I have to rewrite and word-grade my stories? Not because the authors should have written them in a different style, God forbid! No, it was because the subject matter, generally informational, appealing to the "poor" reader, did not exist at his level of ability—the same reason why the United States Army had to create new primers for grown men. The problem demanded a tool-book. I, in my little study, and the Army with all its brilliant resources, discovered the same thing; the *style,* the *words,* of these tool-books can be at a high level. It can have dignity and variety, and not insult an adult taste. (Many children have a very adult taste and sense of style. That is why they hate most primers.)

But we of the book world do not need to confuse a tool-book with a real book. Do you editors impose on all your books a style like that of, let us say, *Time* magazine? Of course not, any more than you model them all on the style of the King James Bible. Nor do you try to remember in editing adult books that the average mental age of our army is fourteen. I think probably a large per cent of children's books should be considered as tool-books, in other words, books to prepare children for reading real literature.

Do not fool yourself into thinking you create an audience for good books by turning them into baby books. If a book is a tool, call it one. Leave it to the specialists to make them. And leave the work of a real author as he wrote it, keep it alive as he wrote it, do all you can to help the slow readers get through with their tools and ready to share the minds of adults.

I recommend now a book I have been talking about since 1942. But I have yet to meet one parent, one librarian, or one bookmaker who has read it. It is *The Training of Secondary School Teachers, especially with reference to English,* the authors a joint committee from the faculty of Harvard College and its graduate school of education. I quote: "There is no value in reading as such. . . . To place a book, any book, in a pupil's hands merely because he likes it amounts to educational nihilism. . . . The pupil who is taught that all print must give him pleasurable emotions is not being taught. . . . Reading, if it is to develop an intelligent citizenry, cannot safely remain what it is so often called, a worthy leisure-time activity. . . . Children's minds are so absorbed and perverted by movies, radio, comics, that *the channels of communication are clogged.*"

I urge everyone who has a real interest in the future of American education to read this book, to know by first-hand report our English teachers' problems and point of view. Besides the criticism I have arbitrarily chosen to quote, there is optimism, and there are the stirring words of good teachers. They, too, you must remember, are booksellers.

Plans to indoctrinate elementary school teachers with "children's literature" are on the way. They would be helpful indeed. But the reading problem there, as in the high schools, must bite upon method as well as material. Read the delightful analysis of a child's reading in *Pursuit of Understanding,* by Esther C. Dunn. She raises fundamental questions about a young child's relation of books to immediate experience, the importance of giving them early "emancipation of mind and being by spiritual kinship with other beings." She says, "There is not only pleasure in such parallels; but power to reassure and stabilize one's life. Could this pleasure not be felt sooner? At eight instead of eighteen?" I say, it can only be felt at eight if at eight one is a good reader, not just a picture book reader.

V. AUTHORS AND ARTISTS

When you are writing for children, do not assume a style for the occasion! Think your best, write your best. Let the whole thing live!

—Anatole France, *Le Livre de Mon Ami*

Intelligence consists in having read the heart and deciphered the promptings latent there; and then, in reading the world, and deciphering its laws and constitution, to see where the heart's ideals may be embodied.

—George Santayana, *Reason in Art*
(The Life of Reason, v. 4)

What difference does it make to the youngsters if the style repeats itself sometimes, if it says what it wants to say without much ceremony? If, instead of wornout and artificial words, it uses words that are picturesque and genuine? If it is clear? In short, children reading remind us that the simple forces of the soul, like the simple forces of all art, contain the values that endure eternally.

—Paul Hazard, *Books, Children and Men*

I give the authors and artists my central place and my shortest message. Their work springs from what has been said before of the public, the children, the schools. They are conditioned by the bookmakers, the bookshops and libraries.

They stand not only in the center, but at the peak, for without them none of the rest exists. They are closer to the heart of the child than all the rest of us. To the genuinely creative person, each facet of experience, each ordinary fact of the outward world, has, as for the child, the impact of surprise, the aura of wonder. Their agonizing trouble is to find the suitable style, most suitable to themselves, in which to state what they have seen. We want them to search honestly for this style, not to judge themselves by routine or mass standards, not to copy each other.

True genius has been lavished on the world of children's books. Genius has met it on the part of many editors. The crafts of bookmaking have reached a high level. Often as soon as they reached it, the effect was lost in a flood of poor imitations. But the increased sales resulting should have and did lure more good writers and artists into the field. The fact that some of them wrote and drew purposely for children, others worked with never the sight of a child, made no difference, if the spark of genius was there, if the artist had something to say. Today, the great variety of the audience of children is his opportunity. The new adulthood of the modern child is his challenge.

What a blessing it is that there are forty-six of these publishers for the authors and artists to approach. How brave and independent it should make them feel! Surely among so many, there must be enough diversity of taste and opinion so that a unique idea could somewhere find a home. That is very healthy.

To the authors and artists, I say, be brave! Badger the publishers, worry them, terrify them! Write lots of books one year and none the next year. Scream with rage when they do bad printing. Pester them about your royalty reports. Call them up and wail if they let your books go out of print. Let them bribe you with advances, let them feed you good lunches—ask for a second helping of dessert. Dare all—even to leaving one of them for another—dare anything, if you, in your heart, know you have done your best. All the publisher has is nothing compared to ideas, and to that style which every publisher's reader should pray to find leaping out like a new sun from the new manuscript.

If only, during the war, it had been the plates that were lacking and not the paper! Think of the glorious children's books that would have come back into print, the faith in life restored to many an author, the new generation of children meeting wonderful old books because the shops had no new ones to sell! Alas, it was not the type and the plates that went to war. And so, many new artists and authors did get a hearing, which after all was most necessary.

There must always be that new chance, for every kind of book-making. In the welter that results, in the printing that seems bad taste to you and me, the children are gradually learning to protect themselves. And some day criticism will rise to better levels, children's book reviewing will be given more space and be done more critically. Some day the work of author and artist in this field will be properly related to the several worlds of the child and the adult, not kept in a tiny special corner alone. It is no solution occasionally to have a famous name review one book. What we need is continuous professional criticism of the whole field, and evaluation of art by artists and writing by writers.

VI. LIBRARIANS

The growth of mental activities is independent of formal teaching . . . From the development of a latent psychological energy comes the inner life. This private, hidden, not-to-be shared, undemocratic thing . . . remains the source of all originality, of all greatness. It permits the individual to retain his personality, his poise, and the stability of his nervous system in the confusion of the modern world.

—Alexis Carrel, *Man the Unknown*

American libraries are the defenders of the children, the authors and the artists, and the whole pro-book, anti-materialist world. No one knows better than the publishers how much librarians have counted in the development of children's reading. Besides filling out the card at the desk, shepherding the hordes of children, answering questions, filling out book orders and reports, they have found time to teach new librarians, to support and spread Book Week, tell stories, write book reviews, and sometimes to do both research and creative writing.

The children's librarian is in several senses the defender of books. She judges them both by her own trained judgment and also by their direct appeal to children. Through her buying and display of them, her selection also suggests book purchase to the public.

Above all, on her depends the life of the older book, in a very real sense.

The children's librarian is also the defender of the individual reader against standardization. Here is a place, in the well-stocked children's room, which also necessarily includes selected adult books, where the child can roam and select as he wishes. Here too is the one place, as opposed to both school and home today, where the great classic tales in their original best forms are still read or told, where any age is free to listen to the immortal folk and fairy tales, and where, supposedly, a child can be led to read "good" books.

If parents, teachers, publishers, bookshops, really knew what librarians can do for books, such salaries would be paid them, that many more of our best young people, both men and women, would go into this field. In 1945, registration at library schools was falling off, and many city library systems lacked a third or more of the necessary workers. Where a worker such as a librarian is overwhelmed with physical labor, how can she keep her mental poise? How can she go home at night to judge the floods of books? For it is only at night she has time to read them. And at night the children's librarian also must keep balanced by reading adult books.

In the matter of children's reading, we could ask more of our librarians. We could beg more of them to reach out into their communities; to show and use a greater variety of books than just literature, that is, the "tool" books of information, art, music, that have first appeal to modern boys and girls. We could beg them, being mostly women, to have more men volunteer to help them talk books, especially with growing boys. It is so easy to think up things for librarians to do—but *when* would they do them? Each new idea we have is meant to lure the 80 per cent non-book people and children into the libraries, where there are, at the moment, neither books enough nor people enough to take care of them.

But it is an aim worth fighting for—to see that our children's library rooms, and the whole library, are so well supported that the librarian is one of the most important people in the community, and that *all* the community knows it.

Fortunately, the tastes and standards of our American librarians differ greatly. Let them differ and argue loudly with each other. Let us all hear their arguments. For at the moment when the book order is made up in every small town and great city, one of the greatest acts of a free democracy takes place. Your money, my money, is waiting there to be spent; every writer and artist has a stake in that act.

We demand more than we know of such book orders. For instance, a village librarian brought me the problem of younger boys and adult war books. Her policy, by agreement with her board and her local school, was to forbid them to boys under twelve. I said the problem meant, "what boys and what books?" Her boys were the little toughies of the neighborhood who seldom used the library. Here was her chance to use the heroes of today to lead back to classic heroes. Who is to say that Ernie Pyle and John Mason Brown would not give these boys a great deal more than current boys' books? I pity any boy who has been denied such books, who has had the war only in the movies. My librarian, who is not a children's librarian, had not time, courage, or imagination to start a club about war heroes, to begin with the contemporary, to create a few more readers of the real book. But it takes a very special sort of person, with plenty of background, both in child psychology and in adult literature, to handle such a problem. "Who are your heroes?" That question is at the very core of adolescent life today.

One of my war heroes is a librarian. It is one Madame Kessels in Brussels, who once studied at Pratt Institute. For two years she worked daily at the university library in the midst of German soldiers. They had "commandeered" expensive reference books; she ferreted them out, presented them with loan cards, got the books back. Day after day, she faced those stupid beasts who she well knew had burned books, appropriated whole universities, hung and tortured those whose minds were unlike their own. But to Mme. Kessels, the defense of her books was her duty, and day by day she risked her life for a book. Today, she is alive; the library of the University of Brussels is intact. Let the boys and girls hear of more kinds of heroes like this librarian. Let the adult world give greater respect and devotion to all librarians.

VII. BOOKSHOPS AND PUBLISHERS

"Il est toujours l'heure de faire le bien." (Every moment is the moment to do one's very best.) Engraved on Saint-Méry's watch.
—Henry W. Kent, "*Encore Moreau de Saint-Méry,*"
in *Bookmen's Holiday*

So, I come at last to you, the people who make and sell the books. You are only a part of the whole seven, you too are the product of the schools and libraries, the atomic age, the war neuroses, the muddle of tastes, and the thin-spread culture of America. You are naturally busiest finding out what sells best. In the golden era of the twenties you lavished forth many a book on a dare, on a slim chance of breaking even. Those glorious moments of courage seem to come less often nowadays. Yet forty-six of you have entrusted your children's bookmaking to specially chosen people, and many bookshops have entrusted that selling to special people. The sales figures show you that this meant sense, rather than courage. And there is great hope in the quality of your recent appointments in this field.

As I sit alone in my little book room in the country, the effect of your publishing is very puzzling. I see, in newspapers, in *Publishers' Weekly,* that there are over 600 new children's books in the fall of 1945. After thought, I check about fifty that I would like to own perhaps, to recommend at least, but only after I see them. I go to our excellent local bookshop, find it flooded with new children's books, but only a few of my fifty. I make Book Week speeches in the midst of most lavish displays—again, very few of my fifty. Well! my taste is a special taste, a trained taste, surely it means little that the fifty I guess to be best are not evident. But it is true that in spite of *The Horn Book* (which after all has under five thousand subscribers all over America and still is run with no profit), in spite of the columns of reviews, in spite of all the library lists, parents and booksellers are pretty well lost in the flood of new books. I still think *having* such a flood is healthy for America—but I leave with you the idea it is terribly puzzling to the bookshop and the book buyer. If there *is* a good new children's writer—and Mr. Melcher says *where* is a good one—his book certainly is easily lost sight of in the shuffle. *You* are not going to solve this, for to each of you, your writers are good, if not the best. Oh, if only you had printed *only* the best!

Since my time, however, many fine things have happened in "the trade." One is the two-year-old Association of Children's Book Editors. This was much needed. It should develop in the nature partly of a discussion club and partly of a medieval guild. I think it has not yet grasped its possible power for good. Another is the Children's Book Council, which supports Book Week and also a year-round children's book promotion agency. The Council admits besides the editors, many other trade people. This Council's secretary is properly concerned with production of cheaper books—all power to her! If many books of only passing value were experimented with first in cheaper form, the floods of books might be reduced. Conversely, to print "good" books in cheap form, without sacrificing either text or taste in bookmaking, is a great need. The recent plan of the New York City Board of Education to put into circulation 600,000 paper-bound non-copyright books is exciting, and a clear indication to the publishers of a definite need. The books have gone to press and will probably be ready for distribution in September.

Other hopeful experiments are the Junior League Book Recordings and the A.L.A. Storytelling recordings. I suppose if these pioneers are successful, we shall have floods of records, done without the care and good taste of the originals. Another helpful note is in the treatment of material for children at our great museums, both in teaching, in exhibits, and in material for sale. It is not only in New York that such work and such museum publications reach many children. As to the recent innovation of book reports by a clinic of children, I am skeptical. Like the publishers' children in *Publishers' Weekly,* as soon as they make several reports, they are a conditioned group. Free experiment in publishing will reflect more aspects of the world than any single child or group of children could be expected to like at a given moment.

There are always signs of hope in the books themselves. One of mine is E. B. White's *Stuart Little.* I hope it gets all possible awards and medals, for its text and its bookmaking. Another is E. W. Teale's *The Lost Woods.* Mr. White and Mr. Teale always give of their best, let the audience fall where it will. I admit to liking very much two of the new Heritage children's classics. And I congratulate the young firm of William Scott for continued courage and intelligence in the difficult field of preschool books.

It is very hopeful, too, to see how well many of our schools do other things than reading and writing. Take science and music. They are impersonal, in them the idea alone is shared, the emotion subordinate to a group emotion or to a classic thought. How well our young people do in these fields. Their mechanical and musical skills are adult, and may be channeled later into writing forms we do not foresee today.

I dare to prophesy that the postwar flood of civilian goods will not help the "real" book. But it will mean revaluation, and a return to something better all along the line, if the writers and publishers keep up with the children. Television, radio, movies, comics cannot eliminate the reading child, if the creative person still is encouraged to tell his story. It is the story that is the source of all that comes over the air and goes into the movies and the comics. There is always a new generation to read and to hear the story, before the mechanized world takes hold and gives it back secondhand.

I have drawn up a few questions for book publishers to ask themselves. They may focus the generalities I have used so far. They seem to me the same problems as those of 1929, but today they have much greater urgency.

Questions I.—About the "good" book

1. Are you really working, outside of libraries, to see that the good book reaches its widest audience?

2. Are you neglecting the real writer, the good writer, in favor of the stunt book? Do you lose sight of the author in making up the package?

3. Do you expect the good book to pay for itself in one year? Or do you realize that only the good book will live and make you money for many years?

4. Have you considered the average quality of your list and of the total new titles for 1945? Do you think it reached an all-time low, since 1920, or was there a worse year?

5. How many books have you published recently cut to a pattern

because you knew the pattern would sell? This happens to career books, biographies, picture books, and, alas, to the so-called "classics."

Questions II.—About children's book editors

1. Is there any reason why they should all be women? Would it not be better for the children if more were men?

2. Do you hesitate to put a man in this department because you would have to pay him more and let him be a director of your firm?

3. Are your editors paid as much as your sales people?

4. Can your children's book editors both write and edit good English? Are they really editors as well as package producers?

5. Can your editors distinguish between a propaganda book and an opinion-forming book? Can you?

6. Do you demand of your editors, once a year, a written survey of the status of their department? This should be included with their next year's budget, and should give you an idea of their ability to guess the needs of this special field.

7. Editors, draw up your report whether it is asked for or not. Are you satisfied with your firm in its cooperation with you and your books? Your field still is special, and it changes rapidly. Do not suffer in silence! Draw up in writing your hopes, prophecies, complaints, send the top copy to your president, carbons to the heads of sales and advertising and anyone else you wish. If your document is well done, the writing of it will give you yourself new ideas, even if the men take no action on it.

8. Editors, do you believe that the average child of reading age, say from eight to twelve, really likes many new children's books? What do you do to find out? Do you realize that this is the key age that creates the good reader? Do you realize how many good books,

old and new, can be appropriated for them from the adult lists?
What do you do in format and editing and in distribution, all three,
to suit the new book and the old book to the *new* children?

VIII. CONCLUSION

American culture today is at a low ebb because it is spread so thin.
Everybody sees too much, hears too much, looks at too many movies,
has the whole world brought in bits close to the eye and ear. Everybody, including the poor little children.

If the book publisher is engaged in a profession, as against a
trade, he is searching for somebody, not everybody. Movies, radio,
comics, pulp magazines are the enemy of the book. Do not fool
yourselves into thinking that the hours children or adults spend
with these other mediums will lead back to books. Their production
is at the lowest point of mass thinking. The harm they are doing
at this minute, taking their untrue suggestions of an American way
of life all over the world, is incalculable. "The channels of communication are clogged." The wonderful folk-humor, the superb
old, classic stories are distorted, simplified, cheapened, to suit
everybody.

It is easy enough to guess how to please everybody. When I
check up on the comics, when I meet that slinky-black girl who
was every soldier's pet comic (and I assure you, I am glad they
had her, if they wanted her), when I hear the children tell why
they love Superman, whose new adventures are dictated by advertising men, I think way back to Mr. H. G. Wells and *Tono-Bungay*:
"The real trouble in life, Ponderevo, isn't that we exist; it's that
we *don't* really exist, and we want to. That's what all this muck
of advertising stands for; the hunger to be for once really alive,

alive to the fingertips. Nobody wants to do and be the things people are. Nobody. What we all want is to be something perpetually young and beautiful, young Joves, Ponderevo, pursuing coy nymphs through everlasting glades."

There is a wonderful golden age when everyone who feels like this can find the answer in good books. It is that golden age of childhood, when minds are only partly corrupted, when individualism is rampant, when the sense of good words is acute, when the world is still surprising, and all good still is possible. This age used to last till people were adolescent. Now the golden age is shorter and shorter, depending on where children live and how much of the mass-culture touches them.

It is our job together to work to prolong it, and to make books that give it a belief in its own best impulses. M. Hazard says, "How would heroism be kept alive in our changing earth, if not by each fresh young generation of the human race? The finest and noblest of the books intended for children tell of heroism. They are the inspiration of those who, later in life, sacrifice themselves that they may secure safety for others."

From Dr. Dolittle to Superman: New Trends in Children's Books

From the Twenty-fifth Anniversary issue of the New York Herald Tribune Weekly Book Review, *September 25, 1949. This was reprinted in* A Children's Sampler, *in a limited edition by the Distaff Side, 1950.*

For children's books the year 1924 came in a period of many beginnings. Special library work for boys and girls was not new, but it was reaching greater effectiveness, with more trained people in charge of children's rooms in public libraries and steady increase in appropriations for purchase of books for those rooms. Progressive education was changing teaching methods and the movement toward social studies had started: this meant a freer use of source materials and of non-textbooks in schools. It suggested different needs for books in homes and libraries, too.

Then after the First World War had come an exciting influx of foreign picture books which was a great stimulus to artists, printers, publishers, and the general public. Wonderful color work, gay new patterns of layout, bold and more original artwork tumbled in from Czechoslovakia, Germany, France, Italy, Norway, and Sweden. Some of those books were printed in English in the lands of their origin and sold here in large editions. And some European artists came here to live and work and bring a different flavor to our illustrations.

In 1924 there were only a few separate departments in publishing houses to produce children's books, but rapidly they increased. This meant not only more new books more thoughtfully prepared for a special market, but new publicity for the old ones. With the increased output there was new reason for special reviewing in this field, which was given great impetus by the appointment of Anne Carroll Moore to do her "Three Owls" page, beginning with the first issue of the *New York Herald Tribune's* weekly review of books. Also in 1924 came the first issue of *The Horn Book Magazine,* the first such medium about books and reading for young people and still the only one. New York as well as Boston had its special children's bookshops, and departments with able people to advise young purchasers were started in the general bookstores.

All beginnings seem golden in memory and those early twenties now remind us of the first times of so many sorts of fun: Hendrik van Loon drawing history with a match, Elizabeth MacKinstry with her quill pens, Vachel Lindsay roaring out the "Congo" to schools and reciting "Johnny Appleseed," Padraic Colum writing his books of classic myths and retelling Cinderella, and all of us over twelve being thrilled by *John Brown's Body.* That golden time was soon followed by the depression, then all too soon by another war. In each calamity it was children's book production that suffered first in any publishing house, and it began to recover only a few years ago.

One cannot here write a real history, but only glance at some changes and tendencies, and remember some books that through these years have been enjoyed with the children. They have been enlivened by a rare lot of humorous writing taken immediately into what seems permanent favor, whether American or English. More than one generation by now has shared the fun of the Doctor Dolittle books, the "Freddy" books, the Mary Poppins stories, *Winnie-the-Pooh, Ferdinand, Homer Price, Rabbit Hill, Mr. Popper's Penguins.*

Then there are the outstanding picture books, beginning, we all agree, with Wanda Gág's *Millions of Cats,* and her *A B C Bunny.* Beside them we might choose for a small shelf: Mrs. Morrow's *The Painted Pig* from Mexico, Ardizzone's *Little Tim* from England, Bemelmans' *Madeline* from Paris, Handforth's *Mei Li* from China, the D'Aulaires' *Ola* from Norway, the Petershams' *Miki* from Hungary. All made in America but originating far away, their happy spirit still adds more to the gaiety of nations than all the purposeful travel-story books so consciously produced between the two wars, that accomplished so little toward international understanding. Picture books about America itself that stand proudly beside them are: Daugherty's *Andy and the Lion,* McCloskey's *Lentil,* Gramatky's *Little Toot,* Holling's *Paddle-to-the-Sea,* Credle's *Down, Down the Mountain,* the Haders' *Cock-a-Doodle-Doo!,* Lathrop's *Who Goes There?,* Sewell's *Blue Barns.*

Today, picture-book makers need to be on their toes for they have new competition from mass-produced color books. So many more books are being made at cheaper prices that it ought to be a happy state of things for the children. Some are good, some are poor, but the discriminating adult buyer finds many treasures among the big-edition books such as *The Golden Egg Book,* the merry box of *Tiny Animals Stories,* and the beautiful *Golden Christmas Manger.* Artists like Leonard Weisgard, Garth Williams, Helen Sewell in these books have reached huge audiences. Also, since the war have come many new cheap editions of various children's classics. To have a great variety of old favorites available from twenty-five cents to a dollar is a blessing. However, they offer a puzzling choice to the buyer in the crowded bookshops where what is cheapest naturally has the biggest piles. One could wish that somewhere, in school or library, selective exhibitions could be held of inexpensive books—classics, toy books, picture books—as a guide to bewildered parents.

The most obvious change in this era is the change in atmosphere created by comic books, radio, movies, picture magazines, and now by television. As every storyteller knows, they have changed the child's span of attention. Picture-mindedness would naturally have an effect on reading. It discourages a lazy child's interest in the act itself; also it offers him in his movies, etc., much more adult material than do most of his children's books, or than his word-reading power can cope with. So of course he likes the non-book mediums better. Also, the tone of the majority of comics and movies has been tough, even though the ending is morally right. This has built upon the children's natural love for excitement, thrills, and action to a degree unknown twenty-five years ago, and has quickened it at an earlier age.

The effects of all this on the children's books have been many. The longer classics no longer are widely read for pleasure. Style has become so simple that in many books it has lost all flavor. Subject matter in picture books and young stories has been a bit slow to catch up with the child who sees and hears so much of the adult world. The wonder science tales have not caught up with Superman. But in one sort of book the mood of the period is answered: in the flood of horse, dog, and cowboy stories. Here are adults with children, here is excitement, and here generally is emotion to match their favorite movies. They are so successful that one wonders whether all young Americans will grow up to be either veterinarians or ranchhands. However, those are not any more unhealthy dreams than dreams of Robin Hood, and many of these books are good. They range from Eric Knight's *Lassie Come Home* to Walter Farley's *Black Stallion,* from Terhune's collie stories to Will James's *Smoky,* and the many books by Thomas Hinkle and Colonel Meek. C. W. Anderson's picture books of horses offer sound information and fine models for those who dream of being horse artists. The days of gentle little *Moor-*

land Mousie seem long ago indeed. One does not just learn to ride today; one must catch and tame a wild horse.

Another tendency in these years has been increasing interest in books for the nursery school age. This field woke up when Lucy Sprague Mitchell wrote her *Here and Now* stories and Mary Steichen Martin published her *First Picture Book* in photographs. Who remembers that famous debate at the old Civic Club with Mrs. Mitchell defending tales of milk bottles, and Lenore Power standing up for the most grisly horrors of Grimm? Today, we have the psychiatrists and the Child Study Association defending the comics, instead, in debates with opponents whose most vigorous representative is John Mason Brown. But to return to the children too small to care about the comics, they have found an interpreter of their moods in Margaret Wise Brown, who has remarkable insight into their ways. Her first *Noisy Book* brought the young listener right into the frame of reading. Soon she turned to such lovely fantasies as *The Little Island* and *The Little Lost Lamb,* and to such original concepts as that of *The House of a Hundred Windows,* the first book to introduce younger children to adult modern art. In the same field, Irma Webber has brought botany to a four-year-old level with her books on roots and seeds.

In recent years we have had an increase, too, in books of American folklore and folksongs. Regional stories, modern and historical, have been better written stories by Lois Lenski and Marguerite de Angeli, for example. Mary Fitch's *One God* was an outstanding contribution to religious thinking for any age of reader. Books of information before the war were a bit slow to be given fine or original format. Now they cover every sort of youthful curiosity, explaining elevators, jet planes, atomic energy, bugs and automobiles, medicine and how a baby comes to be. The imaginative approach to such instruction began long ago with Maxwell Reed's *The Earth for Sam,* Leo Huberman's *We, the People,* and

Gertrude Hartman's *These United States and How They Came to Be*. Recent good writing in this field includes Genevieve Foster's *George Washington's World* and her parallel titles with a fresh approach to history, Katherine Shippen's *The Bright Design,* Wilfred Bronson's nature books, and John J. Floherty's fine reporting of exciting careers for men. Biography has been well served by Carl Sandburg, James Daugherty, Jeannette Eaton, Cornelia Meigs, Elizabeth Janet Gray.

Fiction for older boys and girls has been much affected by the sensibly increased addition of more adult books to the children's rooms of libraries. Many of the romantic older "series" formerly read by teen-agers now are devoured by those in junior high. Titles like those by Caroline Dale Snedeker, Howard Pease, John Tunis; biographies like *The Silver Pencil* by Alice Dalgliesh and *George Washington Carver* by Shirley Graham are enjoyed by all young people over twelve. Girls will pass the time with the newer series by Maureen Daly and Janet Lambert, and boys with the many sports stories; but their chief fiction reading is adult.

So we turn back to the children and come, at the end, to poetry. Exactly twenty-five years ago, we first read Milne's *When We Were Very Young*. Do you remember how cruelly those clever verses were treated by Dorothy Parker and Beatrice Lillie? But they were fun, and wonderfully easy to remember, and have not been matched since. The rare poetry in *Peacock Pie* had appeared in 1920, but in 1923 came De la Mare's superb anthology *Come Hither*. Many other collections offered the child a fresh approach to poetry old and new, such as the popular little *Silver Pennies,* and the more comprehensive books of Auslander and Untermeyer. *A Book of Americans* by Rosemary and Stephen Benét struck a new note. Verse by Rachel Field, Elizabeth Coatsworth, Sara Teasdale, Elizabeth Madox Roberts, and Winifred Welles was outstanding.

Many beautiful, rather special books of the twenties come to mind that are probably out of print today, but they added great variety and distinction to the book world. Many still remember their discovery of books like C. B. Falls's *A.B.C.*, MacKinstry's *The White Cat*, Helen Sewell's *A First Bible*, Gibson's *The Goldsmith of Florence*, Pamela Bianco's *Land of Dreams* from William Blake, Lynd Ward's *Prince Bantam*, and all the distinguished bookmaking of Boris Artzybasheff from *The Forge in the Forest* and *The Fairy Shoemaker* to *Fables from Aesop*. All these books were specials when they came out in the twenties, and would still be outstanding if reprinted today. However, today good taste is more widely prevalent in book design, whether or not it helps a book to sell to a wide public. The Pantheon Press, Holiday House, the Peter Pauper Press, the Heritage Press, all of which have made beautiful books for boys and girls, are not alone in having top book designers. We think of such titles as William Pène du Bois's *Twenty-one Balloons*, *The Royal Game of Chess*, *Amos and the Moon*, the book of Robin Hood ballads illustrated by Virginia Burton, and many others which have been worthy of the annual list of fifty best-made books of the Institute of Graphic Arts. Their occasional shows of children's books have been most stimulating to this field.

Parents who feel overwhelmed by the huge number of children's books published (about one thousand in 1948) can find help in building their home libraries in some fine books that are lasting records of this era. Before the war, we had Anne Carroll Moore's "Three Owls" books, May Lamberton Becker's *Adventures in Reading*, and Bertha Mahony's *Realms of Gold*. Since the war, there have come Anne Eaton's *Reading with Children* and *Treasure for the Taking*, also Anis Duff's *Bequest of Wings*. May Hill Arbuthnot's *Children and Books* is a larger, more formidable affair, meant for students but full of thoughtful advice for the home. Paul Hazard's *Books, Children and Men* touches off the era from an international viewpoint. And there is the monumental work, *Illustrators of Children's Books: 1744–1945,* by Mahony, Folmsbee, and Latimer. Here artwork for children is reasonably connected with art developments in the adult world, which so seldom is done in criticism of writing for children.

On the whole, publishers are responding much more intelligently to the needs of modern boys and girls than they did twenty-five years ago. We cannot take the words "literature" and "classic" too seriously in reading for ages three to thirteen, and must bear in mind that the school and home worlds of the child are integral to his reading habits. We can hope that with all the fine books there are for them, young readers are turning into better adult readers. Whatever the audio-visual tendencies of the age, words still are our basic medium for thought. It is only through increased attention and intelligence as to words that any discrimination as to the other mediums can be developed.

The Children's Librarian

Speech given at the A.L.A. meeting at Cleveland on the Fiftieth Anniversary of the Children's Library Association, from Library Journal, *October 15, 1950.*

A golden anniversary is an event of such magnitude that the speaker can only cheer herself by beginning with a bit of nonsense. These familiar verses apply almost too well, both to me and to you.

"I skip forty years," said the Baker, in tears,
    "And proceed without further remark
To the day when you took me aboard of your ship
    To help you in hunting the Snark.

. . . .

" 'You may seek it with thimbles—and seek it with care;
    You may hunt it with forks and hope;
You may threaten its life with a railway-share;
    You may charm it with smiles and soap—' "

. . . .

" 'But oh, beamish nephew, beware of the day,
    If your Snark be a Boojum! For then
You will softly and suddenly vanish away,
    And never be met with again!'

I venture to guess that the changes of fifty years, for children's librarians, point to the addition of soap to smiles and of forks to hope, and of increased worry lest the Snark of good reading be a Boojum after all.

To talk about these fifty years of books, children, and librarians in so brief a period is not only a Hunting of the Snark—it also evokes "the thunder of the Jabberwocky." In Elva Smith's *History of Children's Literature,* I found an applicable quotation from Agnes Repplier: "Nothing is so hard to deal with as a period. Nothing is so unmanageable as a date. . . . Events will happen out of time. The closely linked decades refuse to be separated."

In thinking of these years, we know that both books and people prove dateless. As to books, consider the dates of some so much alive in the children's book world of today: *Alice in Wonderland* and *Hans Brinker,* 1865; *The Peterkin Papers,* 1880; *Tom Sawyer,* 1876; both *Treasure Island* and Pyle's *Robin Hood,* 1883; *Captains Courageous* and *Master Skylark,* 1897. Surely *The Wind in the Willows* must have existed as long as any of these? No, it came in 1908. But who cares! They all were favorites with children early in this century; they still are today.

It is the same with people. How can we believe that it was about fifty years ago when Anne Carroll Moore was up on that ladder in the Pratt Institute Library, dusting the leaves of the tallest rubber plant in Brooklyn? She may have been dusting it or washing it; anyway, there she was when a shy young lady from Boston appeared, to learn from her about work with children. Miss Moore says she continued her work on the ladder, and called down to Alice Jordan: "Go right to Pittsburgh: all the interesting things are going on there."

In your roster of pioneers, many names are as vivid to me as if their owners were here today, as some of them indeed may be. The fifty years seem very short. Dates and ages have little to do with such a roll-call. They were and are gay, courageous leaders; they were master hands at merry celebrations; it was always exciting to talk to them about books; and they believed in the imaginative capacity of all children. The power of their small band grew like the mustard seed in the Bible. They remind me of lines by Elizabeth Coatsworth:

> As far as the strong-winged eagles fly
> Our frail thoughts climb to reach the sky,
> And deep in the sea as fishes sink
> A child may go—if a child will think.

Suppose we try to put ourselves back into a book-loving home of the early twentieth century. For many of us, this is not too difficult. Besides the older books I have already mentioned, the children may have had the Dotty Dimple books, Eugene Field's verses, *Peter and Wendy*, *Heidi*, *Rackety-Packety House*, and *Little Lord Fauntleroy*, possibly Belloc's *Cautionary Tales*. The girl may have been absorbed in her mother's set of the Elsie books, and the boy may have found his father's Henty books in the attic. They soon went on through the sets on the library shelves, of Dickens, Thackeray, George Eliot, Kipling, and Scott, reading these alternately with the children's books. When the books had been nearly exhausted, Father may have bought Dr. Eliot's Five-Foot Shelf. In this set they roamed a bit unhappily, for the type was horrible, and there were no pictures. They had *St. Nicholas Magazine*, and later the *Youth's Companion*. They could dip into the old *Harper's* or *Century* or *Scribner's*.

Meantime, their social background was leisurely. Re-created today in many children's books, it must seem funny to today's children: those first electric lights, first automobiles, first telephones.

The population was smaller, and a much smaller proportion of it could buy books or did read for pleasure. Reading for fun, a pleasure that everyone had a right to share, was a new conception.

But there were public libraries and in 1900 came, here and there, the first children's rooms in those libraries. When those rooms were about thirty-five years old, Bertha Mahony Miller wrote a moving tribute to them in a supplement to *Realms of Gold:* "There one finds respect for and appreciation of all races; genuine tolerance of varying points of view; unfailing and imaginative kindness; all the sensitive appreciation of genius. . . . The children's rooms have themselves created a demand for fine books. They have become more articulate in their critical appraisal of books. It was from the children's rooms that the first worthy criticism of children's books came." Again writing last year, Mrs. Miller quoted from a man who had used Miss Overton's library at Westbury as a boy: "The atmosphere was one of delight. . . . The fact that I would come into a kind of refuge and really sit still to read, work, or merely to dream, is not without its validity."

The records show the swift spread of these happy places, and the training of special librarians to staff them. In the early twenties, there was an answering renaissance of book publishing for children—no, not a rebirth, for nothing like it had been seen before. It coincided with America's serious preoccupation with child study, the improvement of schools, and the increase of wealth and population. In the twenties, Anne Carroll Moore and Anne Eaton had their reviewing spaces in New York papers, and other newspapers paid more attention to the criticism of children's books. Then came Children's Book Week in which all child agencies gradually shared. The power of the children's work reached a point where library purchases alone could support one edition of a book. And from a handful of special children's book publishers, the list has grown to more than sixty today.

How astounded those keepers of early children's rooms would be, perhaps are, to watch the program of a superintendent of children's work in a big city today. At the risk of boring you, I will put one actual program down for the record. I only wish it would reach an audience far wider than librarians. The children's librarian copes with these tasks: book evaluation of an output of at least one thousand new children's books each year; visiting branches; conducting training groups; talking at a wide variety of clubs, churches, schools; telling stories at schools, settlements, playgrounds, scout meetings, hospitals; experimenting with movies, victrola music; providing, or performing on, radio programs; supervising the printing of lists. Besides, she must find and keep her staff, and attend to her A.L.A. committee duties. No wonder the person whose list I have copied from a report had premature white hair.

To call such a job a challenge to the human mind and frame is to put it mildly. It was women who rose to the challenge and willingly created more and more work. These women became important leaders, with untold influence on the progress of children's reading.

At first it seemed clear what they were after: simply to have more children read more good books. But soon, they were involved in as many battles as the wars they were living through. The book battles were waged but never were wholly won.

There was the question, at what age can children read what books? Shall books have ages specified on them? What about the book that can be read *to* one age, but only *by* a later age? That led to the battle of the rewritten classic, vocabularized according to word lists of the educators. Then came the horrible discovery that some children could not read at all, and we had remedial reading, with its cry for easy books. This led to such simplification of books, even for older boys and girls, that style took a bad beating. Then there was the battle of the *here* and *now* against the fairy tales.

And there was the war against the series books: out with them! Away with Elsie Dinsmore and the Bobbsey Twins! No sooner were they banished than along came the comics. Then came the plethora of children's voting. Shall what they are given depend on what the majority like best? Next, the great increase in home ownership of radio and television changed the child's whole span of attention and range of reference. And these increasingly powerful mass media were also lowering public taste in general, including that of authors, artists, and publishers.

These literate book-lovers, embattled, were taking on new foes, trying to be, all at once, booksellers, nurses of the preschool child, actresses, critics, movie mechanics, and, necessarily, good business women. As custodians of the public taste, their challenge was terrific. For they were living in a new world. The child of today really was a new child. Clinging to certain ageless books, he also needed many new kinds of books, and to the old books he brought a new sort of imagination.

Today we are at last aware of the new, rather sad, complete awareness of all children. I think of a poem called "Listening" by Winifred Welles, a poem about ears:

> There's not a stauncher chink
> In all my tremulous self
> Than these, who can house both
> The giant and the elf,
> The engine and the moth.
> Quieter than the hands,
> Greedier than the tongue,
> Their fragile stuff withstands
> The most destructive song.
> Nostrils quiver, eyes can close,
> But shutterless stand these
> Frail grottoes, white and rose,
> My bravest crevices.

What we adults are pouring into those "brave crevices" today is definitely not worthy of them. No one could fail to have been moved at a recent *New Yorker* cartoon, of a very small boy who has crept down at midnight to turn on the television. He sits there biting his fists, watching an adult murder mystery, eyes and ears both involved, and possibly no adult aware of what he is doing.

Let us turn, however, to a more cheering picture of children of today. In John Mason Brown's *Morning Faces,* you remember the chapter on trying to read aloud from *Treasure Island.* He recalls the books he read aloud when his boys were very little, the books that bored him so much, but that he had to read over and over again: *Peter Rabbit, Gabriel Churchmouse, Little Black Sambo, Uncle Remus;* the ones they read to themselves: *Alice, The Hunting of the Snark, Stuart Little, The White Deer.* Yes, these boys lived in a literate home. But when it came to taking a nine-year-old to *Hamlet,* by then the comics had had their day. What chance, thought this father, has *Hamlet* against the comics? Against Disney, with his creatures "creating pleasure by pain, living only to sock, and having socked, socking again?" He had his doubts.

He prepares by a none too happy reading from Lambs' *Tales.* Then comes the marvelous experience in full. At the end is proof that all those real books really have won. They are going home in the taxi. Father says: "How'd you like it?" "Gee, it was swell. I liked it better than *Oklahoma!*" A pause. "I liked it a little better than Donald Duck." Another pause. "'A little more than kin and less than kind.' Gee! That's pretty, isn't it?" So, once more we are reminded what exposure to the best can do, if it really is the best, and perhaps the adult best. All children might not be as ready for *Hamlet* as the Brown boy. But they should always have the chance to compare their Donald Ducks and their Oklahomas with Shakespeare.

To offer this comparison must be at the core of any work with books. That the librarian is aware of it is obvious. That book called *Youth, Communication and Libraries* showed your thinkers ready to use every possible device to lure the non-reader as well as the good reader, to help the greater mass of the population, who never may be "literary," to know at least the usefulness of books, and to fight the taste of our times which has fallen to a new low. I find another fine statement in the introduction to the new basic book list for high schools, by Dorotha Dawson: "The focus is for the individual these books can serve. . . . The titles had to throw some light on the world's heritage, or create new channels into which divergent interests might run, or to give increasing depth to maturing personality."

But the challenge will always be thrown back to those working with younger children. In their increasing millions, many may never reach the high schools where such standards prevail. It is easy enough to awaken their wonder, to share their fun, when they are very young. How are they to be held? The task has been increasingly difficult. If one could find any criticism to offer, it might be in the fact that the children's librarians remained childish too long.

The first Newbery Medal was given to Van Loon's *History of Mankind*. Such books do not appear often. But how seldom since then has a creative, informational book, appealing to the growing intelligence, either been given an award or been featured. A younger child can read and love fairy tales and be absorbed in his comics, and at the same time be pursuing some serious hobby or some line of factual reading. He needs that basis in world folklore and fable to which the library clings. But in this modern world he will not return for it at ten to twelve, for he has found his modern folklore in media other than books. Many a poor reader of that age refuses a piece of good fiction which looks too long, but *will* read well enough if the matter concerns baseball, electricity, jet planes, the anatomy of a horse, the way an owl's eye winks, or the causes behind an election. The publishers have provided such books in wonderful plenty. They sell. But perhaps they have been too seldom featured by the children's room. When one considers the list of "distinguished children's books of 1949" chosen by the A.L.A., one sees that it is the much younger child who is borne in mind. Outstanding, creative, informational books are not admitted.

It is easy to criticize the children's librarian for being more faithful to what she calls literature than to modern life, and certainly all are not open to this criticism. Besides it is hardly her fault that the world of the child so suddenly changed. But it is true that in a period while the librarians continued chiefly to serve the younger children, and overemphasized the purely imaginative and poetic, the average child had fled to the adult fantasy of Superman and to the dream of taming a wild stallion. Too late they put up pictures of baseball heroes and an exhibit of modern machinery. As the first publisher of a book about a derrick, I speak out of my own experience: libraries would have none of it twenty-five years ago; but it appears on some lists today. This is putting one aspect of a broad picture in too brief a space. But it is true that neither librarians nor schools, for a long while, coped with the world of the modern child.

In this last decade, it is much more than the child's increasing sophistication that has conflicted with traditional library work. There has come the tremendous increase of other mass-produced books besides comics. Those charming folk tales were taken over by Mr. Disney, and the tie-up of his mangled movie versions with mass-made, colorful books made them hideously familiar in a form unrecognizable to the librarian. You have heard the tale of the poor little girl who took the big Italian *Pinocchio,* with the Mussino pictures, to her school, and was told by her teacher to take it home, they had the Disney book.

In 1950, the publishers are well aware that there will be

29,517,000 new children of reading age. They announce the figure, and say they will be ready with editions of 100,000 of such books as the *Lone Ranger* and *Hopalong Cassidy* series, with their radio and television tie-ups for sales. The little picture books, sometimes good, sometimes not, are sold along with the groceries. But at the same time, the editions of what we like to think of as better books have also increased.

There is no use fighting the machine age we live in, and there is great use in having millions of cheap books available. They increase the challenge to the librarian, however, to teach the public comparative values and to help the parent who faces the great piles in bookshops to select wisely.

And as to public taste, we must remember the dime novels. Writing recently in *Publishers' Weekly,* John Winterich says of the Beadles and their books: "Today we take stories like these and put them in hard covers and call them historical novels. Sometimes we call them detective stories and get them from lending libraries. Sometimes we call them westerns and see them in the comics and movies. The Beadles set the reading habits of millions of Americans. In one way or another, they go marching on."

Is it better to read something than nothing? Who can say? This sort of reading has been called "sub-literature." Was it, or is it, very much better than some of the books children today are most fond of? The ones they vote for?

Let us stop to consider the word "literature" as applied to children's books. Would it not be healthier to talk about children's reading? In a recent *Atlantic Monthly,* Lord David Cecil said: "To enjoy literature as it should be enjoyed is a task of immense difficulty, requiring, in addition to common sense and uncommon sensibility, faith, hope, charity, humility, patience, and most of the other Christian virtues. It also involves a long process of self-training." Let us be honest enough to admit that very few of the books with which children prepare to enter this great world of adult reading are literature. This is no reason why they should not be read by them. But it is one thing to make a list of readable books children should not miss—and quite another to lead them into the great adult books. Revaluation of what we call children's classics is long overdue.

What do we all agree upon as great literature? Fifty years ago, an agreement was more taken for granted. Today, people are much franker about what bores them, and more disinclined to agree that anything is great. May Lamberton Becker has said: "There is no such thing as a best book; there are books that are best for you." Many great books bore many intelligent adults, just as many so-called children's classics bore many intelligent children. What about the Bible, Homer, and Shakespeare? Think what a wonderful reading and teaching program could be devised, with dramatic publishing to present it, based on these three great books. They could be offered in various stages of selected age appeal, to follow the reading of Mother Goose, and lead up to high school. Here would be every sort of reading—folklore, adventure, history, poetry, romance, in great style, and with great thoughts. Here would be literature and the adult content children really want. When and how do our younger children of today meet these books?

Alas, I do not foresee that any such program could ever be agreed upon. If not these three books, which others would you suggest? In this wonderful Cleveland Library, we find the words of Shakespeare used as posters in the general literature room. Whose words do you display in your children's rooms?

The children's librarian alone cannot restore these sessions with sets of the classics which offered a transition to children in the homes of fifty years ago. Nor can she restore the parents who used to read aloud from these three great books I have mentioned. Is she, or is she not, to be the one who really leads into literature?

Any talk of literary standards leads us, of course, to our schools. One of the greatest changes in recent times is the better work being done in school libraries. Here the work of the children's rooms had a most flourishing offshoot. Only within the last twenty years has the separate room for books in the school begun to call upon trained children's librarians and to prosper. In the same way, one believes that the new children's books affected the school books. Certainly text book publishers made a remarkable change, from the dull to the attractive, and they quickly used the new authors and artists discovered by the children's book publishers. To be sure, they reworded some of the stories, they offered them piecemeal, but they did introduce better writing into all the readers. Because of that division between school sales and trade sales, the new books, whole, did not get into the schools as fast as they should have. But the demand for the better book has so increased that in your index of subjects for schools half of the books are trade books, and a large proportion are fiction. Times have changed indeed.

But the ideals of school and public librarians for children should remain the same. The teacher may emphasize what she knows the child *can* read; the librarian may know better what she *hopes* the child will read. Both must continue to offer all kinds of children all kinds of reading, hoping for the awakening to real literary values that probably will come long after the child has left the elementary school and the children's room.

Walter de la Mare, writing a preface for *The Insect Man*, said: "What matters in learning—and this is Fabre's sovereign wisdom— is not to be taught but to wake up. . . . This book reveals a joy in acquiring knowledge which even the youngest children may have in fountainlike abundance." And Anne Eaton has said: "The problem is to awaken the imaginative and the unimaginative child alike to a larger world than the one he instinctively knows; to give to one the wonder of reality, to the other the wonder of romance. It is hard sometimes to draw the line between them, and perhaps it is not necessary to do so." I add to her wise words, that the children's room is the ideal place for both kinds of awakening to happen, the place where both can appeal as reading for pleasure.

We are together upon a long, long road. We know that more than one-third of our children either live in towns with no libraries or go to schools with no libraries. We know that there are at least two million children in our country who do not go to school at all. We know about the one million school-less migrant children. It will take many kinds of librarians to take care of them all. With so great a need, with so difficult a challenge, what is most important is a growing conception of the child's needs, and greatly improved training to meet it.

When one reads in your reports the sort of discussion you are holding today, all over this great country, it is clear that you are now awake to the need for new approaches to the children of this new world. Such a meeting, for instance, as that of the Southwest Regional group in 1949 at Fort Worth, where those thirteen significant questions were asked; the 1947 meeting in California called "The Crisis in Children's Books"; the report by Dr. Robert D. Leigh of the Public Library Inquiry—all these show foresightedness and hope for your profession. Dr. Leigh said that "children's library service is the classic example of successful library work." His figures showed that the largest proportion of library users are children. You could hardly ask for brighter laurels for your fiftieth year than this.

So, what of the future of the children's room? It must always exist, if only as a happy retreat, a place for any sort of child to roam in freely. It is the place for that accident in reading, that chance discovery which no one can ever prescribe, the discovery of a book that sometimes changes the whole of a child's reading

life and growing ideals and imagination. It is the place for all the
"special" books, and for all kinds of children's reading.

Everyone who talks about children's reading admits that the
ideal introduction to books would be that home library of the early
century, much improved, of course, where the transition to adult
books would be natural and inevitable.

Several famous writers have told me that, about forty years ago,
they didn't like those new children's rooms because they kept
them out of the adult rooms. Those critics do not know your
present children's rooms. But it is possible that the bright child
of today has the same feeling, for segregation and classification
always irritate the bright child. At what age does one stop being
a child? Some of you may have heard my story of that bright
boy George, aged six, in my home book room, who threw his
borrowed children's books on the floor, demanded the ladder, and
said he wanted to go up to those grown-up shelves, to get a book
he could share with his father. That summer, George took out
The Bright Design, The Stars for Sam, the *Big Book of Railroads,
Homer Price,* and the *Rootabaga Stories,* and loved them all, with
or without his father. To let my George, however bright, roam
freely amid most of the adult fiction of today would not be too
happy an affair.

Librarians are coping with this problem with many admirable
lists—and especially those suggestions for a basic home library.
When the best modern reference books, and attractive, readable
editions of the Bible and Homer and Shakespeare are to be found
in more homes, this transition to adult reading will again be easier.
This building up of good home libraries has to begin all over
again.

The children's librarian of the future will cope with all this.
Perhaps she may have to be less sentimental, more tough-minded,
more aware of the whole world of the children. She will celebrate

the beloved fairy tales and legends, but also the marvelous bright designs of the miracles of our new age. She will light candles for Shakespeare and De la Mare, but also for Edison and Marconi; and perhaps for Marshall and Eisenhower and the UN, as well as for Washington and Lincoln. She will be an even greater leader because the children know that she knows their present world as well as its past. She will continue, as she has begun, to work with mass communications of all sorts, to improve them. She will stretch the child's mind, besides charming and amusing it. Let us hope that, even before she accomplishes all this, she will receive that public gratitude and recognition she has so long deserved.

Let us end, not with books, but in my garden. Stoop to watch a snail, and think of Father Feeney's couplet:

> Snails obey the holy
> Will of God slowly.

And remember it to cheer ourselves in the world of the sub-literary and the non book readers.

Let us think of children and books as we watch a man training his hedges, in V. Sackville-West's "The Garden":

> Level your hedge by pruning to the spur,
> But here and there, at intervals designed
> Let a strong tree go up, in loftier
> Canopy hung with fruit, a spreading cry;
> As from the tedious level of mankind
> Once in a generation rise the high
> Lanterns of the imaginative mind.

To summarize: The fifty years of library work with children rose to a definite height in the twenties, to which both publishing and the public responded. In the thirties, financial depression affected both libraries and publishing, and in the forties a second World War changed public attitudes. With the rise of new mass media of communication came a great change of values, moral, spiritual, literary. Population had a huge increase, and the average taste affected the whole. The fact that children clung to certain old books, good or bad, proved nothing in particular, except that these were what we had offered them; especially it did not prove that these books were literature. The voting taste of average children remains low.

But we are now at a thrilling turning point. Publishers, authors, artists are well aware of it. New leaders are arising in the library world, with vision, sense, and imagination, at all levels, from young childhood to youth. They will help the children's rooms to win back the parts of their audience they may have lost to the worst forms of non-book imagining. They will help the special child to find his special book. And they will discover new ways to help all children to become better adult readers, and to be better able to explore the best of the world's great literature. The new emphasis should be on all children reading, and the old classics should be reevaluated for the child of today. In the words of *The Hunting of the Snark*, "forks will be added to hope."

Books on the
Ladder of Time

A speech given in 1960 to celebrate the Fiftieth Annual
Exhibition of Children's Books Suggested as Holiday
Gifts at the New York Public Library. Reprinted
in Young Readers' Review (Greenfield Park,
New York), Vol. 2, 1965.

This golden anniversary surely calls for trumpets and drums and
banners, and golden crowns widely distributed. One lone human
being feels most inadequate.

I would so happily have passed out those golden crowns! But
being asked to put the books of fifty years into forty-five minutes—
that seemed impossible. Like the Elephant's Child, I wailed to
Mrs. Spain, "Led go! You are hurtig be!" But she gaily replied,
"Oh, just give us a few trends and high spots."

High spots! A piece I wrote in 1949 for the twenty-fifth anni-
versary of the *Herald Tribune Book Review* was called "From
Dr. Dolittle to Superman." But now, I must jump from 1910 to
1960. How should I do it? "From *Old Mother West Wind* to
You and the Atom." "From A. A. Milne to Dr. Seuss." "From
Peter Pan to *Pippi Longstocking*" "From *Black Beauty* to *The
Black Stallion*."

Then I realized that my own real high spots fitted into no such
"From" and "To" pattern. For, there were *Peacock Pie* and *The*

Wind in the Willows in 1910, and here they still are in 1960, with new editions. So I put such titles aside, and there I was back with trends.

What is a trend? Can this book history be put into capsules to get these trends off our minds? Here is how I came out with them:

1910–1920. The golden age of great classics. The best of the past prevails; new books by the late Victorians; new retellings by our own great Howard Pyle. Influence of *St. Nicholas Magazine*. Effects of pioneer reviewing and library work with children.

1920–1930. A new era in American children's books. Postwar influences on book production. Expansion of sales with new prosperity. Effects of progressive education on subject matter. Effects of separate juvenile departments in publishing houses. First newspaper pages on children's books.

1930–1940. The influences of mass production. After the depression, increased annual output. Many more picture books. New series of fact books, easy books, regional books. Increase in folklore. Accumulating effects of library work, and the propaganda of Children's Book Week.

1940–1950. Coping with a new enemy, mass communication. Postwar changes in reading habits, and in reading ability. Heyday of the comic books; children's use of TV. Growth of school libraries. Further increase of juvenile publishers.

1950–1960. New wealth amid new chaos. Still increasing production, in spite of rising costs and prices. Still more series on history and other facts made easy. Renewed influences from Europe. Diversity plus distinction. New efforts to revalue the past.

Of course, you must have been putting your own trends into these decades. Someone wants to ask, "Where's that influence of Mrs. Mitchell's first 'Here and Now Story-book,' and the arguments against fairy tales?" Well, I know! It was in the twenties. I can see Lenore Power, then head of this room, defending the Grimm Brothers and the princess who married the frog.

We see that trends in reading are tied in with social change. Huck Finn was published in 1885, but it wasn't till about 1910 that Asa Dickinson got it released in libraries to children, or rather to youth. In the fifties, I remember a campaign to get more bookshelves built into new housing: no room there for the old family sets of Scott, Dickens, Thackeray. What did go on the new shelves? Perhaps a new Children's Encyclopedia. Perhaps the new Great Books series, which offer much less for a child's roaming than did Dr. Eliot's Five-Foot Shelf of my childhood.

Then think of the great changes over these fifty years in schools. Back in our first decade, Latin and ancient history were required courses in high schools; one had a full year of English grammar in the eighth grade. Did you do those fascinating sentence diagrams? We thought it was exciting to pursue a stanza from Sir Walter Scott over two blackboards. A school room of 1910 was apt to have on its front wall photos of bearded poets, and between them a big sepia reproduction of Watts's "Sir Lancelot." Every child who looked at it could say, "His strength was as the strength of ten, because his heart was pure." What is on those walls today?

You will find our early decades most vividly described in Miss Moore's first three books, gathered together later in *My Roads to Childhood* (re-issued by The Horn Book, Inc., 1961): Here are her reviews and booklists for *The Bookman*, edited by John Farrar. Here is the real story of that era. Here are the titles, the book experiences with children that bring alive those years. She says: "In 1918, new writers with new ideas and originality of expression were sorely needed in this field. . . . In contrast with the static conditions of 1918, is the rich, varied output of 1922, where illustrators no less than authors, have disclosed new ways of looking at people and things." By 1924 she had started "The Three Owls" page in the new *Book Review* of the *Herald Tribune,* and I was proudly publishing the first "Three Owls" collection. Soon after came Anne Eaton's page in *The New York Times.*

THE THREE OWLS: A Book about Children's Books. By Anne Carroll Moore, Supervisor of Children's Departments in the New York Public Library. Fully illustrated. Probable Price, $2.50.

Here is a new kind of book for everybody with an interest in children's books and reading, edited by a well-known critic and authority on this subject.

The Three Owls is the name given by Miss Moore to the first department of criticism of children's books to appear in a weekly literary review on equal terms with the reviewing of adult books. It is an integral part of "Books" edited by Stuart P. Sherman and Irita Van Doren for the *New York Herald-Tribune.*

Many interesting people are among the contributors to The Three Owls—authors, artists, critics, booksellers, librarians. The result is a varied and stimulating treatment of the outstanding books of the year, a fresh approach to the seasonal holidays—Hallowe'en, Twelfth Night, St. Valentine's Day, and the rest—and a series of delightful articles on such popular subjects as Plays to Read and Plays to Act, Books of Ships and Sailors, The Quest of the Perfect Boys' Book.

The book is an important contribution to our talking and thinking on a subject of year-round interest and it is also a practical and constructive guide for parents, teachers, librarians, and booksellers.

A MID-CENTURY CHILD AND HER BOOKS: By Caroline M. Hewins. Introduced by Anne Carroll Moore. Fully illustrated with both color and line drawings from the old American children's books. $2.50.

IN the early fifties a small girl learned to read and spell and count. She had no kindergarten but she lived in a large family of older people, all book lovers. Here she gives us her reminiscences of childhood, of the books she grew up with, of the people and events that shaped her later years. This new book will combine a record of the children's books of that period with a delightful picture of child life.

Miss Hewins' many friends among book lovers have often heard her talk of these things. They have heard her recite the old Peter Piper alphabet, which is included entire in this book, with many of the illustrations from the first edition.

Other old books are represented by the most interesting color plates, steel engravings, line drawings, title pages, decorations, etc., to be found. To all older people, the book will be a reminder of treasures of long ago. To younger readers it will give an unusually colorful picture of the child-life of that day.

From the 1925 catalog of Macmillan Books for Boys and Girls

A portent of this new decade had arrived at A. C. M.'s office in 1918. A tall, big Dutchman, a history teacher at Cornell, presented her with his *Short History of Discovery, Written and Illustrated with a Match*. She was the right champion for the genius of Hendrik van Loon, and for his next, greater book, *The Story of Mankind*. She wrote: "No boy is likely to skip . . . a single chapter of a history which makes the world he lives in seem so spacious, so teeming with human interest." Reread her astute praise; perhaps you will then reread the book itself. Does its place at the top of the Newbery Medal books find it new readers? Of what age are they, compared to the boys to whom Miss Moore gave it?

The tone of the twenties also was set by another European, another learned *adult* writer—the poet, critic, novelist, playwright Padraic Colum. Before then, he had published his memorable *The King of Ireland's Son*, which I gave a new edition in 1921. Before the twenties a fellow Irish patriot in Macmillan's Educational Department had persuaded him to edit *The Children's Homer*, which he based on the Lang, Leaf, and Myers translation. This school book I gave a trade edition in 1920. And so Colum began his shelf of epics, and the retold fairy tales in which we heard the rhythms of his rare Dublin English, and met his gay mingling of poetry with prose. He was the bardic-fireside story-teller, bringing us "deeds and wonders" of the great, and new images of such old friends as Cinderella. In *The Girl Who Sat by the Ashes*, she became the lovely goat-girl of my first catalog cover.

By now you hear "I" and "my" creeping into my text, for in 1919, there I was, at one of a crowded row of desks in the old Macmillan building. My new department was only half my job; the other half was the whole trade book publicity. So I was chiefly involved, for two years, with adult writers. For a shy young editor, friends like Van Loon and Colum were great good fortune. Theirs was a learning and genius that overflowed gaily into everyday life; they, in the flesh, were as I had imagined the writers I studied at college.

There were many distinguished authors on those spring and fall lists which I wrote. Stefansson had to teach me his new global geography before he allowed me to write publicity for his great book, *The Friendly Arctic.* That led to his boys' story about Eskimos. He brought a friend, born at a Hudson Bay trading post, who was writing for the Yale Pageant histories, to try her first boys' book. That was *Silent Scot,* by Constance Lindsay Skinner. There came to stride about my room on Tenth Street Vachel Lindsay, declaiming "Johnny Appleseed," which he was reciting to huge high school audiences. I put it into our Children's Classics, and lo! here it is today as a "survivor."

A friend of his, and of all poets, a best-seller on our adult list, was Sara Teasdale. She was persuaded to do her very selective anthology, *Rainbow Gold,* and later chose her own poems for *Stars To-Night,* which happily has also survived.

So my editorial angle, at first, was apt to be sternly literary. To ask anyone to write purposely for a child—how horrible! But gradually I relaxed. I visited library schools and found out about their new courses in what they called "Children's Literature." I visited more kinds of schools than those of my own youth, and knew more kinds of children.

These points of view might be symbolized by two books by my college classmate, Elizabeth Coatsworth. She was coming to New York to publish her early books of adult poetry. Looking at one of my new books, she cried, "I bet I could write better for children than that." On a three-day visit, she produced for The Little Library *The Cat and the Captain,* a merry tale with a distinguished style. In it, all unknowing, she had done an "easy reader" which was a best seller for years.

But her heart was much more in a book that reflected her study of Buddhism and her travel in the Orient, *The Cat Who Went to Heaven*. When the first copy, with its beautiful wash drawings by Lynd Ward, reached Mr. Brett, he said, "Miss Seaman, again you have made a handsome book which seems to me more for adults than for children." Soon the children's librarians gave it a Newbery Medal. After thirty-two years, it still is much alive, with a new edition. It seems to me proof that a children's book can be part of the one continuous tradition of art, poetry, learning that I so firmly believed in then, and still do.

My world had changed when the new juvenile department was given its own separate office. The department head decided to find out how children's books were *sold*. She stood in line with the city salesmen, with her briefcase—very unwelcome indeed! This was no place for a *woman!* Then she persuaded Mr. Brett to allow her to make a sales trip across America, and made other far journeys, lecturing with lantern slides. It was a strenuous sort of book education; it was also a wonderful way to know America.

For a year, too, I went every week to a strange loft building in Newark, where that new wonder, radio, was installed. Putting my mouth close to a big flat plate, I read from our books, or told stories, a free half hour.

All this was pioneering. But there was no pioneer spirit, no feeling of being "first" at anything, while I made the first Macmillan juvenile catalog, issued in 1920. Here were over 250 titles, about half from England, half produced in America by editors before me. The headings were much more varied in subject than those in your list today. I didn't notice that there were few picture books, for there were plenty of wonderful illustrations. It was the words that counted most, then.

What I thought was, "Ye Gods! what more could any child need?" Yet by 1930, I was publishing about sixty titles a year; by 1934, when I retired, I had published over six hundred new books.

The catalog grew to be one of eighty-eight pages, with color illustrations, photos of authors, little essays on reading, various book lists based on my lists and also on the great Macmillan catalog.

What caused this outpouring of the twenties, from other publishers as well? Mr. Brett foresaw, in an era of peace and prosperity, expanded sales for children's trade books, along with sales of school books. Of course, his first interest was in my putting together the many "Macmillan Children's Classics," a series which grew in that decade to over fifty titles. Some of the texts of my time are preserved in the new classics and some are lost, with my introductions and others by the eminent editors.

Their new format was brightened by artists from Europe, with a fresh sense of book design, such as Artzybasheff, Hedwig Collin, the Petershams. They came here along with the new European children's books, which we discovered eagerly in bookshops. New York in the twenties seethed with all sorts of new art, anyway. There was the new percussion music by Edgar Varese; there were the fun of "Charlot's Revue" and the new rhythms of "Lady Be Good." There was the new idea of book clubs—I listened to Van Loon and Carl Van Doren argue about it. There was such new writing as that of Virginia Woolf; I heard Elinor Wylie and Edmund Wilson argue about that. Even women's smoking was new—the reviewer for the *Boston Transcript* and I were put out of the Copley Grill for smoking there at lunch!

Fine typography was far from new, but it then had an exciting revival. The first Nonesuch Press books arrived from England. Bruce Rogers and Goudy and others created new types. I looked at the run of the older American Macmillan trade books for children with sorrow. I decided to try to learn typography, studying Updyke at midnight. To design my own books—that was a challenge. Today, most juvenile editors can turn over book design to type specialists. Good typography, good printing, now are almost taken for granted.

So it is impossible for younger editors today to imagine the impact of the ten or more books I had printed in English in Europe. How proud I was of books like *Spin Top Spin,* from Germany, with its delicate hand lettering; of the brilliant peasant colors in books done in Prague; and even of the old-fashioned art in the so-called "Big Pinocchio" printed in Florence, which I discovered in this room.

Here, too, were shown the originals of such lovely books made by me in America as Rachel Field's edition of D'Aulnoy's *The White Cat,* with its MacKinstry pictures taking us to the court of Louis XIV; and of Pamela Bianco's edition of Blake, *The Land of Dreams,* the first children's book to have a limited, signed, boxed edition. Here, too, the fine art of Helen Sewell was shown, and today you see her special "survivor," the picture book of some geese she knew well, *Blue Barns.*

Then there were books like *The Goldsmith of Florence, All the Ways of Building,* the Hines photo-book of *Men at Work,* the children's writing and painting in *City Stories* from the Lincoln School. Some of these books, though out of print, are by no means forgotten.

Some long survivors, not honored on your list today, are Jennie Hall's *Buried Cities,* a pioneer book in archaeology, and Alice Dalgliesh's *The Little Wooden Farmer,* a pioneer too, in real child-language play stories. It is natural for replacements to have come for my early books on machinery, though Artzybasheff's big diagrams of dams and dynamos are by no means out-of-date today, nor is the still surviving Lent *Diggers and Builders.*

I would put Boris Artzybasheff, Helen Sewell, Lynd Ward, at the top of those illustrators who changed the appearance of our books in the twenties. Many more helped and are still making lovely books today—the D'Aulaires, the Haders, Dorothy Lathrop, Pamela Bianco, Marguerite de Angeli, Henry Pitz, James Daugherty. They will remember well the sudden flood of full-color picture books toward the end of the twenties. Now came cheaper new processes in color lithography and bigger editions. My thousands of little Happy Hour Books at fifty cents were soon pushed aside by the millions of Little Golden Books at twenty-five cents. Mass production at first had a sameness which by now has more or less been conquered. One cannot complain of such processes as have given us the varied, distinguished, beautiful color work of Leonard Weisgard.

With this, I must leave the twenties, the story only partly told. You will have gathered that when I became a reviewer, in 1949, I brought a peculiarly critical eye to bookmaking. I had followed it after retiring in 1934 as a book buyer, lecturer, and judge at several Graphic Arts shows. I knew that good taste had persisted, especially under editors who had started in the twenties. I knew that fine bookmaking had increased. Since the end of the last World War, I had felt a wind of revival blowing. The early fifties seemed to me a time when all the good trends of the past were coming together in children's bookmaking.

The horrible surprise for a reviewer lay in the quantity of titles. It had reached over 1,400 a year by 1950. Children's books had become "big business."

There was really too much of a muchness. And reviewing too was different, with new kinds of promotion involved, all very exciting but greatly increasing the reviewer's work. Why complain of all this, when out of it came the publishers' support of big spring and fall newspaper sections on children's books? And why moan over too big an output, if, out of it, came more than before that was good?

By 1958 the decade did not look so admirable to me. Experiments with modern art were stimulating; but there was too much un-facile caricature. There were too many thin books with too slight text; too many history and fact series, an exploitation of realism in teen-age novels; too much imitation of every new success; and poor proofreading, too. More Oz books, more Babars, new Pollyanna books, new Tom Swift books, when their originators were long since dead!

On the plus side of the ledger, one found much to admire. Some children still might cling to the more sentimental classics, but editors had mostly broken with sentimentality. They welcomed more varied styles, more authors from grass-roots America. The honest portraits of foreign lands in fact and fiction, very few in the twenties, now were a great stream. There was more experiment, more fun in bookmaking itself. There was a general use of really modern art, some good, some meaningless to children.

Probably most of our creative people, among whom I include publishers and librarians, were reflecting the deep social changes that had begun in the thirties. Their symbol perhaps was the advent of the American folk hero. These tough, swaggering big-talk giants stood for the American working man. They fitted both the comic-book aspects of heroism and a changing concept of the fairy tale. They loosened up our use of a truly American prose. The same social trends led to the increase of regional books, and to more proletarian children in all story books.

All this was to the good. But as Pecos Bill and Davy Crockett came in, the epic hero left the scene. Before their brash humor, even the humorous doings of the classic gods and heroes faded and epic series in oral library storytelling ceased. Toward the end of this last decade, these epic heroes of the Old World were being introduced, again, in new kinds of retellings. The whole hero concept was diffused. War heroes, space heroes, Dr. Schweitzer and Dr. Carver and Amos Fortune types of heroes, had to be sorted out from the great wealth of new biographies.

We cannot stop today to speculate on the odd survival of one

English folk hero, not exactly epic, to be sure, Robin Hood. Sir Osbert Sitwell, who grew up in Sherwood Forest and owns Robin's own bow, thinks we like him for social-economic reasons. So did the lady who recently attacked him as communistic. I doubt that children have any such ideas about those old ballads Pyle put into prose so long ago. Anyway, Robin has had a special honor in a book which is a very high spot in our modern bookmaking, *The Song of Robin Hood,* so miraculously decorated by Virginia Burton.

Looking carefully at the plethora of easy fact books, one could find outstanding, original ones. More important, one still saw, looming above them, as in the twenties, the longer, bigger books where facts gathered toward wisdom, where the older child could stretch his mind. How many fine writers have rearranged facts on the Ladder of Time in new ways. A few are: Bronson and Holling, with their imaginative picture-stories of nature and science; Gertrude Hartman, Katherine Shippen, Elizabeth Baity, Genevieve Foster, with new concepts of history; and such brilliant biographers as James Daugherty, Esther Forbes and Elizabeth Gray Vining. Such books as these need more continuous new introduction to parents, teachers, and children.

We had new thinking, too, in significant religious books like *The Tree of Life, One God,* and *The Good Ways.* We had a splendid new editing of the Bible for the young or for families, Sypherd's *The Book of Books.* And all along the way, poetry was offered in striking kinds of anthologies for all ages, freshly chosen from the new and the old. Think of such old treasures as the still loved *Winged Horse, Come Hither, Silver Pennies,* and such later fine collections as *An Inheritance of Poetry* and *Imagination's Other Place.*

Let us remind ourselves of just a few of those seemingly accidental works of genius for which an era, a trend, a decade, give no explanation. Think of *Homer Price, Charlotte's Web, The Twenty-one Balloons, All Kinds of Time, The Tree of Freedom, The Bells of Bleecker Street.* America can be proud of such books, and also of editors who offered our children books from abroad like C. S. Lewis's Narnia series, *The Caves of the Great Hunters, The Defender, Treasure Trove of the Sun.* All those books have something special to say in a new way; whether fact or fiction, they lift both the mind and the heart. Each had also beautiful, original book design and production.

With 1960 we may be facing an era of greater change than ever before. You may have read an article called "From Quality to Mass Production," prophesying the doom of the individualistic, "quality," trade editor. You may have heard the remarkable TV panel program "Trends in Publishing," which followed it. When that moderator brought up the intrusion of Wall Street into bookmaking, reaching toward the coming increased profits in text books, he added softly, "and juveniles."

A new sort of commercialization of juveniles has taken them into schools as paper books. Surely new ideas are needed to reduce the prices of children's books, since labor costs obviously will not go down. The question, as in the adult field, is how all this will affect editing.

We must take cheer in the fact that in the juvenile field, the lucrative back log of best sellers looks far different from that of current adult lists. These are the books kept alive chiefly in libraries, where children and youth are now 48 per cent of all borrowers (a 1959 figure). One must remember that they include those long series not found on library shelves. In all honesty we must admit how little we know *what* titles young readers borrow most often. Nor do we really know which juvenile best sellers make the field financially alluring. The truth about sales is seldom told. This field too has its very successful non-books.

In this chaos of trends and portents, I see more than one hopeful sign. The long overdue reform in the teaching of reading and writing in public schools is on the way. Many educators are working toward it. I reported on some whose criticism had had little effect, in my Bowker speech here in 1946. By the time of my speech for the fiftieth anniversary of library work with children, in 1950, the situation was no better; in fact, the increase of school libraries had increased the use of the trade book that was thin and easy. But this was a wedge toward freer use of non-text books in schools.

Today, there seems to be a new urge toward the use of the whole book, not snippets. Well I remember Padraic Colum making a speech on this at the first Book Week in the twenties! Now, at last, we may see preference for excellence purposely cultivated, even as the population explosion engulfs us. For ability to read with comprehension is at the base of education.

Isn't it up to us all, but especially up to the publishers' advertising and the library list-makers, to believe more in that core of good readers among children which has always existed? In children's rooms, supposedly books are offered without age levels, freely available to all ages. Do they really spread out alluringly the harder-to-read books, new and old? Are there enough selected adult books shown? Can the *able* younger reader find there what he is ready for?

I have spoken of the persistent publications of the longer factual books, where text still predominates over pictures, the *words* with which we still must think. It cannot be only teachers who buy them! That such books continue to exist at all, is proof of that core of good readers who need more help and encouragement. They can be increased, whatever happens to the teaching of reading.

I am also reasonably hopeful, as you have heard already, that whatever happens to the commercialization of publishing, there will always be new, experimental, individualistic publishing done. Think of Harold Monro's Poetry Bookshop of the twenties in London, and of Bill Scott beginning in the thirties in his barn in Vermont. This tantalizing profession, with its peculiar demand for people who combine literary flair with commercial sense, feeds best upon the same creative instinct which has always given us new authors and artists. It is a very personally expressive matter.

Perhaps we shall see the Miss Moores, Mrs. Sayers, Mrs. Spains, Miss Mastons of the future broadcast books to half a continent from a space station. Whatever the undreamed-of changes in book promotion, one special skill of theirs surely will continue and prevail. That is, the seemingly simple matter of personal introduction of the child to the book.

Adults can touch greatness, can discover it for themselves, in so many ways. But children today seem to have few such chances, and to be even more lost than their elders in the masses of new books. They now seem outwardly sophisticated when so young, they "take in" the adult world so soon. Don't we overrate the inner effect this has on them? Don't they need more than ever the balance given by the sort of reading we here today call "best"? How do they discover it? Not by lists, nor by huge exhibits, nor in big bookstores; and seldom, alas, through their teachers, who haven't time or training to be selective about trade books.

No, it is still up to the librarians. We must see that more of them have time to express their personal book enthusiasm to all ages of children. They must discover, also, more people, not necessarily either librarians or famous authors, who can lure others into books they truly love, and let the children hear them. I found the recent TV program of famous people reading children's books aloud a fearful bore. The trouble was, those adults *didn't seem to love the books*. Dozens of librarians I know could have done better.

How well I remember a day in the twenties, in this room, when

FOLK-LORE AND FAIRY-TALE

WITH ARTHUR RACKHAM'S PICTURES

From English Fairy Tales

ENGLISH FAIRY TALES

By Flora Annie Steele. Ill. by Arthur Rackham. *16 color plates, and many line drawings. Dec. cloth, 8vo, $4.00.*

Miss Steele and Mr. Rackham have given satisfying spirit and form to the old English stories that are the rich heritage of Anglo-Saxon children. The humor of Lawkamercyme, Nix Naught Nothing, and Master of all Masters, is irresistible. Here are our old friends St. George, Tom Thumb, Jack the Giant Killer, The Three Bears, Little Red Riding Hood, Henny Penny, and Dick Whittington. The Wise Men of Gotham and Cap o' rushes, Catskin and Tattercoats, are the most beguiling new friends. A book for mothers to read aloud, and for children to read in as they begin to learn. (4-7.)

IRISH FAIRY TALES

By James Stephens. Ill. by Arthur Rackham. *16 color plates, and many line drawings. Dec. cloth, 8vo, $4.00.*

The very wind of the land of faery is in this book. It is hearty with the laughter of those epic days when priests must be warriors, and each hero stood almost alone in his world. So it was with Finn, until he built up the band of the Fenians whose exploits are recorded here. Great fights and great races, great magic and madness, all described by Stephens as only the author of The Crock of Gold can tell a tale. There is all the beauty and humor and courage of those ancient epics in this new book, and older people should not miss it. (12-16.)

(See color plate, facing p. 9)

¶ These two books are ideal for reading aloud to all the family. The English stories, based on simpler folk lore of the country side, come to their point quickly, and are told in a style suited to little children. The Irish stories come from the cycle of the third century, and are more complicated in plot and more sophisticated in point of view. Many of them, however, can be read to younger children.

From Irish Fairy Tales

THE ILIAD FOR BOYS AND GIRLS
THE ODYSSEY FOR BOYS AND GIRLS

By the Rev. A. J. Church. *Dec. cloth, colored ill., 12mo, $1.75.* (7-9.)

From the 1921 catalog of Macmillan Books for Boys and Girls

Miss Moore lit the candles and introduced that rare Irishman, James Stephens. He was famous for his adult poetry and novels like *The Crock of Gold*. We had just published his robustly retold *Irish Fairy Tales*, and I hoped he would tell those stories.

There were mostly children present, who seemed awed at Stephens' gnome-like figure and that long, dour face of his. Then, in his beautiful Dublin-English voice, he began reciting his adult poetry. He said poems like:

> Come with me, under my coat,
> And we will drink our fill
> Of the milk of the white goat,
> Or wine if it be thy will.

He gave them "The Goat Paths," "The Green Billow," "What Tamas an' Buile Said in a Pub." You remember that Tamas had seen God.

Next to me sat a rough-looking boy of about twelve. At the end of each poem, he gave me a dig with his sharp elbow. Once he muttered, "I *never* heard *nothing* like this!" At the end, he seized my arm. "Gee!" he cried. "Gee, what a *man!* He sure does know his onions!"

To see that boy touched by genius, surprised by greatness—I shall never forget it. It was your great city library system which, not at all by accident, brought him here to receive this gift. I pray that you librarians continue doing such miracles. It is up to all the rest of us to see that you have more time to do it, and more honor, and greater reward than your own joy in helping to create the book-lovers of today and tomorrow.